Praise for

THE COLOR COMPLEX

"*The Color Complex* is a much needed and insightful examination of color prejudices which persist among African Americans. It illustrates how deeply white racism continues to intrude on the black psyche and behavior."

—Alvin F. Poussaint, MD, Harvard Medical School

"Should make it easier for artists, writers and thinkers who want to probe deeper, examine new truths, and most of all, heal the wounds." —*New York Newsday*

"The authors—a black woman, a white woman, and a black man—ably survey the highly charged issue of discrimination among blacks on the basis of skin color." —*Publishers Weekly*

"Long overdue. . . . Far too much time has been spent worrying about what to call ourselves—Afro-America, black, African-Americans, people of color—and not enough time learning how to understand and reconcile the ma̶̶̶̶̶̶̶ hues."

̶̶̶̶̶̶̶Veekly

Kathy Russell-Cole, Midge Wilson,
and Ronald E. Hall

THE COLOR COMPLEX

Kathy Russell-Cole is Vice President of Sales for Omar
Supplies Inc. and lives in Plainfield, Illinois, with her
husband, photographer James M. Cole. Midge Wilson
is an associate dean and a professor who holds a joint
appointment in psychology and women's and gender
studies at DePaul University, in Chicago. Ronald E. Hall
is a social work professor at Michigan State University
in East Lansing.

— THE —
COLOR
COMPLEX

*The Politics of Skin Color
in a New Millennium*

— REVISED EDITION —

Kathy Russell-Cole,
Midge Wilson, PhD,
and Ronald E. Hall, PhD

ANCHOR BOOKS

A Division of Random House, Inc. | New York

SECOND ANCHOR BOOKS EDITION, JANUARY 2013

Due to limitations on space, permission to reprint previously
published material can be found on page 288.

Library of Congress Cataloging-in-Publication Data:
Russell, Kathy.
The color complex : the politics of skin color among African
Americans/Kathy Russell, Midge Wilson, Ronald Hall.—1st
Anchor Books ed.
p. cm.
Includes bibliographical references (p.) and index.
1. Afro-Americans—Race identity.
2. Black race—Color—Social aspects—United States.
I. Wilson, Midge. II. Hall, Ronald E. III. Title.
[E185.625.R79 1993]
305.896'073—dc20 93-13294

Anchor ISBN: 978-0-307-74423-4

Book design by Joy O'Meara-Wispe

www.anchorbooks.com

Printed in the United States of America
10 9 8 7 6 5 4 3 2 1

Kathy Russell-Cole dedicates this book to the love of her life, her husband, James McArthur Cole II, and to the world's most amazing parents, Will and Dorothy Russell.

Midge Wilson dedicates this book in loving memory of her longtime partner Michael Abramson, who passed away from kidney cancer on March 21, 2011, and to her mother, Marge Wilson, whose continuing achievements in publishing two books when well into her eighties keeps Midge inspired.

Ronald E. Hall dedicates this book to Marsha, Karen, and Crystal for what might have been.

— Contents —

— Introduction —

A lot has changed in the twenty years since *The Color Complex* was first published. During the intervening years, we've crossed into a new millennium, and an entirely new generation of Americans has been born and come of age. It is a generation that is so much more racially diverse than any other before it that some have said we now have, in place of Generation X, Generation Mix. While many Americans still cling to racial prejudices and fear of immigration, there is on balance more racial tolerance in America today. White Americans are more likely today to live and work near those whose racial makeup differs from their own. However, the most striking evidence of racial attitudes' having evolved since publication of the original *The Color Complex* has been the election in 2008 of an African-American man as president—a man light skinned and fine featured enough to be acceptable to Whites, and, in having married a darker-skinned woman, racially identified enough to be acceptable to Blacks. Throughout this revised edition there are references to this historic, touchstone event in America.

For readers not familiar with the 1992 edition of *The Color Complex,* it is worth noting that at the time of its publication it was the first nonfiction book devoted solely to the topic of colorism. Since then, there have been other books published on the topic of skin-color prejudice, some in memoir form, like Marita Golden's *Don't Play in the Sun: One Woman's Journey Through the Color Complex* (2004), and others that are edited collections of stories, poetry, and essays on the subject, from *Skin Deep: Black Women & White Women Write about Race* (1995) to *Shades of Difference: Why Skin Color Matters* (2009). But no other book has been able to capture the spirit or duplicate the interdisciplinarity, easy readability, and multiperspective sensibility that only three authors from different backgrounds and of different genders can bring to a project like this. Readers of the present edition—which we like to call "CC 2"—will find that the authors have kept the formula intact.

Of course, much has occurred since 1992 that is relevant to the issue of skin-color prejudice. Among the developments, in no particular order, are the following: (1) Internet access through handheld communication devices; (2) social media; (3) video-sharing websites; (4) the emergence of economic powerhouses such as India, China, and Brazil; (5) the appearance of additional multiracial categories on the U.S. Census form; (6) the emergence of the new critical mixed-race-studies discipline; (7) greater acceptance of cross-race (and same-sex) relationships and marriage; (8) the death of pop star Michael Jackson; (9) more legal recognition of color as a separate category for protection in Title VII workplace-discrimination cases; (10) greater workplace diversity; (11) proportionately more communities of color living in poverty; and (12) less optimism overall in America. These topics will be discussed in this new, extensively updated edition of our book.

When *The Color Complex* was originally published, the term "colorism" was only beginning to come into popular usage. This is not to say that the prejudice of skin color itself wasn't intimately known and personally experienced, especially among African Americans. But various attitudes relating to skin-color differences tended to be looked at more as problems of individuals, as in "He's just colorstruck" or "She's too color conscious." It was only after Alice Walker used "colorism" to describe the phenomenon that its more systemic nature, intimate relationship to class, and historical development could be better recognized and studied. Today, the term is widely used to refer to the prejudices and discriminatory practices surrounding skin-color differences that occur not only among African Americans, but also among other populations of color such as Latinos and Asians, both in this country and around the world.

Other terminology that has changed over the years is the greater usage of "African Americans" as the descriptor for those of African descent living in this country. In 1992, the preferred term was "Blacks," although by then "African Americans" had been proposed as a preferred descriptor, one that put the emphasis on culture instead of color. Today, there exist both those who eschew the name African American and those who do the name Black. In *CC 2* we chose to use the two descriptors interchangeably in the hope that readers who do the same conversationally will outnumber any who are offended by one term or the other.

A new term the reader will find introduced in *CC 2* is "the bleaching syndrome." As coined by coauthor Ronald E. Hall, the concept reflects not just the literal act of rubbing bleach on one's skin, but the internalized ideal held by people around the world that being lighter skinned and more Western looking is better. Because of the recent dramatic rise seen in the number of products sold and the diverse procedures performed globally associated with imitative cosmetic practices, we decided to include a new chapter exclusively devoted to what is also sometimes called "cosmetic Westernism."

What hasn't changed since the original *The Color Complex* is that no unifying theory has emerged in the literature that could neatly explain and address the many nuanced and complicated issues associated with colorism. There is simply no easy way to resolve questions regarding whether hair-straightening and skin-lightening practices are expressions of personal preferences or reflections of an unconscious enslavement to Western values. In trying to answer the many questions raised by this topic, we make every effort, as was the case in our first edition, to provide a balanced approach to all sides of controversial issues so that readers may form their own opinions based on the evidence presented.

Perhaps the best rationale for issuing a revised edition of *The Color Complex* is to answer the simple question, "Has colorism gotten better or has it gotten worse?" Starting from the assumption that improved awareness leads to positive behavioral change, one could make the case that colorism's influence has declined over the last twenty years because many more Americans, including Whites, now know something about the subject. Articles about intraracial color prejudice regularly appear in mainstream newspapers and magazines; throwaway references to colorism crop up in sitcoms, movies, and song lyrics; and the topic is even central to the plot of Dael Orlandersmith's extraordinary play *Yellowman*, which in 2002 garnered a nomination for the Pulitzer Prize for drama. Intimate disclosures about skin-color issues now freely flow on social media sites; rants on the topic appear in various blogs; and articles posted on Wikipedia explain in detail how colorism is a form of prejudice separate from that of racism. There also have been several documentaries made on the topic of skin-color prejudice, including *Skin* by National Geographic (2002), *The Skin Quilt Project* by Lauren Cross (2010), *Dark Girls* by Bill Duke and D. Channsin Berry (2011), and, on colorism's sister issue, hair, Chris Rock's most notable and commercially successful film *Good Hair* (2009).

Skin-color prejudice is now routinely discussed in social science and humanities courses in the academy. The number of peer-reviewed scholarly publications on skin-color prejudice has gone from one in 1989, by Angela Neal and coauthor Wilson, to more than three thousand such publications today. Colorism has become a legitimate field of study, as well as a recognized class of protection in the area of employment discrimination, one that is separate from (but still related to) racism. Some scholars even argue that colorism is the more legitimate form of prejudice to empirically investigate since skin tone is at least a visible and measurable attribute, whereas race is largely a social construct. Critical mixed-race studies, which includes scholarly inquiry into color-class hierarchies, cosmetic Westernism, and media representation, is also an emerging discipline, with its own conferences, journals, and books. Relevant updates from these new areas of scholarly research are included throughout the present edition.

At the same time, a case can be made that colorism has *gotten worse* since 1992, exacerbated by the same technologies that served so well to raise awareness of the issue. We now live in an era of global wireless Internet and instant access from small handheld devices with enhanced video software. The current digital revolution means that a greater number of people from what used to be considered remote places on earth are now seeking to emulate the looks of Westerners. What else can adequately explain the rapid rise in the number of cosmetic practices, skin-bleaching products sold, and procedures performed, all designed to achieve a more Caucasian-featured appearance? The Internet allows individuals to see firsthand the imagined (and sadly sometimes real) social and career benefits associated with having a more Western-like appearance. Social media outlets are making the globe smaller, and populations more homogenous. One has to wonder: If colorism continues unchecked, will it result in the genocide of very dark skin, a kind of evolutionary removal of a biological trait through the force of social attitudes? It would seem that greater awareness is a double-edged sword.

The authors hope that you, the reader, will be informed and enlightened by our inclusion of new perspectives and scholarship in this revised edition of *The Color Complex*. If you learn as much in reading the new version as we have learned in updating its content, then our ultimate goal of furthering dialogue and discussion on the topic of colorism will have been met.

— THE —

COLOR
COMPLEX

Chapter 1

The Emergence of Modern Colorism in the Americas

We begin in Europe in the late 1400s, when seafaring countries such as England, Spain, and Portugal were financing merchant voyages to find new trade routes to the Far East. The men returned instead with exciting tales of faraway places that were rich with gold, spices, and silks. The very notion that there existed unknown lands beyond the horizon set off a frenzy of empire building on the part of many European nations. This would later be known as the Age of Discovery, and it lasted well into the seventeenth century. After Christopher Columbus reached what he mistakenly believed were the Indies, and it was realized that vast new lands were available for plunder and colonization, European nations began financing more ship captains for even more expeditions with orders to stake claim to as many territories as they could find. It mattered little to the Europeans if indigenous peoples already were living in these "discovered" places. Europeans believed they were the superior race. As such, they saw it as their Christian duty to tame the "savage" natives and bring them civilization, a self-serving rationale that would persist for centuries—Rudyard Kipling would call it "the White man's burden" as late as 1899.

During the early 1500s, the islands of the Caribbean—or "West Indies," as they were mistakenly named by Columbus—were popular destinations for Portuguese and Spanish explorers, and other areas of Central and South America soon followed. While the hoped-for gold rarely materialized, it was recognized that the warm climates and rich soil in these new lands had the potential for growing cash crops like sugar and coffee. The crops were labor intensive, however, and for them to be profitable, a source of cheap labor was needed. At first, local indigenous people were captured and forced to work in the colonists' fields, but there were not enough of them. Some White indentured servants from Europe ventured over, but again, not enough. The Portuguese, who already had explored the east coast of Africa, found the solution by bringing over the first slaves to the New World. This nation would continue to be the largest importer of slaves during the era of Atlantic slave trading.

African slaves poured in to work in the Americas during the seventeenth and eighteenth centuries. Throughout the Caribbean, the British, French, and Dutch had also claimed islands of their own, and they, too, needed slaves to work the sugar plantations. Conditions were ideal for race mixing to take place. Large numbers of individuals from different racial backgrounds were living and working side by side, and doing so under the rule of White plantation owners who were greatly outnumbered. In fact, it has been estimated that throughout the Caribbean, there was an average ratio of one White to ten Blacks and/or mulattoes, and in some of the most remote rural areas there could be as many as fifty slaves and/or mulattoes for every one White male. Finally, there was a significant gender imbalance. During the early years of slave trading, far more African males, with their greater upper-body strength (relative to that of females), were brought to the New World to clear the fields, but females were valued as well, and albeit in smaller numbers, they came too. Predictably, under the extreme conditions in many of these settlement outposts, the White men in charge raped the women who worked for them. But, to be fair, we should note that many romantic relationships and successful unions also came into existence during this time.

Racially mixed individuals, called "mulattoes" (a term considered derogatory by many today), began to make up significant segments of the population throughout Central and South America. They were people of every conceivable variety: those of mixed European and African blood, those of mixed European and indigenous blood, those of mixed African and indigenous blood, and subsequently every combination and permutation created by the mixed-race offspring of the first unions.

In Central and South America, many of the mulattoes lived free and enjoyed a certain status in the society, one that was certainly lower than that of Whites but also much above that of the darker-skinned slaves. Many mulattoes acquired their free legal status from being the direct descents of wealthy White plantation owners, some of whom openly accepted responsibility for their mulatto offspring and made provisions for their future, including an education and land of their own. And when the White owner had no other progeny, his mulatto offspring inherited the family wealth and were expected to continue the family line. These racially mixed islanders enjoyed what American historian Carl Neumann Degler has called "the mulatto escape-hatch." Though not as fully privileged as Whites, most mulattoes were not subject to the restrictions of slavery. It is interesting to note that later, when revolution rocked many of the Caribbean islands, it was the more recently arriving slaves who tended to be the most rebellious; the better-situated mulattoes were often quite satisfied with the status quo. When it became clear to the rebel slaves that the old mulatto families were not joining in the fight for freedom, they too came under attack along with White owners. As a result, many Caribbean mulattoes fled for safety elsewhere, with a majority going to New Orleans, where they would generate their own brand of colorism, a topic that will be discussed later.

Today, the persistence of a mulatto-based color-caste hierarchy is perhaps most evident in Brazil, a country that prides itself on being free of racism. Brazilians proudly refer to themselves as "*café con leche,*" and they have close to forty different racial names and categories with which citizens may identify. But in reality, social stratification follows color: the lighter the skin, the wealthier one is likely to be, and conversely, the darker, the poorer. Lighter skin, and in some cases the socially constructed label of light skin, is preferred for what it signifies. Two commonly heard expressions in Brazil are "Anyone who escapes being an evident Negro is White" and "Money whitens," meaning that the wealthier a Black man or woman becomes, the lighter his or her racial category becomes. Today, lighter skin is so preferred that there are those who fear Black features will eventually disappear altogether from the Brazilian population. In short, one might say that there is a consciousness about—even a preoccupation with—skin color in Brazil, but to the Brazilians' credit, their country never developed the kinds of exclusionary laws and blatant racist practices that plagued and continue to influence race relations in the United States.

According to social historian George Fredrickson, race in Brazil became more "biologized" than socially constructed, meaning that a difference between actual ancestry and observable phenotype came to be recognized. That is, a Brazilian child would never be automatically identified with the racial status of one or both parents, but instead how the child looked physically would become the determining marker of his or her racial identity. Interestingly, a plausible hypothesis regarding why Brazil and other South and Central American countries never adopted the rigid rules of racial classification that developed in the United States is that the somewhat darker skinned Portuguese and Spanish people who settled these areas were more comfortable with living among those of varying skin color, as a consequence of their homelands' having been invaded by Moors from northern Africa centuries earlier. Those Moors who stayed behind mixed racially with the local population, which over the years became on average somewhat darker skinned than their neighbors to the north. In contrast, the British tended to be more homogenously pale and certainly more supremacist in their attitudes regarding the value and meaning of white skin.

We now turn to the United States to explore its history and the events that led to a significantly different societal structure based on skin color. In particular, we will examine how economic and social concerns resulted in the passage of certain laws that produced the seemingly intractable discrimination we still see to this day.

In 1607, three small ships, financed by the venture capital of the Virginia Company of London, sailed into Chesapeake Bay to set up camp in an area that would be named Jamestown. The settlement would become the first English colony in the New World that would continuously flourish. As local inhabitants watched, pale-skinned strangers cleared the wilderness, built a fort, planted crops, and settled down for the duration. But the colony struggled mightily, especially during the winter of 1609–1610, known as "the starving time," when natives surrounded the fort and the settlers had to barricade themselves inside without food or supplies for months. Deep despair set in. The hoped-for gold was nowhere to be found and the Indians—as the confused Englishmen called them—who initially had presented themselves as friendly trading partners had suddenly become murderous foes, with the help of firearms obtained earlier in exchange for food. Of the original 500 settlers, an estimated 440 died during that terrible winter. The remaining 60 or so were barely alive but in May of 1610, two new ships,[1] loaded with fresh supplies, arrived and soon were followed by others. The weakened settlers who had decided to sail back in defeat to England were made to try again. It was a smart decision, as from that point on the colony successfully grew, both in population and in claimed land.

Attacks by natives—American Indians or Native Americans, in present-day terms—continued, but the colonists improved the defenses of their forts and began to expand their territory. However, they did have a problem common to all colonial settlements, and that was the lack of young women with whom the men could marry and settle down. Not that there hadn't been any women in the Jamestown fort. We now know from newly discovered settlement graves that there were at least two

---

1. These ships were built by survivors of the shipwrecked *Sea Venture,* from whom one of the passengers coauthor Wilson is descended.

Englishwomen who lived in Jamestown as early as 1608. A few other women, already married to newly arriving colonists, followed. But it was evident that if the tiny new settlement was to thrive and become a permanent outpost, a shipment of unmarried women needed to arrive soon.

Thus it was that, in 1619, the Virginia Company of London ordered that "a fit hundredth might be sent of women, maids young and uncorrupt, to make wives to the inhabitants and by that means to make the men there more settled and less movable." In 1620, ninety women, some of whom had been living as prostitutes on the streets of London, were rounded up and given a choice between prison and free passage to a strange New World. During the long transatlantic journey, those who had chosen the latter must have questioned their own sanity. But once they arrived, they no doubt quickly realized that the gamble had paid off. The women had barely stepped ashore when eager bachelors surrounded them and proposed marriage on the spot. Old street identities were shed and new respectable ones were assumed. Soon there were families with children and a growing sense of optimism that the colony would make it after all.

Not every man was lucky enough to secure a wife, however, and the resulting gender imbalance led many Englishmen to turn to indigenous women for sex and marriage. While some White colonists and Native American women, most notably John Rolfe and Pocahontas, formed true romantic relationships, other local women bore the brunt of violent rape and forced marriages. In either case, the first generation of blue-eyed children of Indians and Whites began appearing in the local population.

Little is known about how the offspring were received by

either indigenous relatives or colonial settlers, except that these mixed-race individuals were never as frowned upon as were the children born of African and European parents. Sadly, we do know that over successive generations, attitudes of color prejudice spread among Native Americans. By the mid-nineteenth century, the Cherokee Nation, for example, displayed a clear preference for those among them with a mixture of Cherokee and European blood—and lighter skin color.

The English, like the Spanish and Portuguese much farther south, never found a wealth of gold and silver for the taking; instead, they turned to planting cash crops. In Virginia, the tobacco plant, having gained popularity in Europe, promised to be the most profitable. But like the sugar and coffee crops of the Caribbean and South America, tobacco was labor intensive and therefore an expensive crop to grow. Labor needs—for the work of planting and harvesting—were generally met by what seemed like an endless supply of lower-class white male and, increasingly, female Europeans who came to the New World as indentured servants. Some had prior arrests and a few were court ordered to go to America, but for most others, the exchange of free passage (and sometimes land, too) for a mere seven years of indentured servitude was a deal worth taking. It is estimated that prior to the American Revolution up to 80 percent of all immigrants to America arrived as indentured servants.

In early seventeenth-century Virginia, English immigrants were not the only ones who arrived under contracts of indentured servitude. There were also an estimated forty to fifty Africans, men and some women, who did so as well. In light of newly discovered legal documents, scholars now have a different understanding of what happened to the first Africans to arrive in the Virginia colony. Before this discovery, and for close to four hundred years, it was commonly believed that "20 and odd" slaves were transported to Virginia on a Dutch warship that had sailed from the West Indies. It is now known that this account, written by John Rolfe, was not accurate. In fact, the first Africans to land in Virginia came directly from Angola in 1619, having been kidnapped in their homeland by Portuguese slave traders intent on selling their human bounty for profit in Mexico. The Portuguese ship, carrying an estimated 350 slaves, was itself captured by pirates from two English vessels, the *Treasurer* and the *White Lion* (which flew a Dutch flag). The English vessels each took on twenty to thirty slaves stolen from the Portuguese and found their way up the coast to Jamestown. The pirates needed food and other provisions, and the colonists needed labor, so deals were struck and the Angolans were released to come ashore.

Unlike the many thousands of slaves to come who tended to be from more remote areas of Africa, at least some of the Angolan men and women who were aboard the pirate ships were urban, literate, and Christian, their homeland having been converted to Christianity during the late fifteenth century. The fact that some of the Angolans were Christian and literate impressed neither the Portuguese slave traders nor the pirates, but to the English settlers, the Africans' Christianity did make a difference. After some discussion as to what to do with the unexpected visitors, a decision was made to treat the Angolans no differently than White indentured servants were treated. So it was that after seven years of labor, these first-arriving Africans were granted their freedom in the strange new land.

As a labor arrangement, indentured servitude worked well enough for both the colonial planters and impoverished Englishmen wanting passage to the New World. Yet many indentured servants were treated no better than the slaves who would follow. In fact, some of them were denied their freedom after seven years of work, and beatings and rapes by planters were not uncommon. But it was the planters, not the abused servants, whose complaints were heard. From the planters' perspective, the constant turnover of labor meant time wasted in constantly having to train new arrivees. Seeking a more permanent labor solution, some planters even tried enslaving the local natives, but that generally did not go well. The indigenous people knew the land far too well, and, if captured, found it relatively easy to escape and hide.

Early Christian concerns about the morality of slavery seemed to ebb as demands for cheap labor continued to rise. The colonial planters were well aware that plantation owners in Central and South America were economically advantaged by the importation of slaves from Africa, and they began asking why they couldn't do the same. A series of laws were thus passed, progressively leading to legalized slavery. By the second half of the 1600s, it became legal for colonists who wished to do so to keep for life their indentured servants who were dark skinned. In 1667, Virginia declared that a person could legally be both Christian and enslaved, thereby discouraging slaves from converting solely to gain freedom. Three years later, the colony ruled that any non-Christian servant arriving in Virginia by ship would immediately be subject to lifetime enslavement. Since Africans were the only non-Christians traveling to the New World, the law was specifically aimed at them. By the 1700s, slavery was an established fact of life in the colonies, and statutes regulating its practice were no longer oblique. In 1705, for example, the Virginia General Assembly declared:

"All Negro, mulatto and Indian slaves shall be held, taken, and adjudged to be real estate, in the same category as livestock and household furniture, wagons, and goods."

In colonial America, especially in the areas around Chesapeake Bay, White indentured servants were still being hired, and many ended up working side by side with Black slaves. Since men and women of the two races generally shared the same lifestyles, privileges, and restrictions, it is not surprising that cross-race friendships and romances developed. Such interracial relationships might have been unthinkable in Europe, but in the New World things were different, and miscegenation, or race mixing, came to be widespread. Given the harsh realities of frontier life, mate selection tended to be more pragmatic than passionate. Offers of marriage were often opportunistic, and were made and accepted on perceived abilities to protect and procreate.

Again, it was the shortage of women that made it more likely that cross-race intimacies would develop. Among Africans there were only about three men for every two women, and among Whites, there were as many as three to four men for each woman. A free White man might gladly marry a female African slave if she was the only woman around he actually knew. More rarely did White female servants accept the proposals of Black men, but that, too, did happen. Given that the already short supply of African females was being further drained by marriage to White men, the African males turned to Native American women for love and marriage. Although the Indians had initially feared the Black man and called him "Manitto," a word meaning both god and devil, the two groups eventually came to regard each other as equals.

Colonial Whites tended to ignore the sexual affairs of Indians and Blacks. Both groups were considered of lesser status, and as long as they did not interfere with daily life in the colonies, they were left alone. But Indians and Africans did seem to be consolidating their hatred of the White man, as evidenced by the fact that Africans were usually spared when Indians exacted their revenge on White settlements. In the Virginia massacre of 1622, not a single one of the more than twenty Africans present was harmed. Years later, Indians would provide safe refuge for runaway slaves, who then sometimes stayed to marry and raise a family. So much interracial mixing was occurring with the native population that entire tribes are thought to have been genetically absorbed into both the Black and White populations, a trend aided by the fact that it was those natives with a mixture of European blood who were more likely to survive exposure to smallpox and other deadly diseases brought to the New World by the colonialists.

Today, anthropologists calculate that as many as one-fourth of all Blacks in America have Indian ancestry, a convincing estimate when one examines the features and skin color of many African Americans. Yet among Whites, especially those with ancestral roots reaching back to the seventeenth century, an equally high proportion are likely to have some Indian ancestry, too. And many anthropologists also believe a respectable percentage of Whites with roots in colonial America likely carry African genes as well. Stories about having some "Indian blood" in one's family past may well be true, but a tinge of color to the skin might also be due to prior White-Black admixtures. In other words, saying that one is part "Indian" may be more acceptable, and even carry cachet, among some Whites, than claiming Black roots in the old family tree.

Unlike the American Indian and African pairings, the rapidly proliferating White and Black racial mixing was causing great consternation among the wealthier English colonists, especially those advocating for their colony to adopt slavery. They believed that in order for slavery to gain moral acceptance on the part of the "civilized" Englishmen lawmakers, it was essential to foster a belief that Africans were less than fully human, despite evidence to the contrary already provided by the Angolans. The proslavery men feared that if sexual relations between Whites and Africans continued unchecked, moral and ethical questions about slavery would surely follow.

Contrary to practices in Central and South America, where Africans and Europeans were freely having conjugal relations and forming families, the English wanted any such pairings to cease. They got their way. As early as 1622, a little more than two years after the first Africans had stepped ashore, Virginia legislators were passing antimiscegenation statutes. The statutes were written so as to imply that Africans were a lower life-form than Europeans, and therefore that sexual relations between Whites and Blacks were twice as evil as fornication between two Whites; far worse, sex with Blacks was equated with bestiality.

Despite strong public condemnation, early colonial males and females, White and Black, continued to fall in love and intermarry. Historical records document the complaints of White masters when this happened among their own slaves and servants. In 1720, Richard Tilghman of Philadelphia filed a protest when his mulatto slave, Richard Moslon, escaped with a White woman. And in 1747, a White servant named Ann Wainwright, of New Castle County, Delaware, reportedly ran off with a "Negro" man. Concern was greatest when the interracial relationship involved a White woman and a Black (or racially mixed, with Black blood) man. There were far too few White females in the colonies for White authorities to tolerate any sexual activity with Black men, and lawmakers meted out stern punishments for such transgressions. In Maryland, for example, any White female servant who had sex with a Black male slave was subject to a lifetime of enslavement. Unfortunately for many poor White women, this law had the peculiar effect of influencing White slave owners to encourage their male slaves to rape their White servants so that these women would also become their slave property.

A White master having sex with his own female slaves was yet another matter, one that required a certain degree of vigilance and delicate attention. Although the topic was one that many White men might rather have avoided altogether, it was evident from the growing number of mulatto offspring that the practice was common enough to have become problematic. A central question for colonial lawmakers to settle was whether an owner's mixed-breed offspring should have the free status of the White father or the slave status of the Black mother. Not surprisingly, legislators in Virginia found a solution that worked to their own advantage. Departing from traditional English law, in which the status of the child was always determined by that of the father, the legislators voted in 1662 that children born in Virginia would have the same status as their mother. Not exactly a victory for women's rights, this statute allowed—even encouraged—owners to increase their slaveholdings through sexual misconduct. The law also dashed slave women's hopes that their mulatto offspring might go free.

The colonial mulattoes who lived free before the passage of such a law were increasingly treated as outcasts, visible reminders of the state's failure to keep the races apart. Certain rights, like holding property, running for office, and voting, were reserved exclusively for Whites and denied to "Negroes." It was also becoming evident to the White colonists that the growing population of free mulattoes required legal definition, and preferably in a way that would grant superior status to the Whites. In seeking a solution, the colonial legislators could have looked to see how their White European neighbors in Latin America were handling the situation, which was to mostly ignore the rampant race mixing and passively accept free mulattoes into the population. But the English colonists chose a different path by approving a law declaring that any person with even a drop of Black blood would have the same legal status as a pure African—which is to say they would have no legal rights at all.

This early statute became the basis of the "one-drop rule" (also called the "one-drop theory" of racial identity), and it persists, at least informally, to this day. It has meant that in the United States, no matter how White-looking or White-acting someone of mixed ancestry was, or how little Blackness was actually in the person's genetic makeup, that individual was to be considered Black. More than anything else this curious law shaped the emergence of an entirely different color-caste system than what developed throughout Central and South America. Its long-standing legacy is summed up by sociologist Edward Telles, who has written that "miscegenation tends to whiten the population in Brazil whereas in the United States the same process blackens the population."

By the early 1700s, this curiously inclusive definition of Negroes was firmly entrenched in the upper South. The one-drop rule also spread to the North, where it, too, became widely accepted, even after industrialization made the demand for slavery less necessary, and later still when during the early 1800s slavery was declared to be no longer legal. By then, though, the Northern mulattoes, most of whom were the offspring of poor White indentured servants and Black slaves, shared the same bottom rung of the social hierarchy as those of pure African descent; superficial differences between the two groups mattered little.

In the region below North Carolina, and especially in the Deep South, race mixing occurred somewhat later and treatment of mulatto offspring followed a slightly different path than elsewhere in the country; in fact, it showed a pattern that was more akin to what took place in the Caribbean Islands. The continuing shortage of European women in sparsely populated agricultural areas in the South led many White plantation owners to become sexually involved with their Black female slaves. Many White men saw this as their right, and if children resulted from these sexual relations, so be it. Many White plantation owners viewed the offspring strictly in terms of increased slave property, but there were others who lovingly freed and educated their mulatto sons and daughters, some of whom might have been the only children the owners ever had. When this was the case, it was not unusual for White fathers to help these racially mixed children get started in a business, trade, or farming. There were even White slave owners who provided their mulatto offspring with slaves of their own. Mulattoes in the Deep South then were often the beloved progeny of the finest families and typically not the descendants of lower-class servants and slaves, as was the case in the North.

White legislators in the South, some of whom had themselves fathered such children, were inclined to be more liberal regarding the legal status of the mulatto population. Consequently, mulattoes of the Deep South were assigned the status of a separate "Colored" or "Creole" class, the latter being defined as those who were of French, Spanish, and African descent. In some colonies, including South Carolina, mulattoes who were "proper acting"—a quality determined by their wealth and education—could even apply for legal standing as "White." Those with light-enough skin and fine-enough European features commonly got around the law by simply passing themselves off as White.

A three-tiered social system thus evolved in the lower South, with mulattoes serving as a buffer class between Whites and Blacks. Members of the White elite found advantages in this arrangement. Necessary business transactions between the races could be conducted through mulattoes, whose presence reduced racial tensions, especially in areas where Negroes outnumbered Whites.

Prior to the Revolutionary War the free mulatto population of the Deep South was quite small, but it grew after the war. Ironically, the British, in seeking to defeat America's drive for independence, guaranteed freedom to any slave who escaped and joined their forces. Some slaves took advantage of the offer and remained free when the British surrendered. Other Negroes served in the Continental Army, since masters who were drafted were allowed to send their slaves as substitutes. Still other slaves took advantage of the wartime confusion to escape and hide among free Blacks. And finally, a few owners, caught up in the patriotic spirit, freed all their slaves when America declared its independence from England.

The resulting flood of manumitted and escaped Negroes darkened the free Black community. Accustomed by now to their unique status as a buffer class, the privileged mulattoes worried that Whites would associate them with these poorer, darker-skinned new arrivals. Social distinctions within the Colored and Creole communities were increasingly made on the basis of skin color and length of time a person had been free. Mulattoes living free in Charleston, South Carolina, and other cities intermingled and intermarried only with one another, and actively discriminated against those who were darker.

When revolutions rocked the West Indies in the 1790s, a wave of Creoles—also called "Creoles of Color" or "Black Creoles," depending on the extent of their African ancestry—fled to America, settling predominantly in Charleston and lower Louisiana. They came mostly from Haiti and Santo Domingo (formerly Saint-Domingue), and they brought with them their French Catholic culture, still evident in New Orleans today. A few were even wealthy, having benefited, like the mulattoes of the old South, from being members of a buffer class separating masters and slaves in the West Indies.

The color-conscious Creoles quickly rose to positions of power and influence within the Colored community, and before long being Creole in itself garnered respect. Outsiders found it difficult to penetrate the Creole population. Creoles' marriages were arranged so that the "purity" of their bloodline could be maintained. To this day, many older-generation Creoles see themselves as separate from other Blacks in America. In general, they resist the one-drop rule of racial identity, preferring a three-tiered system of racial classification in which they place themselves well above others considered simply as Black.

Free persons of color—the vast majority of whom were racially mixed—in the South were an unusual and often elite group prior to the Civil War. Some became leaders of the Black community, often with the sponsorship of a White parent. Throughout the era of slavery there were occasional masters who risked arrest by providing for the education of their mixed-race offspring or by arranging for them to escape when they were old enough. Some of these masters sent their mulatto children abroad, to the finest schools in Europe, and on their return the children became some of the earliest Black educators, doctors, and lawyers in America.

While before the Civil War the majority of those of African descent living free in the South were mulatto, most mulattoes of that era and region remained enslaved. Approximately 10 percent of the more than four hundred thousand slaves in the South before 1860 had some degree of White blood. Even among slaves, those with the lightest skin had the highest status, especially on the larger plantations. Coveted indoor assignments, including those as artisan, driver, valet, seamstress, cook, and housekeeper, were nearly always reserved for mulattoes, while the physically grueling fieldwork was typically left to slaves who were dark skinned. Masters considered mulattoes more intelligent and capable than pure Africans, who in turn were thought to be stronger and better able to tolerate the hot sun. Mulattoes also brought the highest prices on the slave market. As color increasingly divided the slave community, frictions developed in the cabins. Light-skinned slaves returning home from their days in the "big house" imitated the genteel ways of upper-class White families, and the mulatto offspring of the master often flaunted their education. Many field hands both envied and resented the house servants. Yet working in daily close proximity to a White master had its own risks, especially if one was female.

Rape was a fact of life on the plantations. At any time and in any place, female slaves were subject to the drunken or abusive sexual advances of a master, an overseer, a neighbor, or a master's son. Few Black women reached the age of sixteen without having been molested by a White male. Many White men longed to escape the suffocating effects of a Christian ethic that equated sex with sin. For many, the African women's dark skin was a fetish. Southern White males, who had nursed as infants at a slave's bosom, often later experienced their first real sexual pleasure as men in the arms of Black women. They fantasized about and fetishized these women's "animalistic" nature.

In some parts of the South, female mulattoes were actually bred and sold for huge profit on the female-slave market. Called "fancy girls," pretty quadroons (one-quarter Black) and exotic octoroons (one-eighth Black) were in especially high demand, and were quickly sold at "quadroon balls," auctions held regularly in New Orleans and Charleston. A respectable White gentleman might buy himself a concubine, and when he tired of her, six months or so later, he might get himself another one. Sometimes he found one he liked so much he kept her for life.

Some Whites lived openly with their Black female mistresses. One southerner, a man named William Adams, stipulated in his will that his Black concubine, Nancy, be set free upon his death and awarded a portion of his property. He even left money for the children he had fathered by her. However, Adams's White son was outraged by this directive and successfully contested his father's will in court. The judge declared Nancy and all of her children to be part of the son's estate.

The most famous and controversial case of a "White gentleman" keeping a mulatto concubine was that of Thomas Jefferson, principal author of the Declaration of Independence and third president of the United States. The concubine, Sally Hemings, was a light-skinned slave who worked for Jefferson, and was actually related to his wife, who passed away before Jefferson's alleged affair with Sally began. Sally had six light-skinned children altogether, and among her generations of descendants, it has long been accepted fact that Thomas Jefferson was one of their ancestors. From the Jefferson side of history, however, the rumors were always denied. In 1998, DNA tests were conducted to see if there was any familial link. We now know that some in Jefferson's family do share DNA with Sally Hemings's descendants, and while most believe that Thomas Jefferson was the one who fathered Sally's offspring, there are also those who continue to dispute this proposition.

In 2000, the Thomas Jefferson Foundation formed a research committee consisting of nine members of its staff, including four with PhDs. The committee looked at original documents, written and oral historical accounts, and statistical data and concluded that there was a high probability that Thomas Jefferson was the father of Sally's youngest child, Eston Hemings, and that he was perhaps the father of all six of Sally Hemings's children listed in Monticello records. But the Thomas Jefferson Heritage Society, an organization whose primary mission is "to further the honor and integrity of Thomas Jefferson . . . ," reviewed essentially the same material and reached a different conclusion, namely that Sally Hemings was only a minor figure in Thomas Jefferson's life and that it is very unlikely he fathered any of her children. Most scholars today support the findings of the Thomas Jefferson Foundation committee.

In the patriarchal South, the White wives and daughters of many plantation owners led lives in some ways almost as limited as that of a slave, although they were much better fed, clothed, and sheltered. In rebellion, some White women took secret lovers of their own. Less has been written about White women crossing the color line for sexual excitement, but there are known cases, and more than a few who even abandoned their husbands for dark-skinned men. Some White women even flaunted such affairs, talking openly about the Negro male's sexual prowess. In 1837, a Kentucky minister named John Rankin disclosed that the daughters of some of the finest White families had had affairs with their fathers' male slaves. Some White women also became involved with free men of color. One African man who lived in Louisiana, and who was described as having the "body of Hercules and . . . eyes as black as the moonless nights of Africa," kept two White concubines who produced a total of nineteen mulatto children.

Unlike the mulatto offspring of slave women, White women's racially mixed children disrupted the patriarchy. Mulattoes in the slave quarters were an economic asset, in the form of slave property, but a racially mixed child in the "big house" created havoc and shame. Because of the one-drop rule, the child was considered Black, but because the law defined a child's status as that of its mother, the child was also free. If the woman was married, her husband almost always filed for divorce. If she was single, her options were few: send the child away, usually north, to be reared by someone else; give the baby to a local slave family; or flee to the mountain country. Support for the existence of the latter choice comes from recent DNA evidence indicating that at least some Melungeons, an isolated population of non-Whites still living in Appalachia, were originally descended from the unions of White women and Black men, who then mixed with Native Americans, and are now believed to have then later mixed with Romani immigrants from Eastern Europe.

As the South came under increasing criticism from the North for its refusal to end slavery, racial and sexual tensions mounted. The former alliance between free mulattoes and Whites weakened, and in the Deep South, support for the three-tier system of racial classification crumbled. State after state moved in the direction of a two-class society racially divided by the one-drop rule.

By the time of the Civil War, sexual relations between Whites and Blacks had become less common in the South. The social upheaval and economic devastation brought on by the war did nothing to reverse the trend. Even after the war, when there was a shortage of White men, few White women turned to Black men as lovers or husbands. Vigilante groups like the Ku Klux Klan also had risen up, determined to keep the races apart.

Yet even if Whites and Blacks could be kept from ever intermingling again, "White genes" would continue to be disseminated through the Black community via the marriage of mulattoes to unmixed Blacks. Only a few Negro groups living in the most isolated rural areas, like the Angolan Blacks near the coast of South Carolina, would escape the dilution of their African genes. More than two centuries of race mixing between masters, slaves, and lovers, both White and Native American, had already produced a population of African Americans, Whites, and indigenous people who are all more racially mixed than they are pure.

Chapter 2

The Global Rise of Colorism

Color classism is a phenomenon that exists worldwide, with multiple root causes and consequences. Its beginnings can be traced back thousands of years, to the time when humans first began to transition from being nomadic to being agrarian. As crops were harvested and animals domesticated, land was increasingly claimed as personal property. Before long, differences in the amount of crops, animals, and land some individuals owned compared to others began to emerge, and those people with the most assets started farming out the chores to others. Spared from having to work in the hot sun all day, the wealthier landowners began to lose their tans, and to tout their lighter, tan-free skin as a sign of their greater wealth. Those who were more suntanned and thus of darker skin came to be stigmatized for their lack of resources. This is the story of how skin color became a highly visible and reliable indicator of social status, especially useful since it was a feature that was hard to fake.

By nature, we are status-seeking creatures, and thus it is not surprising that individuals with skin tones in the middle range began to emulate as best they could the looks of those with greater means. The status strivers became more conscientious about covering themselves up before going outside, but the permanent tattoo of tanned skin is hard to hide. The prejudice against tanned skin served the high-status people well. Proof of its effectiveness as a marker of status is that it evolved independently and concurrently in vastly different cultural regions around the globe.

From the earliest times, then, skin color has maintained an intimate relationship with class. Today, societal patterns involving skin color and class are better known as "color-class hierarchies." More precisely, that term is defined as a social, economic, and political societal framework that follows skin-color differences, such that along a continuum of possible shades, those with the lightest skin color enjoy the highest social standing, and those with the darkest skin color are among the poorest.

Color classism was ensconced in agrarian societies everywhere, but other, more insidious forms of prejudice and influence subsequently began to circle the globe on ships carrying the European explorers. In the wake of their imperialism there emerged what coauthor Hall came to name "the bleaching syndrome." Like "cosmetic Westernism," it reflects an internalized belief that having light skin and more Western-looking features makes someone more attractive. At first glance, the intense desire to emulate European features sounds like a larger and more encompassing preference under which the emergence of global color classism could be subsumed. However, the concepts differ in a crucial way. Preferences around skin color evolved slowly over thousands of years, and did so among vastly different cultures around the world because of the status associated with being spared from outdoor labor. But in the wake of

European conquerors, the bleaching syndrome swept through cultures worldwide like a giant tsunami washing out long-existing feature preferences that had nothing to do with skin being tan free.

To illustrate the difference, consider the fact that thousands of years ago, hundreds of different human groupings, with their own cultures, lived independently on every continent around the globe. Over centuries, each culture would have developed its own distinct preferences and criteria for what was deemed attractive among its members. The criteria would have taken into account race-related features such as eye shape and hair texture, and would have included the preference for having skin a shade or two lighter—or some cases darker—than the next guy, along with what evolutionary psychologists have identified as universal markers of attractiveness like feature symmetry and body proportions. Yet beyond the basics, each group also had its own culturally constructed notions of what makes for an attractive person and a desirable mate. In one culture, hair that was the most tightly curled might have come to be valued for its ability to support elaborate hairstyles; in another culture, eye color that was the darkest might have come to be valued for its contrast with White facial tones; and in yet a third culture, a nose with the widest structure might have come to be valued for its suitability for decorative piercing. While these invented examples are offered for purposes of illustration, we know from anthropologists and others that criteria for attractiveness varied significantly from one culture to the next, and that preferences did not mirror the features of Western populations.

Just one of the many devastating effects on indigenous populations that occurred when Europeans took over was that long-held culturally distinct values and preferences rapidly collapsed, to the point where even features unique to a people's own race began to be discarded and even hated. This is the legacy and ideology of the bleaching syndrome. In the name of survival, indigenous people learned it was better to abandon their ancestors' cherished beliefs, so as to resemble as much as possible those now in control, than it was to maintain the traditional ways but be ostracized and possibly made destitute as a result.

To summarize, thousands of years ago tan-free skin became a common marker of status in agrarian societies across diverse regions of the world. When indigenous populations were conquered by people from the West, who just happened to have lighter skin, the importance of having light skin color took on even greater significance. And then other cosmetic features associated with White Europeans came to be admired, internalized, and imitated.

We now turn to evidence of color classism across different continental regions. In this chapter we will identify some of the specific imitative cosmetic practices and procedures found in diverse populations. Discussion of how issues of color classism developed among African Americans, and what African Americans' unique cosmetic practices have been, is reserved for the next chapter.

We begin in Europe, a large continent with some fifty different countries or independent states. One might initially believe that the people of this continent would be exempt from the prejudices of colorism, as these individuals already possess the envied light skin color. But the truth is that, both historically and continuing into modern times, Europeans have displayed the same issues with color and class that have been observed in populations elsewhere in the world.

Given Europe's size and geographic spread, and its long history of human migration, it is not surprising that regionally based differences in physical attributes and appearance developed. For example, in the Scandinavian countries, as well as northern provinces of mid-European countries like Germany, individuals are frequently born with pale skin, blond hair, and blue eyes. To this day, the northernmost reaches of Europe remain the primary producer of "Nordic" traits, as collectively these attributes are called.

In western Europe, where England, Ireland, Scotland, and Wales are located, the most commonly shared physical feature would have to be very pale skin. Red hair and green eyes may be prominent among the Irish, but for most others born in the United Kingdom, hair is often a dirty-blond color and eyes may be hazel, green, or brown.

Traveling southward, completely different looks can be seen in the local populations. In southern Europe, in countries such as Italy, Spain, and Portugal, and in the Balkan region, which includes Greece and Turkey, people are more likely to have olive skin, brown hair, and brown eyes. Within a single country, geographically based differences can also appear. For many in Italy, it is the northern-born women with their blond hair and blue-green eyes who are to be considered the country's most beautiful. Southern Italians would naturally disagree with this assessment and assert instead that their women are not only the most beautiful but also the most representative of the Italian ideal of beauty.

Across eastern Europe, including parts of the Soviet Union, there are pockets in which the population has blond hair, blue eyes, and fair skin. Most of the eastern European populations do possess fairly light skin, but other features, such as hair and eye color, range widely. Women in this region seem to most prefer the Nordic features, and if they aren't born with them themselves, they often envy those who have them. It should be noted that wanting to possess certain features is not in itself evidence of color classism, but preferences can quickly turn into prejudice against those who lack the desired look.

This is nowhere better illustrated than in the negative attitudes that developed toward the distinctive features and slightly darker skin of many Jews, who, as a result of the Jewish Diaspora, had spread out around the world, with a critical mass settling in eastern Europe. Their slight difference in appearance, along with their "strange religious beliefs" and "curious customs," made them easy targets for discrimination, persecution, and ultimately murder. Jews fortunate enough to be born with lighter skin, hair, and eye color can sometimes pass themselves off as Christian, and those who could during World War II had greatly improved odds of surviving the Holocaust.[2] But confounding the usual pattern of color classism, prior to that sad chapter in history, Jews who were slightly darker skinned (relative to Europeans in general) were often far from poor. In fact, many were quite wealthy, as well as highly educated, cultured, and refined. Jewish people then were an affront to the "class" aspect of a traditional color-class hierarchy. It didn't seem to matter, or maybe it mattered more that Jews weren't properly poor; Hitler declared their continued existence a threat to the purity of the "Germanic race," and ordered them exterminated. The anti-Semitic views of Hitler and his followers were driven partly by White color-class prejudices, although that driving force is seldom recognized.

---

2.   To this day, the comment "You don't look Jewish" is nearly always intended by others to be a compliment and is sometimes received that way as well.

The Romani Gypsies, or Romani people, as they are known today, are another diasporic population living mostly in eastern Europe but also scattered elsewhere across the continent of Europe. They tend to have darker skin, darker hair, and darker eyes than the majority population, and like the Jews, they, too, were among the first populations to be marked for extermination by Hitler. It is estimated that between 250,000 and 1 million Romanis were killed in the Holocaust. Unlike the Jews, though, the Romanis were adrift in poverty before World War II, and have been afterward as well. In fact, for hundreds of years the social and economic circumstances of the Romani population as a whole have never been great.

Centuries of harsh treatment of the Romanis by lighter-skinned Europeans is a form of White colorism. And because of the Romanies' lower-class status, the prejudices did display the classic pattern of a color-class hierarchy.

Unlike the European Jews, many of whom gained sympathy after World War II, the Romanis, shockingly, faced continued efforts to exterminate them. In Scandinavian countries, where many of the Romanis had migrated during the sixteenth century, state-sponsored compulsory sterilization programs, some of which ran as late as the 1970s, forced "Gypsy-featured" women to undergo the procedure against their will. It is estimated that as many as sixty thousand Swedes, two thousand Norwegians, and six thousand Danes were made infertile by these countries' quest for Nordic "racial purity."

Today, throughout Europe there is rising discrimination, some of it violent, against darker-skinned immigrants. It is nearly always referred to as a form of racism, but a more accurate description is color discrimination. An ethnic group like the Algerians, with their slightly darker skin, is not a separate race—which is a social construct anyway. But that hasn't mattered to an anti-immigrant movement fueled by Islamophobia; the Algerians were just different looking enough to be marked as targets for hostility and resulting discrimination.

We now turn to the continent of Asia. Beginning with India, we don't have to look hard to find evidence of color-class hierarchies. For centuries, India's population practiced a rigid caste system that in some cases trumped differences in skin color. Across all castes of Hindus, there have always been dark-skinned people. Even the god Vishnu was praised for being "black as a full raincloud," and his incarnation Krishna is always depicted as having black or blue-black skin. That there was a distribution of skin colors across different castes is not to say, however, that skin color didn't matter to Indians. For example, as a group northern Indians are generally lighter than southern Indians, but within each of those two regions, the upper class tended to have relatively lighter skin color than others in the population. Thus skin color did have some associations with status, and skin lightness for women has long been a valued attribute. But as India fell under British rule in the eighteenth century, skin color assumed an even more significant role in the culture. As noted earlier, when White European imperial powers arrived, preexisting local customs and societal structures were rarely honored. Ignoring caste, the British simply gravitated toward those Indians of higher status, who also happened to have lighter skin color. In that way, lighter-toned skin increasingly became associated with the upper classes, and light-skinned individuals began to become more upwardly mobile, while the darkest-skinned Indians fell to the bottom of the economic ladder.

Though the caste system has long been legally abolished in

India, it should be no surprise that color prejudices persist. The most negative attitudes are reserved for the Dalits, who live not just in India but also in Bangladesh, Pakistan, and Nepal. Also called "Outcastes," and even more derogatorily "Untouchables" (as if dark skin were dirty and contagious), the Dalits are also among the darkest-skinned people in the Indian subcontinent.

Fear of being perceived as someone with unacceptably dark skin persists. Among many adult Indian women, memories of mothers warning them to get out of the sun remain vivid. The harsh reality, according to Indian parents, is that it is simply harder to marry off a darker-skinned daughter, especially if she is poor. So worried do some parents get about a daughter's dark skin ruining her chances for matrimony that they are willing to spend what little family money there is to buy skin lighteners for her to apply.

Over 30 percent of half a billion females in India admit to using skin-lightening products on a daily basis, and many more say they have tried them within the past year. As of 2010, the skin-lightening market in India alone was estimated to be worth well over $432 million, with 80 percent of that market controlled by Hindustan Unilever, the India-based division of the massive European corporation Unilever, which makes Fair & Lovely "fairness cream." While emerging market sales were less than expected in 2012, Unilever attributes the reduced profits to the worsening global economy, and certainly not to any increased consciousness about color prejudice.

An India-based company named Emami saw an untapped male market for skin lighteners, and in 2005 put out a product named "Fair and Handsome." Sales soared. Wanting in on the action, a year later Hindustan Unilever launched "Fair & Lovely Menz Active," which actually uses the same formula as its women's lightening cream but with a more masculine-sounding name. In July 2010, Vaseline, a division of Unilever, further cashed in on expanding sales for men worldwide with a new skin-lightening cream called "Vaseline Men." Aiming for a more urban and sophisticated male market, Unilever hired such celebrities as Shahid Kapoor, an Indian actor and star of many Bollywood films, and Michael Strahan, a former NFL football player, to endorse the product. But what was rather unsettling about the launching of "Vaseline Men" is that it came with the added feature of a skin-whitening app, whose download pitch is, "Transform your face on Facebook with Vaseline Men."

Critics of the skin-lightening industry claim that its advertising campaigns prey on fears of being dark skinned and left behind in a booming economy. The ads have been denounced as racist by activists who believe the emphasis on having light skin not only is a painful reminder of India's colonial past, but also serves to further marginalize and stigmatize Indians with darker skin. To these criticisms, manufacturers of products that Westernize features give a familiar response: that they are only responding to market demand. The entrepreneurs also typically claim they did not cause the desire, in this case a light-skin preference or a dark-skin prejudice. Ashok Venkatramani, a former vice president of Hindustan Unilever, views the profiting from skin-lightening products as being no different from making money off antiaging creams that prey on women's fears of looking old. "The definition of beauty in the Western world is linked to antiaging," he says. "In Asia it's about being two shades lighter."

But there also are those Indian women who view skin-lightening products as empowering. No longer will girls have to stay inside waiting for some future husband to find them acceptably light enough in skin color. Instead, modern Indian women (of the professional and middle classes) are stepping out into the world and claiming control over their bodies and lives. Indian feminists do not agree with this assessment of the massive popularity of these products and worry that women especially are being further manipulated into believing that light skin is the only acceptable skin color to have.

Despite such criticisms, skin lighteners continue to fly off the shelves. The products sell because they are effective. The melanin-suppressing property of hydroquinone (HQ) was accidentally discovered in 1938 by workers at a tannery in Waukegan, Illinois, when they noticed their skin turned blotchy after the company introduced a new leather-softening agent for them to use. HQ's potential market as a skin lightener was soon realized. Most skin-lightening products on the market today contain varying amounts of HQ, which is now known to be carcinogenic. Because of health risks associated with this chemical, skin-lightening products are required by law to contain no more than 2 percent HQ in their formulas. Still, some countries like Thailand and South Africa have assessed the risks and decided to legally ban sale of all HQ-containing products within their borders, though Internet and black-market sales have made enforcement of the ban close to impossible.

In East Asia, most notably in China, Japan, and the Philippines, light skin color has long been prized, especially for women. Near-white skin is an ancient feminine marker of beauty. But in what must have been a whiter-than-thou mentality, Japanese women took the light-skin beauty ideal all the way to no color at all. To properly achieve the desired alabaster look, women had to cover their faces in a powder. In having the whitest-skinned wives possible, peacock husbands could show how deep their financial pockets were in being able to afford the daily applications of cosmetic powder. The costs of creating the infamous white faces on geishas have also traditionally been covered by male clients.

Like India, Japan has had a class of citizens derisively called "untouchable." The official name of this minority group is Burakumin, and predictably the Burakumin are the ones with the darkest skin. The Burakumin were actually once slaves in Japan, assigned in the feudal Japanese caste system to jobs associated with death—as executioners, butchers, and undertakers. They were officially liberated in the nineteenth century. Nevertheless, prejudice against them remains.

Unsurprisingly, in Japan there continues to exist a strong desire to be lighter than one naturally is. White powder makeup is still popular, and according to a Nielsen global survey in 2007, 24 percent of Japanese women report having used a skin lightener at least once during the past year. Being sensitive to the desires of its many Asian markets, Unilever advertises the same ingredients found in Light & Lovely not as skin lighteners but as skin whiteners. The market is expected to grow.

The Philippines has a somewhat different history than other East Asian nations, as it was settled thousands of years ago and then again more recently by multiple ethnic groups. The earliest indigenous peoples were followed by East Asian immigrants, predominantly from China, who came ashore and mixed their blood with that of the natives. Then, much later, in the 1600s, White European explorers began colonizing Filipino territory, and bloodlines were mixed further still. Unlike China and Japan, the Philippines during the Age of Discovery endured more than three hundred years of colonial occupation, first by the Spanish and then later by Americans. The country did not gain full independence until 1946.

Like many other places around the world, the Philippines had in place an ancient system of color classism, inspired by prejudice against tanned skin, that preceded the arrival of European conquerors. But during the most recent four hundred years, the preference for lighter skin color took on greater meaning, as political power became aligned with the interests of White Europeans.

That preference has not lessened today, as evidenced by Filipino women who continue to avoid direct sunlight for prolonged periods of time. In America, many newly arrived female immigrants from the Philippines report being shocked by American attitudes toward tanning. They have just come from a place where getting tanned by the sun leads to a good scolding from older relatives, only to arrive in a country where the sun is worshipped. Then, when they return to their native country with suntan intact, an explanation for how they could let such a thing happen is demanded. It is time for skin lighteners to be applied. About 50 percent of Filipino women already report using a skin-lightening product in the past year; it is the population with the highest-frequency usage.

The first decade of the new millennium witnessed a rise in sales of skin-lightening products not only in Japan and the Philippines, but also in Korea and China. A 2007 Nielsen global survey found that 29 percent of South Koreans and 46 percent of Chinese had used a skin-lightening product within the past year. Unilever believes that China has even greater market potential than India for selling its skin-lightening products, perhaps up to $2 billion. And, like India, China is a country on the economic move, with a growing middle class and a rising number of professional working women with disposable incomes of their own to do with whatever they want.

In addition to using skin lighteners to "enhance" their attractiveness, many East Asian women (and a growing number of Asian men as well as Asian Americans) get double-eyelid surgery. Blepharoplasty, to use the medical term, is a cosmetic procedure that converts the one-fold eyelid into a structure with two folds. According to the International Society of Aesthetic Plastic Surgery in 2010, blepharoplasty, at 13.5 percent of all plastic surgical procedures performed worldwide, moved into third place behind only liposuction (18.8 percent) and breast augmentation (17 percent). (Not all blepharoplasty procedures are done on Asians, though, as many older White women also undergo the surgery in order to lift eyelids that have drooped from aging.) Contrary to many Westerners' beliefs, not every East Asian is born with the single-fold eyelid. In fact, only about half the population is, and even within the same family, some children may have one fold while others have two. Those who undergo the surgery say that the choice to do so is no different from that of a Westerner deciding to get a nose job. Among the reasons Asians (and Asian Americans) most commonly cite for getting double-eyelid surgery are a desire for eyes to look brighter and larger, for eyelashes to be more prominent, and for makeup to be applied more easily; a desire to appear more alert, intelligent, and outgoing; and a desire to avoid prejudice related to being perceived as lazy or sleepy. The results are referred to as "round eyes." On surveys and interviews, people never say the reason is that they want to appear more Western-like. And they may well be right about their motives; the first known double-eyelid surgery was performed in Japan in 1896, long before the influence of Western media.

Historically, the countries with the highest percentage of the population getting double-eyelid surgery are Japan, the Philippines, and South Korea, which now holds the dubious distinction of having the highest number per capita of its citizens who go under the knife. But as with the fast-growing market for skin lighteners across Asia, the procedure's popularity in China is also on the move. A recent survey of nearly sixteen hundred Chinese aged eighteen to fifty-five from Shanghai, Tianjin, and Shenzhen found that 29 percent of the women (and 33 percent of the men) either wanted or would consider double-eyelid surgery.

For the many Asians (and Asian Americans) who desire the surgery but simply cannot afford it, there are cheaper alternatives for achieving the same effect. There is a noninvasive technique that relies on stitches to raise the lower part of the eyelid to the top part, thereby making two folds appear. It's still rather expensive, though, costing about $1,000, and it has to be redone every year or two. And for those who can't afford even that, or who just want to experiment with how they might look with double eyelids, there is an over-the-counter product. About $10 will get you fifty pairs of clear-colored tiny strips of double-faced tape that can be applied daily to glue the lower part of the eyelid upward to create the desired fold.

There is no doubt some merit to arguments that skin lighteners and double-eyelid surgical procedures are not always due to colonialism or White-dominated media influence, but it is more difficult to swallow explanations given to account for other trends in cosmetic adjustments among Asians. In the survey mentioned above, about 30 percent of Chinese women said they wanted their faces to be more oval (and less round), and their breasts to be larger, legs to be longer, and bodies overall to be skinnier. Put all these attributes together and you have yourself, as Adam Sandler might sing, one fine-looking European. Or as a Beijing-based cosmetic surgeon bluntly put it, "Chinese women just want to look more Caucasian."

In the Arab world, preferences and prejudices around skin color date from ancient times to the modern day, with the lightest-skinned women long serving as the gold standard of beauty. Several expressions capture attitudes about skin tones. The highest admiration is reserved for women who are "as white as snow," a curious descriptor in a land where snow rarely falls. Beneath them are women called "golden," followed by "wheatish," and so on, along the spectrum until you arrive at "*akhdhar,*" a polite term for "black." Yet there also is an ancient Moroccan proverb that warns young men against the superficial attractions of the pale-skinned wife: "A fertile Negress is better than a sterile White woman." Throughout the Muslim world, the upper class is generally likely to be light skinned and the lower classes are likely to be dark.

Products and procedures that can render women more Western-like are gaining in popularity in the Middle East. As *Al-Ahram,* the Arab world's most influential news medium, recently reported regarding the trend:

> *An ever-increasing number of well-heeled Egyptian women are desperately resorting to skin-lightening creams, light-tinted contact lenses and hair-bleaching dyes in an often farcical attempt to attain the golden-locked look. The Whitening of Egypt has become a lucrative industry.*

Al-Ahram blames this desire to be lighter on a color hierarchy imprinted in our psyches through centuries of White colonial supremacy. Thus even in countries generally hostile to Western culture and capitalism, there still can be found women chasing Eurocentric ideals of beauty.

Within Africa there are indigenous populations whose skin color is the darkest on earth, but there are also regions of the continent where the current population has skin color that is light enough to pass as White European. It is ill advised, then, to make any generalizations about a continent with fifty-five countries and an estimated three thousand different "people groups" (the preferred term for tribes) who dwell in landscapes that include deserts, plains, mountains, and rain forests. But there are growing urban population centers as well. With all this cultural diversity, it seems likely that there were many places in Africa where light skin developed an association with high social standing, especially for females. And we can further assume that it was the arrival of White colonists during the Age of Discovery that stirred up a hornet's nest of new feelings about skin color.

Typically, when European imperialists came across people groups of differing skin colors, they treated those with lighter skin better, falsely assuming them to be more intelligent. Many historians believe that the European colonists who until the early 1960s occupied the land now called Rwanda are partly to blame for the tensions between the Hutu and Tutsi peoples, which erupted in the 1993–1994 genocide that resulted in the death of a half million Tutsis. At the time of the genocide, the Tutsis were only about 15 percent of the population, but due to a legacy of preferential treatment from the German and Belgian colonists who had controlled that part of central Africa for centuries, the Tutsis held much of the land, wealth, and power. This did not sit well with the majority Hutus, who initially staged a rebellion in 1959, and then after years of ever-increasing conflict between the two groups eventually ordered the mass killing of Tutsis that took place in 1994.

Ironically, Americans of African descent also contributed to the development of color classism in Africa, in particular in

Liberia, where some had resettled during the nineteenth century. While many of the original American Blacks who went to Africa were dark skinned themselves, some of their offspring started defining social class by relative lightness of skin color. Those with the greatest proportion of European ancestry began to assume higher positions of power and status. To this day, Liberia's two political parties reflect a difference in average skin color, with the Republicans generally being more light skinned and the True Whigs generally being more dark skinned.

Unsurprisingly, skin lightening is practiced and gaining in popularity across Africa today. For most African women, though, the starting point from which the pigment-suppressing chemicals are to achieve their desired effect is significantly darker, and thus instead of simply brightening a light brown skin color, the products can turn very dark skin a yellowish orange. Africanist scholar Alice Windom, who served as the coordinator for the James T. Bush Center at the University of Missouri–St. Louis, has studied how the arrival of Europeans in Africa began to affect the indigenous cultures. While in Africa in the 1960s, Windom observed a number of dark-skinned African women, mostly in countries formerly under British rule, using bleaching creams and special soaps so that they, too, could look "English." Some urban Zambian women began applying bleaching products so strong that government officials criticized them for having "Fanta faces and Coca-Cola bodies"—Fanta being a popular orange-colored carbonated beverage.

Nonetheless, skin lighteners are lucrative business on the "dark" continent, a region of the world that also has become a dumping ground for products banned elsewhere because of their dangerously high (4 percent) levels of HQ. Even more harmful than using a 4 percent HQ solution is the practice followed by some very poor African women desperate to look lighter, who are creating their own homemade preparations, into which they mix everything from toothpaste, shampoo, and milk to household bleach, cement, and brake fluid. Just about anything that has a corrosive effect on the skin will do. During the early 1990s, coauthor Hall named this intense desire to lighten one's skin "the bleaching syndrome." Kelly Lewis and three of her research colleagues recently published findings from interviews with forty-two women from Tanzania who practiced skin bleaching. While the African women's motivations for bleaching varied, it is indicative of the nation's colonial roots that one of the reasons offered was "to be White, 'beautiful,' and more European looking."

Also increasingly common in modern African cities is the use of hair-straightening products, along with hair weaves and wigs. There is even a line of African hair care products called Nairobi, after the capital of Kenya, which is considered by many the best place in all of Africa for hair straightening. When asked why she goes for the scalp burn, a process described more fully in our chapter on hair, a customer at Queens Hair Designers in Nairobi says, "It's so easy to manage because I have a lot of hair. I love it." She makes no mention of wanting to look like a White woman or to have more European-textured hair.

Throughout Central and South America, color-class hierarchies similarly formed in the wake of conquering colonial imperialists, who claimed for themselves vast areas of land previously held by brown-skinned indigenous people. The White Europeans imported thousands of dark-skinned Africans to work as slaves, and the predictable result was a lot of race mixing. The history of how color classism developed in Latin American countries was discussed more fully in the first chapter, so here we confine our discussion to evidence of its continued existence and current cosmetic practices.

Brazil, a country whose population reflects the African Diaspora, has the world's second-largest population of Blacks, and provides strong evidence of persistent patterns of color classism. The southern parts of Brazil are where the descendants of the original European immigrants settled, and the inhabitants are generally far wealthier and lighter skinned than most other Brazilians. By one estimate, close to 80 percent of that region's population consider themselves "*blanco,*" or White. Brazil's industrial economic base lies in southern Brazil, and much of the area is urbanized. Nearby southeastern Brazil, where the capital city, São Paulo, can be found, along with the number one tourist destination of Rio de Janeiro, is also dominated by a majority of Whites, although there is much greater diversity here than in southern Brazil. In the northern and northeastern regions of Brazil, where the highest proportion of African slave descendants now live, there are some small pockets of extreme wealth where Whites and racially mixed individuals dwell, but much of the population living in these regions is mired in extreme poverty. In fact, northern Brazil has the dubious distinction of having the country's highest index of inequality, meaning that the wealth gap between those with the highest income and those with the lowest income is the greatest. To no one's shock, those with the absolutely darkest skin color are the poorest of the poor.

South America has been curiously resistant to widespread use of skin lighteners. Products like Fair & Lovely that sell well in Asia are not that popular in this part of the world. Some race activists fear, however, that a strong advertising campaign by a big corporation like Unilever, always primed to profit more, could create a demand for skin-lightening products where none existed before. This is not to say that skin-lightening products are making no inroads into Latin America. In fact, in the West Indies such products have been used for years. When former Major League right fielder Sammy Sosa, who hails from the Dominican Republic, suddenly appeared to be much lighter skinned in November 2009, it was obvious that he had used some product or procedure. By May 2010, media reports indicated that Sosa was back to his original color. But Jamaican reggae musician Vybz Kartel, whose own skin has become progressively lighter over the years, celebrates his use of a skin-lightening product known as Cake Soap[3] in a song of the same title. While Caribbean studies scholar Donna Hope finds this appropriation by men of the light-skin female aesthetic to be an interesting phenomenon, Kartel seems not to care that he is crossing gender boundaries. In fact, he once asserted, "When black women stop straightening their hair and wearing wigs and weaves, when white women stop getting lip and butt injections and implants . . . then I'll stop using the 'cake soap' and we'll all live naturally ever after."

Dyeing one's hair lighter seems to be a growing practice in countries like Brazil, Chile, Argentina, and Venezuela, although no statistics for this observation can be found. But the percentage of blond Latin American women in the media is far above that of natural blondes in the population. Examples include television stars like Venezuela's Carolina Tejera; like Cristina Saralegui in Cuba, Luisana Lopilato ("Luli") in Argentina, and Maria da Graça Meneghel ("Xuxa") in Brazil; models such as

---

3.   Cake Soap is manufactured by the Jamaican-owned company Blue Power Group Limited, which claims its product was developed for use as a laundry detergent, and denies any association with the dancehall artist Kartel.

the Colombian Sandra Muñoz and the Argentinean Valeria Mazza; and others, like Paulina Rubio, the Mexican singer-actress. The relatively high frequency of Latina blond-haired celebrities like these women sends a strong message to others about what it takes to be successful in the media. But when it comes to well-known U.S.-born Latina actresses—beauties such as Eva Longoria, Jennifer Lopez, and Rosario Dawson—dark brown hair and eyes would seem to be preferred, perhaps to more clearly mark their "exotic" credentials. Apparently, though, looking exotic is a minus for some media purposes. In a 2012 casting call for a promotional film for the New Mexico Office of Tourism, the announcement specified that one of the requirements for auditioning was that actors look "Caucasian or light-skinned Hispanic."

In what would appear to be a radical departure from cosmetic Westernism, the most popular surgical procedure among Brazilian women involves a lifting of the buttocks. If ever there was a body feature that had zero ties to a White European beauty aesthetic, this would be the one. Yet the typical Brazilian female desires a round, taut rear end and is willing to pay good money to achieve the look. And apparently, so do an increasing number of others; the procedure has become so popular in Miami, Beverly Hills, and elsewhere in the United States that it is now called a "Brazilian butt lift."

Another fascinating factoid about Brazil is that it is the country with the second-highest percentage of its population who undergo plastic surgery. So popular and inexpensive has plastic surgery become in Brazil that thousands from around the world go there for the sole purpose of having a procedure performed. The medical tourism trade is lucrative business for the country. Not far behind in the acceptance and popularity of plastic surgery are Venezuelan women. Since 1979, they have won the Miss Universe title six times. Since padding, cosmetic dentistry, and plastic surgery are now being permitted in this beauty pageant, there is no doubt that at least some, if not all, of the Venezuelan contestants underwent the knife beforehand.

In our global review of color-class hierarchies, we now head northward to the United States. Starting in the 1600s and continuing well into the next two centuries, waves of immigrants from western Europe and especially England started coming to the new country. With the start of the Industrial Revolution in the 1700s, England itself was also undergoing major changes. It was during this period of history that new attitudes of White colorism began to form among the English, especially the new urbanites. Prior to the Industrial Revolution, there was basically a two-tiered class system in England, the upper class with its relatively small number of titled families and members of royalty, and the common class, made up of the rest, the large number of farmers and servants. The Industrial Revolution opened up new opportunities for members of the less-privileged class. Families that for generations had tilled the land, raised livestock, or practiced a trade began flocking to the cities to find work in newly opened factories and merchant shops. England began to develop a substantial middle class, and newly belonging members sought ways to distance themselves from their recent humble past, through cultivated prejudices against those still working the land. When farm families came to the cities to sell their produce, they were easy to spot because of their suntanned faces (even in cloudy England). Before long, pale skin came to signify the more prosperous middle-class people who largely worked inside, or at least not under the hot sun all day. For the reputation-conscious Englishman, having pale-skinned family members, especially a wife and daughter(s) who were additionally fragile appearing, was an effective way to broadcast his new financial viability. After all, if a man's family was free of suntan, it meant no one except himself need be providing for them, unlike those hearty but sunburned families living down on the farm, where everyone had to contribute to the family's survival. Albeit for slightly different reasons than what had developed in the global agrarian societies, skin that was tan free in England similarly came to represent prosperity.

The idealization of pale skin was imported to America—where it may have developed in any case—especially in the antebellum South. Farmers there, increasingly called "plantation owners," similarly made a living off the land, but unlike their farming cousins back in England, some of these men became quite wealthy from owning huge tracts of land, raising profitable crops like tobacco and cotton, and, most important, having slaves perform all the labor. As has happened many times elsewhere around the world, skin that was not tanned emerged as a signifier of higher social standing.

What has not been mentioned thus far is the relationship between patriarchy and color-class hierarchies. Color classism flourishes best in societies where men own women, where daughters are little more than burdens to unload, and where women's opportunities for advanced education are limited. In such cultures, a man calls all the shots, and if having a light-skinned wife and a pale-skinned daughter is what it takes for him to be noticed as successful in society, then female offspring will have no choice but to fall in line. Across history and geography, it has mattered little whether a young woman was the daughter of a wealthy colonial landowner in Latin America, a brown-skinned ruler in the Middle East, an ebony king in

Africa, or a lowly sunburned farmer just about anywhere else; it fell on her pale shoulders to preserve the family's perceived societal status by staying as light as possible. That was the patriarchal structure under which she lived until the day she married, at which time control of her life would be transferred from her father to the new husband.

White plantation owners in the American South were no different; southern ladies stayed indoors during daytime hours, while proper gentlemen, liberated from the demands of plantation labor, were free to engage in various leisure activities such as riding, hunting, and fishing. In fact, a certain amount of tan on the men's faces was fine—even good—as it demonstrated their vigor and sportsmanship. But skin touched by the sun was decidedly not acceptable on women and especially on daughters as they approached marriageable age. If a girl did have reason to venture outdoors during daytime hours, she had to carefully cover herself from head to toe. Anyone who has seen the film *Gone with the Wind* (1939) likely recalls the famous scene in which Mammy, played by Hattie McDaniel, fusses at Scarlett, played by Vivian Leigh, for not properly covering herself, saying, "Keep yo' shawl on yo' shoulders. Ah ain' aimin' fo' you to git all freckled after de buttermilk Ah done put on you all dis winter, bleachin' dem freckles." Daughters in less-affluent farm families had no mammies covering them with buttermilk, and no exemption from working the fields like everyone else in their family. But the poorer girls did what they could to distance themselves from the stigma of suntan, so they too wore hats and long sleeves when outside, even though they could never truly emulate the pale skin color of those plantation girls who seemed to have life so easy.

Today, prejudice against tanned skin has abated. In fact, the relationship between perceived social class and tanned skin among Whites seems to have reversed itself. But while it may seem odd that many Whites want to darken their skin with a suntan, the underlying status-driven motive to emulate those who are wealthier than themselves remains intact. Pale skin may once have meant someone was spared from outdoor labor, but after the Industrial Revolution, when much of the working class left farms for factories, paleness came to signify being a lowly indoor factory worker. Meanwhile, those financially able were enjoying greater leisure time, and when the jet age arrived, the wealthiest of the wealthy began to migrate to warmer climates during cold weather. Suddenly, having a tan, especially during winter, signified one had both the time and the money to go elsewhere to do nothing more than lie out in the sun all day. Now, of course, a tan on someone in the dead of winter may only mean he or she has enough cash to visit the local tanning salon.

Even while attitudes about being suntanned were undergoing revision, prejudice against Whites whose skin was slightly darker than that of most Western Europeans was on the rise, as evidenced by the passage of the Immigration Act of 1924. Its primary agenda seems to have been that of limiting the number of immigrants from eastern and southern Europe, who often had olive-toned skin (and were often poor), and who had been pouring into the United States after World War I. Given the already huge influx of poor Irish coming to America since the mid-nineteenth century, anti-immigration attitudes were on the rise. And while the Irish certainly didn't darken the overall population, the old prejudice against those who potentially could was being activated.

To this day, many White Americans, especially women, still

strive to achieve a western European look, specifically one that is northern European, or Nordic.[4] Even at a time in history when the criteria for defining beauty have been expanding, it would seem the pinnacle of ideal feminine beauty remains that of a White woman with pale skin, blond hair, and blue eyes. Other than perhaps the rarity of such features in the human gene pool, it is hard to pinpoint exactly why this particular combination of physical attributes, out of all possible others, became the gold standard of femininity. Whatever the reason, White women are "dyeing" to be blond. One survey found that among White college females who chemically alter their natural hair color, 48 percent self-reported that they dyed it blond or blonder, 8 percent said that they dyed their hair to make it darker, and the rest said they did so for reasons of maintenance. The high number of "suicide blondes"[5] remains steady, but the percentage of natural blondes in the American population has been dropping in recent decades. In 1980, the figure was 25 percent, but in 2003, it was only 16 percent, with one study putting the percentage of natural adult blondes in the American population as low as 4 percent.

In addition to lightening their hair color, White American women also like to lighten their eye color. Less than 20 percent of Americans have naturally occurring blue eye color, but sales figures from International Lens Incorporated, a company that sells tinted contact lenses directly to doctors, suggest that a very high percentage of its business comes from the sale of blue lenses alone.

---

4. Light skin, blond hair, and blue eyes are features that most commonly occur in the Nordic region of Europe where the Scandinavian countries are located.

5. A "suicide blonde" is someone who must dye/die her hair blond—a double entendre made popular in the 1990 hit of the same name by the rock band INXS.

Yet there is no known economic advantage in having blond hair or blue eyes in this country. Think of impoverished pale-skinned girls with blond hair living in Appalachia. The Nordic preference is neither institutionalized nor political (except perhaps by White supremacists who are alarmed at the decline of blond hair and blue eyes in the American population). Thus while certain similarities may exist between White women and women of color in chasing a particular look, the intensity of motives or consequences for not achieving the preferred look are not the same. The average American man is not going to refuse to marry a woman because she has brown hair and dark eyes, but in India, a prospective husband in an arranged marriage might very well reject a bridal candidate simply because her skin is thought too dark.

As long as the Western world controls economic and primary media resources, preferences for lighter skin will continue to organize into color classism. Once these prejudices infect those in the upper echelons of society, they spread to others wishing to move upward socially. The result is like an illness contaminating one population after another with unhealthy attitudes of color classism.

Chapter 3

The Tiers of Color Prejudice in America

The pattern of color classism that emerged in the United States was profoundly different from what developed in other countries around the world. The primary reason had to do with how racial identity came to be defined in America. In other nations, looking White was enough to make one White, but in the United States, a person who had even a smidgen of African ancestry was legally defined and expected to socially identify as Black. The result was that instead of the more commonly observed single continuum of color classism in which skin color ranged from dark to light along with correlating low and high economic and social status, the United States developed a curious two-tiered system. Occupying the top tier were White Americans whose average income and status were higher than those in the lower tier, and whose range in skin color was fairly minimal, with no observable differences in income or status based on color alone. In contrast, African Americans were forced into a lower tier where large variations in skin color existed, even to the point where some of its lightest members were as light or lighter in skin color than a small percentage of those in the top tier. It was only within this lower tier that the more classic pattern of color classism emerged in this country.

Over time, this curiously defined two-tier system of race and color managed to create both racial disparity and racial solidarity. African Americans had to contend with and figure out how to respond to not only brutal racism from above, but also issues of color prejudice from within. In short, the original one-drop rule of racial identity turned into a storm of issues that has rained down upon this country ever since.

The resulting societal problems began—as so many others have—with slavery and colonialism. Initially, Africans were captured by fellow Africans through local tribal warfare, and then subsequently sold to European sailors who brought them to the New World to sell again to White plantation owners. The captured Africans were stuffed into small ships with unimaginably filthy conditions. A death rate of anywhere from one-quarter to one-third of the slaves on board was expected and taken into account when figuring profits of each Middle Passage journey. The Africans who did survive the long crossing disembarked into a strange new world, and while they were perhaps grateful to be alive, their cultural roots were for the most part dead. It is hard to imagine any other experience being more emotionally uprooting than what these brave Africans were forced to endure in coming to America.

Once onshore, the Africans probably experienced a shared sense of having survived the horrible journey together, and once sold, they likely were united in their opposition to the White slave masters. But as a result of the White masters' actions, cracks in any once-held feelings of solidarity among the Africans and their descendants started occurring in the slave cabins of the antebellum South. Slave owners began to favor the lighter-skinned slaves, some of whom were actually the owners' own progeny from prior sexual assaults. The preference for lighter-skinned slaves was displayed in their master's choosing of them to work in the "big house," an easier work assignment than cultivating and harvesting crops under the hot sun all day. That kind of hard labor was reserved for the medium- and darker-skinned slaves, as well as any light-skinned slaves not among the chosen few. For the slaves who were the master's offspring, assigning them to work in the house enabled him to keep a close eye on them, but even when that was not applicable, most Whites in the era assumed, wrongly of course, that slaves whose blood was mixed with that of Whites had greater intelligence, and thus were better able to learn the more nuanced chores of indoor work. It did not take long for the lighter-skinned house slaves to internalize certain assumptions about themselves, and more than a few did begin to internalize this sense of superiority about themselves relative to their darker-skinned compatriots. But at the end of the day—every day—they were still the property of someone else. From the point of view of the light-skinned slaves, the truly fortunate racially mixed Blacks were the free mulattoes.

Living mostly in the seaport towns of Charleston and New Orleans, mulattoes came to serve as an economic bridge between Whites and slaves. Necessary transactions between the two races passed through the mulattoes' hands and generally did so without incident. Sometimes mulattoes even purchased homes and set up businesses not far from where Whites lived and worked. In the shadow of the "peculiar institution" of slavery, then, there existed this curious society where Whites and Blacks largely interacted with decorum and civility.

Everything changed when the Civil War broke out, and especially afterward during Reconstruction. Tensions grew between the races, and it was as though overnight all the Whites who before the war had treated free mulattoes with a modicum of respect were now blaming them as much as the newly freed slaves for the South's defeat and resulting misery. But the frustrated free mulattoes felt they actually had more in common with White southerners, who had similarly lost property, prosperity, and profession as a result of the war, than they did with the uneducated slave masses. However, not shared with White southerners was the growing backlash of racism and pure hatred directed at free mulattoes, as much at them as at the recently freed slaves.

The mulatto elite no longer had the distinction of freedom to separate them from the generally darker-skinned slaves, and they no longer enjoyed support from White southerners who used to treat them decently. What they did still have, and very much clung to, was their former elevated status. They thus sought ways to preserve it, such as making a distinction between what they were to be called and what Negroes newly freed by the Emancipation Proclamation were to be called. The mulattoes referred to those freed by the proclamation as "sot-free," while for themselves they reserved the title of "bona fide free." They also started referring to themselves as the mulatto elite to further distinguish themselves from other mulattoes who were among the "sot-free."

To secure their status, the mulatto elite began establishing their own private social clubs, churches, neighborhoods, educational institutions, and business organizations. Most notable among the social clubs, whose stated purpose was to provide opportunities for the mulatto elite to exclusively meet and mingle with one other, were the Bon Ton Society of Washington, DC, and the Blue Vein Society (BVS) of Nashville. The mulattoes actively promoted the idea that only they possessed the finest of bloodlines, and being a "blue veiner" or a "bon tonner" was an enormous honor. In reality, admission to the clubs depended not so much on bloodlines, although family membership did count for a lot, as it did on skin color, the visible marker of the mulatto elite's higher status. To join a BVS, an applicant's skin had to be fair enough for the spidery network of veins at the wrist to be visible to a panel of expert judges, hence the name. Mulatto elite offspring who happened to be born somewhat darker skinned than other members of the family no doubt had a harder time being accepted into such a highly color-conscious environment.

People today look back on these social clubs and see them as preposterous. But in defense of the mulatto elite, it needs to be said that they only did what other high-status people have always done in establishing their own exclusive social clubs, business organizations, and congregations. Prosperous White Protestants have long built private country clubs and restricted membership on the basis of social connections, wealth, and religion. The primary difference was that, unlike Whites, upper-crust Blacks used the immutable physical characteristic of skin color to screen membership.

During the early decades of the twentieth century, an ever-increasing number of Blacks—mulattoes and otherwise—did begin to see the blue veiners as ridiculous. They derogatorily referred to their clubs as "blue *vain* societies." Some, like African-American writer Wallace Thurman, were actually quite alarmed by the groups' racist agenda. To raise awareness of what he saw as these clubs' real intention, Thurman mocked their existence by including a fictitious credo for a Blue Vein–like club in his 1929 novel *The Blacker the Berry:*

> *Whiter and whiter, every generation. The nearer white you are the more white people will respect you. Therefore all light Negroes marry light Negroes. Continue to do so generation after generation, and eventually white people will accept this racially bastard aristocracy, thus enabling those Negroes who really matter to escape the social and economic inferiority of the American Negro.*

Not until after the Black Renaissance of the 1920s did the influence and prevalence of the mulatto social clubs begin to weaken. By the end of the 1970s, all but a few had fallen into disfavor. But what is interesting is that some of these social clubs have enjoyed a resurgence of sorts among African Americans, especially those living in predominantly White suburbs. Founded in 1938, Jack and Jill of America is one of the social clubs that used to regularly exclude darker-skinned applicants from membership, but no longer do. These clubs appear to be serving a need for professional and upper-middle-class families. Suburban African-American parents in particular worry that their children, who mostly attend predominantly White schools, are not being sufficiently exposed to African-American culture. Nor are their children properly meeting other nice young men and women of the same race and socioeconomic class. But they can do just that at various Jack and Jill social functions.

Many historical African-American churches similarly had congregations with noticeably lighter skin tones, and were known to actively turn away darker-skinned Blacks. Even though such discrimination doesn't sound very Christian, given the social importance of churches in the Black community, it is not surprising that they, too, functioned not dissimilarly from the exclusive social clubs.

During Reconstruction, Black families interested in joining a congregation—or an individual simply wanting to set foot inside a particular church on Sunday morning—might first be required to pass a paper bag test, a door test, and/or a comb test. The paper bag test involved placing an arm inside a brown paper bag, and only if the skin on the arm was lighter than the color of the bag would a prospective member be invited to attend church services. Other churches painted their doors a light shade of brown, and anyone whose skin was darker than the door was politely invited to seek religious services elsewhere. And in still other "houses of worship" throughout Virginia, and in such cities as Philadelphia and New Orleans, a fine-tooth comb was hung on a rope near the front entrance. If one's hair was too nappy and it snagged in the comb, entry was denied.

Although qualifying tests for church membership have long since disappeared, the congregations of some Black society churches remained noticeably lighter than others. Inside these churches one hears none of the loud gospel singing, hand clapping, or foot stomping stereotypically associated with Black churches. St. Mark's Episcopal Church in Charleston, for example, was where the mulatto elite went, and to this day, lighter-skinned African Americans can still be seen going to this church on Sunday mornings. (In the past twenty years, St. Marks's congregation has become more racially mixed with close to 20 percent of it now being White.) Meanwhile, across town there was the Emanuel African Methodist Episcopal Church, where those deemed too dark (or for any other reason) to join St. Mark could go for services. Similarly, in Atlanta there is the St. Mark United Methodist Church, where proportionately more lighter-skinned African Americans attend. Some locals there even joke that no one can join the St. Mark Church unless the person's skin is as light as the lightest faces in the stained-glass windows. And in Savannah there is St. Stephen's Episcopal Church, which used to be described as a BVS (Blue Vein Society) church, where exclusively lighter-skinned African Americans attended.

The congregations of many White Protestant churches are similarly very class conscious. There is always at least one church in any large city where the "very best people" go, meaning those who are the wealthiest in town. This is true for Jewish synagogues, as well, with some of them catering to the most affluent, and possibly costing a lot more to join. The only difference between these practices and what the Black community did is that the latter denied membership on the basis of skin color or hair texture.

The mulatto elite began to segregate into their own neighborhoods, and to this day, virtually every major urban center across the country has a section where predominantly light-skinned and wealthier African Americans reside. In Philadelphia, they live in areas unofficially called "lighty bright" and "banana block." In Chicago, the Black bourgeoisie can be found in Chatham and East Hyde Park (where the Obamas have their home), and in New York, descendants of the original light-skinned mulatto elite can still be found among the residents of certain sections of Harlem, including Sugar Hill—so called because the people who live there are said to lead such a "sweet" life—and Strivers Row, located between West 138th and West 139th Streets and Seventh and Eighth Avenues. Harlem Congressman Adam Clayton Powell Sr. wrote of living there in the 1940s, when that neighborhood was still very much in vogue:

> [I]n Strivers Row . . . were the dowagers of Harlem's society. These queenly, sometimes portly, and nearly always light-skinned Czarinas presided over the Harlem upper class. . . . There was an open door for all who were light-skinned and for most of those of the professional group. The entire pattern of society was white. . . . [And] if invited Harlemites brought with them [to a social function] their dark-skinned friends, they were shunned and sometimes pointedly asked to leave.

Perhaps the most insidious form of color-class discrimination that took place was at the educational institutions established by the mulatto elite. Dark-skinned Blacks were routinely denied admission to these schools regardless of their academic qualifications. According to Stephen Birmingham, in his book *Certain People*, headmistress Dr. Charlotte Hawkins Brown of the Palmer Institute in Sedalia, North Carolina, one of the more prestigious Black preparatory schools in the country, was careful to avoid using the terms "Black" and "Colored" in discussions with or about the light-skinned, fine-featured students who went there. Instead, Brown would always say "one of us" or "our kind." Although having light skin and certain features might signal illegitimacy in one's slave past, Dr. Brown apparently thought it was not such a bad thing to have a White ancestor or two somewhere back in the family tree. A similar attitude prevailed in New Orleans at St. Mary's Academy for Young Ladies of Color, a finishing school for the daughters of well-to-do Creoles. The occasional dark-skinned student who did manage to get accepted at these schools was often ostracized. At the legendary M Street High School (later renamed Dunbar High School) in Washington, DC, a graduate of 1905 claimed that while a dark-skinned youth might receive a good education there, the children of the old mulatto families would never accept him as a social equal. These schools were extremely important, since friendships formed early in life were often the basis for useful political and business contacts later on.

Biased admission policies prevailed at many historic Black colleges and universities (HBCUs), such as Wilberforce in Ohio (1856), Howard in Washington, DC (1867), Fisk University in Nashville (1866), Atlanta University in Georgia (1865), Morgan State (today Morgan State University) in Baltimore (1867), Hampton Institute (today Hampton University) in Virginia (1868), and the Atlanta Baptist Female Seminary (today Spelman College) in Georgia (1881). In their early years, some of these institutions also had skin-color tests for applicants to pass. In 1916, it was estimated that 80 percent of students attending HBCUs were light skinned and/or of mixed ancestry.

A principal mission of an HBCU was to groom the mulatto elite in the genteel mores of the bourgeoisie, while delivering a strong traditional liberal arts education. Many academic administrators of these schools considered it a waste of time to educate dark-skinned Negroes for paths in life that would be closed to them. Denied a liberal arts education, dark-skinned students would turn to schools like Tuskegee Institute in Alabama, founded in 1881 by Booker T. Washington, if they wanted to pursue education beyond a high school degree. But Tuskegee offered Black students a strictly vocational curriculum of "industrial education" because Washington thought that Negroes, particularly those who were not members of the elite, should concentrate their energies on becoming skilled workers. Another college president who rejected the model of a liberal arts education in favor of vocational training was Mary McLeod Bethune, a woman of blue-black coloring who established the Bethune-Cookman College in Daytona Beach, Florida, in 1927. Her institution, originally called the Daytona School for Girls, was founded expressly for "Black girls," and not the fair-skinned daughters of doctors, lawyers, and clergymen who attended Palmer. Bethune students took a curriculum of basic skills, including home economics, cooking, and even housekeeping, so that upon graduation they would be fully prepared to do real work in the real world.

Advocates of industrial education were likely to be darker skinned, while proponents of a liberal arts education tended to be light skinned. Sadly, even as evidence mounted that industrial training did nothing more than channel dark-skinned Blacks into low-paying menial jobs, the separate educational paths taken by light-skinned mulattoes and dark-skinned students were already laid out, reinforced by the existence of a color-class hierarchy.

Although skin color no longer determines which college one can attend or what kind of education one can pursue, it still seems to affect the educational and occupational aspirations of African-American college students. In 1980, coauthor Hall surveyed students from comparable social and educational backgrounds attending a predominantly Black university in the South about their career plans to find a strong correlation between skin color and occupational goals: the light-skinned students aimed for far more prestigious jobs than their darker-skinned peers. A qualification of Hall's research, however, is where it was conducted. According to a 2005 study by Richard

Harvey and colleagues, skin color is actually a more important factor in the lives of Black students attending a predominantly African-American university than it is for those attending a predominantly White university.

Black business organizations that formed in southern cities like Charleston and New Orleans tended to be exclusively for men whose skin color was light to medium, at most. The Charleston-based Brown Fellowship Society, for example, was established in 1790, well before the Civil War, by free people of color to facilitate business contacts among "a certain kind of people." Although skin color per se was not mentioned in the society's mission statement, in reality admission into the Brown Fellowship Society was restricted.

When it came to political activism, though, light-skinned African Americans seemed to put aside their issues of colorism and fight for the rights of all Blacks. This was true except perhaps for the right of dark-skinned Blacks to become leaders themselves. Throughout American Black history, it has been almost exclusively lighter-skinned African Americans who have led the charge toward civil rights progress. It turns out that "one drop" produces a large pool inside a big tent of dark-, medium-, and light-skinned people, and that those in the last group, who also happen to be the most highly educated and economically successful people under the tent, speak for all. A few examples of past historical figures will illustrate the light-skinned-leader tendency.

Frederick Douglass was born in 1817, the light-skinned offspring of a White Maryland slaveholder and a slave woman. He was raised in slavery, but in 1838, at the age of twenty-one, he escaped north to freedom. Within two years he had become known as a stunning lecturer as well as a leading abolitionist.

By the end of his life Douglass had been a newspaper editor, the president of the Freedman's Bank, the U.S. minister to Haiti, and a U.S. marshal for the District of Columbia.

Another light-skinned leader was W. E. B. Du Bois. With his mixture of French, Dutch, and African blood, Du Bois was so light skinned that some said he could easily have passed as White. At the end of the nineteenth century, he called on the Negro community to "produce a college-educated class whose mission would be to serve and guide the progress of the masses," and even named twenty-one other men and two women in the Black community to help lead the way. Perhaps satisfied with the existing color-class hierarchy, he didn't question, or maybe even notice, that all but one on his list—aptly named the Talented Tenth—were mulatto.

Educator Booker T. Washington, who had not only light skin but reddish hair and gray colored eyes, emerged as an important figure in the Black community at around the same time. Although named on Du Bois's list of Black leaders, Washington strongly rejected the notion that a few shining examples of successful, well-educated Blacks at the top would in any way help the average Black person at the bottom.

Another important crusader for Black rights near the end of the nineteenth century and into the twentieth century was the light-skinned Ida B. Wells. She was a respected journalist, an antilynching activist, and an early suffragist. Together with Frederick Douglass and other Black leaders, she helped to organize a Black boycott of the 1893 World's Columbian Exposition in Chicago, after it failed to collaborate with the Black community on exhibits representing African-American life.

The Reverend Adam Clayton Powell Jr., with his dark eyes, White features, White hair texture, and old-family background, was also one of the Black community's light-skinned leaders. During the 1930s he was the pastor of the Abyssinian Baptist Church in Harlem, and he used his pulpit to create a political base that won him election to the New York City Council and later to the U.S. House of Representatives. As a congressman, he was not afraid to attack the White power structure, and he lobbied hard for the passage of antidiscrimination legislation.

And then there was Walter White, who is surely among the most interesting of the historical Black leaders. White served as executive secretary of the National Association for the Advancement of Colored People (NAACP) from 1931 to 1955, yet he was so White-looking that he was able to "pass" while personally investigating lynchings in the South. Anthropologists have estimated that the blue-eyed, blond-haired, white-skinned Walter White was no more than one sixty-fourth Black in his racial makeup, yet he identified himself as Black, and did much to champion Negro causes. But when he traveled abroad, he had to contend with puzzled Europeans who kept insisting that he was not Black. The "rule" that racially mixed Americans had to identify with the minority racial status, no matter how White in features or light in skin they might be, greatly influenced the social and political experiences of these Black leaders.

It is interesting to contemplate the different path in life someone like Walter White might have taken if America had never adopted its one-drop rule of racial identity. With his leadership qualities and passion for justice, would Walter White have become someone equally prominent in the White community? Might he have been elected to the U.S. Senate or appointed to some high-level government position? Would he then have similarly championed racial equality, and helped the Black community fight racism? Would he have been able to make more progress in that regard as someone associated with the White power structure than with the Black community? In being someone in the lower tier who rose to the top, did he ultimately become a better-known and more important historical figure than if he had lived his life as a White person?

To this day, a persistent "light at the top" phenomenon is not hard to see, especially when looking at a list of which African Americans became "firsts," meaning they were the first one to hold a prominent position that was previously occupied only by Whites. To name just a few, there is Robert C. Weaver, the first Black U.S. cabinet member, secretary of the Department of Housing and Urban Development (1966); Edward W. Brooke, the first Black senator since Reconstruction (1966); Thurgood Marshall, the first Black Supreme Court justice (1967); Andrew Young, the first Black U.S. ambassador to the United Nations (1977); David Dinkins, the first Black mayor of New York (1989); Douglas Wilder of Virginia, the first Black governor (1989); General Colin L. Powell, the first Black chairman of the Joint Chiefs of Staff (1989) and first Black secretary of state (2001); Ron Brown, the first Black to chair the Democratic National Committee (1989); Condoleezza Rice, the first African-American female secretary of state (2005); and, of course, Barack Obama, the first African-American U.S. president (elected 2008, took office 2009).

All of these "firsts" were either top appointments made by a White person (e.g., the president) or by a White majority vote. In a society politically and economically controlled by White people, it makes sense that others who most resemble the majority group would become the "firsts."

Of course, not every Black leader has been on the lighter side of the color scale. Going back to the nineteenth century, there were the darker-skinned Sojourner Truth and Harriet

Tubman, who emerged as leaders of the Black community. Fast-forwarding to the twentieth century, we had Shirley Chisholm, the first Black congresswoman (1968); Barbara Jordan, a congresswoman from Texas (1972); Harold Washington, the first Black mayor of Chicago (1983); Maxine Waters, a sitting congresswoman from California (1990); Supreme Court Justice Clarence Thomas (1991); and Michael Steele, first Black chairman of the Republican National Committee—all relatively dark skinned. Nonetheless, the perception lingers among many darker-skinned African Americans that skin color still determines how wide the doors of opportunity will open.

As in other color-class hierarchies found around the world, population members with lighter skin and more European-like features fared better in society. And again as in other countries, those individuals deemed not light skinned or fine featured enough did what they could with what they had. And one sure way to make one's life journey a bit easier is to try and approximate the looks of those with the greatest power and privilege. In America, African Americans who were medium to dark skinned thus aimed to appear more like African Americans who possessed lighter skin. And sometimes they attempted to emulate the beauty ideals of White people as well. We will now explore the beauty practices and procedures of African Americans, along with evidence that they, too, may have fallen victim to the ideology of cosmetic Westernism.

Changing the color of one's skin, the largest organ and most visible feature of the body, has proven to be a challenge, but over the years that hasn't stopped a lot of people from trying. American Negro women of the nineteenth century were known to sometimes rub lye directly on their skin. Others applied harsh acidic products made for removing dirt and grime from floors and walls. It was not unheard of for a mother to try lightening a dark daughter by dunking her every day in a tub of bleach. There also were homemade concoctions of lemon juice, bleach, or urine to smear on the skin and arsenic wafers to swallow, all of which were designed to "get the dark out." None of these methods worked, and all of them smelled, burned, or permanently damaged the skin.

By the end of the nineteenth century, pharmaceutically manufactured skin-lightening products, or bleaching creams, hit the market. They were *un*naturally popular, and just as the advertising of skin-lightening products has been declared racist by Asian and African activists, so were the early marketing campaigns of the new skin-bleaching products in America. One ad for the bleaching cream Ro-Zol, distributed by the Black-owned Overton Hygienic Manufacturing Company, featured a fabulously wealthy Black couple sitting at a table covered with a starched white linen cloth and sipping tea from fine china cups. The woman, who is several shades lighter than the man, is admiring herself in a small mirror, obviously pleased with the results of Ro-Zol. The ad copy reads:

> *Ro-Zol was the first preparation made expressly for bleaching. . . . Ro-Zol does not bleach by destroying the pigmentation. . . . It is received by the pigment and combines and harmonizes to produce a remarkably satisfactory, youthful, wholesome and whitened complexion.*

An even more racist ad for another skin-bleaching product had as its copy:

> *Lighten your dark skin. Race men and women, protect your future by using Black and White Ointment. Be attractive.*

Throw off the chains that have held you back from the prosperity that rightly belongs to you.

Such ads were meant to tap both Black women's and Black men's insecurities about being dark. The ads worked and the products somewhat did, but it didn't matter, as the manufacturers of skin lighteners made a fortune off those insecurities. But after the 1940s, when HQ was added as an active ingredient to commercial skin lighteners, and they actually did become effective to some extent, sales really took off. Such sales have continued to soar, with largely African-American women by the thousands purchasing such well-known brands as Nadinola (which dates back to 1889), Ambi Fade Creme, Esoterica, Porcelana, and Vantex, among many others. Currently, America's skin-bleaching market is estimated to be worth over $5.6 billion.

Since the early 1990s there have been growing numbers of health officials, including Mark Green, former commissioner of consumer affairs in New York, who have requested the Food and Drug Administration to ban HQ altogether from skin creams (i.e., not just limit its formula to 2 percent) because it is a proven carcinogen. Some skin lighteners also contain mercury, another cancer-causing ingredient. Despite the risks and warnings, dermatologists report that African-American patients still request prescriptions for HQ preparations stronger than the 2 percent concentration available in over-the-counter products. And if a dermatologist denies their request, they can always find 4 percent HQ solutions—with who knows what other ingredients added to them—on the Internet.

Beyond just lightening the face, it is also now possible to lighten the entire body with a full bleaching procedure, available only at special salons. The process is expensive, and it requires a shower immediately afterward to avoid burning. Forever afterward, one must be vigilant about avoiding direct sunlight. Some believe that skin bleaching was what the late Michael Jackson did to make himself look lighter, and would explain why he never appeared in sunlight without being completely covered. In 1979, his sister La Toya Jackson claimed, however, that Michael had been diagnosed with lupus, a rare disorder that causes skin lesions and necessitates staying out of the sun.

Another measure for lightening one's skin is a chemical peel, which is extremely painful and may even require hospitalization. The procedure involves burning off the top layer of pigmentation to uncover the smoother, lighter layer underneath. Several follow-up visits are needed, and the entire process can take as long as a year before the skin is fully lightened to the desired shade. And during that time, the patient looks a lot worse for wear.

A third method is dermabrasion, which is considered the most painful. This procedure involves stripping away the uppermost layers of skin with high-speed wire or diamond-edged brushes. New York dermatologist Dr. Robert Auerbach likens the process to "skinning your knee on the sidewalk." But now available are over-the-counter microdermabrasion kits for doing the procedure at home. The process, which can be done either on the face or the entire body, involves scrubbing and sanding off the very top layer of skin.

And finally, a recently developed option is laser skin surfacing, which produces an overall skin-brightening effect on the face by smoothing out areas where color is uneven. Because laser skin surfacing does a good job removing brown spots, it is as popular among White women for its antiaging effect as it is among African-American women for its skin-lightening effect.

Skin is not the only feature that African Americans seek to cosmetically alter. Ever since the invention of the contact lens, there have been Whites, as discussed earlier, and Blacks who have opted to lighten their natural eye color with tinted lenses. It is telling that most ads for tinted contact lenses today no longer tout corrective vision benefits from the product. Instead its value and reason to purchase are pitched as a way to "improve" eye color. The message that brown eyes are less attractive, and that blue, green, or hazel eyes are better, is disturbing to former senior editor of *Essence* magazine Elsie B. Washington, who has written that "the wish to acquire what we were not born with, to adopt the coloring that has for centuries been touted as prettier, finer, better, carries with it all the old baggage of racial inferiority and/or superiority based simply, and simplistically, on physical traits. White America, its institutions, its industrial machine, has always been very clear on the looks that it prizes: in five words, blond hair and blue eyes."

Not every African-American woman with green or blue eyes is necessarily wearing contact lenses, though. There are many African-American women whose natural eye color is not brown. Even so, when the editors of *Essence* and fashion magazines with high African-American readership feature naturally blue-eyed Blacks on their covers, they are typically swamped with letters from angry readers who interpret the magazine's choice of a cover girl as a denial of Black beauty. Clearly, African-American women lacking the more politically correct eye color should not be ostracized, but then perhaps neither should every brown-eyed Black woman who chooses to wear green or blue contact lenses.

Not only are hair texture and eye color loaded beauty symbols for many African Americans, but so, too, are noses. For a few thousand dollars, an undesirable nose, however that may be defined, can be surgically reshaped into a narrow proboscis with just the right upward tilt—something more than a few White women, especially those of Jewish descent, have been known to do. Unlike White women who undergo such procedures, African-American women may be accused of self-hatred. Yet the desire to improve one's looks is universal, and certainly an understandable motivation.

Some Whites don't get what all the fuss is about when an African-American woman does something to improve her looks; they question why African Americans have to be so political and critical about everything they do. After all, Whites point out, when a White woman with brown eyes wears blue contact lenses, she might be thought vain for doing so, but most people would not assume that she was denying her heritage; or if she bakes under the hot sun all day to tan her pale skin, she might be admonished for risking skin cancer, but few would conclude that she hates being White. The important reason why the two choices are different has everything to do with the fact that Whites can dabble in different cultural practices, such as wearing one's hair in dreadlocks for a more "streetwise" appearance, but can always choose to go back to looking "White" if they so desire. African Americans don't have that luxury, nor is what they cosmetically do necessarily a free choice. Sometimes the hairstyle that an African-American woman wears, for example, has more to do with what is expected of her. Imagine Michelle Obama having the freedom in this cultural climate to wear her hair in dreadlocks, or "locs." It simply could not happen. This is understood by other African Americans because everything a Black woman does or doesn't do, and most especially a powerful woman like Michelle Obama or Oprah Winfrey, is going to be scrutinized for evidence of selling out, not accepted as just doing what needs to be done. That subtle difference is not appreciated by Whites who might immediately start saying things like "Well, I can't wear hair that is dyed purple to my corporate job." True enough, but White women can always go back to brunette or whatever anytime they want, and they would probably just get a warning and not a firing if they did show up with crazy-colored hair. As discussed later in the chapter on hair, African-American women can be and have been fired because of a hairstyle.

In conclusion, African Americans in general, and African-American women in particular, are often caught in the space between the two tiers of racism and color classism. It can be hard to decide whether to go for "the burn" from a chemical peel or hair-straightening solution, in hopes of easier assimilation and greater acceptance by those with the most power, or, if born with features at odds with light-skinned and Western-influenced beauty ideals, to not change a thing, in the hope of making a bigger statement about the natural beauty of African-American features. But whatever the choice, it needs to be recognized for what it is by the individual, and honored for what it says to others.

Chapter 4

The Color of Identity

African-American identity is a multifaceted and indistinct concept. Being Black affects the way a person walks and talks; his or her values, culture, and history; how that person relates to others; and how they may relate to him or her. It is governed by one's early social experience, history and politics, conscious input and labeling, and the genetic accident that dictates external appearance. Skin color appears to affect identity, but in complex and seemingly unpredictable ways. Although color has been used as a metaphor for Blackness, pigmentation alone cannot be used to predict the extent of racial identification. In fact, some of the most Afrocentric people in America are those with the least amount of African ancestry.

The effects of skin color on Black identity are far from straightforward. It is certainly not the case that the darker-skinned someone is, the stronger that person's Black identity. There are simply too many influences shaping one's sense of self, most of which have nothing to do with race (e.g., intelligence, personality, talent, height, age), for the result to be that formulaic. However, what is clear is that for persons of color in a dominant White culture, the process of finding a secure and comfortable identity while also having to negotiate societal constructions of race *and* skin color, is all the more challenging. In this chapter, we will look at different factors that shape identity for African Americans. We start with a developmental approach and then segue into the controversy surrounding distinctive naming. We then take a look at how differences in skin color and the centrality of defining oneself as African American relate to the racial identity process. Finally, we discuss how a growing number of biracial and multiracial individuals are questioning the continued application of a one-drop rule that calls for Blackness to trump all other racial and ethnic identities.

We are born psychologically unaware of gender, race, skin color, or anything else that might eventually impact our own identity. Thus, the first step in the identity formation process is to become aware of what and who one is. Over the past four decades, much research has been conducted regarding exactly when children are cognitively mature enough to accurately say what gender and race they are. Because of its longitudinal design, one of the more comprehensive studies on early identity formation was conducted by Phylis Katz and Jennifer Kofkin. The two psychologists began with a sample of one hundred Black and one hundred White children, carefully matched by socioeconomic level, whom they followed (with parental permission) from six months to six years of age. At various periods in their development, the children were asked to respond to different questions, including some about their own gender and racial identity. One experimental task involved two boxes, one filled with photographs of children who were like them and the other with photographs of children who were different from them. Photographs are often used in studies of this type, as they are an effective way to assess children who are preverbal. In studying gender identity formation then, the two boxes, filled with photos of either boys or girls, were placed before the children, along with a photo of themselves. The children were simply asked to place their own photo into the box containing photographs of other children who were similar to them. By thirty months, Katz and Kofkin found, 70 percent of the children were able to accurately place their own photograph into a box of other same-gender photographs, and by thirty-six months, 89 percent of them were able to do so. The researchers concluded that by three years old, a large majority of both White and Black children are aware of their own gender. They attributed the early awareness to the fact that gender differences, from looks to behavior, are constantly being labeled and monitored within the home setting.

When the researchers assessed racial awareness, however, the same percentages did not hold. That is, in a second task, instead of being presented with pictures simply of boys or girls, the children were given two boxes filled with photos of White children or Black children. Katz and Kofkin found that at thirty months, a mere 41 percent of Black and White children were able to choose the right race box (as opposed to 70 percent for gender), and by thirty-six months, the percentage rose only to 56 (as opposed to 89 percent for gender). The researchers attributed the lower rates of successful identification and awareness to the children's not being exposed at home as much to references to gender in comparison to race. But Katz and Kofkin observed an additional race difference between the children that could not be fully explained by the home environment. At thirty months, 61 percent of the White children were accurate in racial self-awareness (or at least knew that they weren't Black), but only 19 percent of the Black children were accurate, with many in the latter group simply refusing to respond to the task. By thirty-six months, 77 percent of the White children knew their own race; however, only 32 percent of the African-American children seemed able to accurately select the correct picture box. Again there was more refusal on the part of the Black children to complete the task, and even when they did do it, they hesitated longer before making the selection. It would seem that these very young children were already trying to decide whether it was better to be right in selecting the Black-photograph box, or wrong but at least be in the box they wanted to be in. This disturbing finding begs the question of how children so young could already have internalized the notion that White is somehow better.

Psychologists Kenneth and Mamie Clark were the first to provide empirical evidence of what was then labeled as self-hatred in Black children. In the late 1930s and early 1940s, the Clarks gave children as young as three, from both the North and the South, the choice of playing with either a White doll or a Black doll. Regardless of geographic region, the Clarks found that Black children nearly always selected the White doll over the Black doll. Furthermore, when asked to explain their choices, the children said things like "The White doll seems nicer and prettier, with better coloring." The Clarks were later asked to appear before the U.S. Supreme Court to testify as expert witnesses about the damaging effects of educational segregation during the landmark 1954 case *Brown v. Board of Education of Topeka, Kansas*. Although the Clarks' original research was later criticized on methodological grounds, its basic findings have been replicated and verified many times over the past fifty-some years.

Little has changed in the intervening years, a sad fact recently brought home by FAO Schwarz's highly successful 2008 "Christmas doll adoption" campaign. A "Newborn Toy Nursery" was built in the company's flagship store, and girls (who averaged seven years old and were predominantly but not exclusively White) were invited to "adopt" a "baby" from a diverse selection of dolls on display. The whole setup, from the cooing of the babies wrapped in blankets behind the glass of a nursery-like viewing station, to the sales associates dressed like nurses assisting the children with their choice, was designed to resemble an actual hospital nursery. Once a girl made her choice, she was even given a little hospital gown to go inside the "nursery" to retrieve her selection, after which a "medical" examination of the doll took place, and adoption papers were signed—and big sales rung up by the cashiers. As a marketing strategy, the campaign was brilliant, and since it received a lot of media attention, even greater demand for the adopted dolls was generated. What was disturbing, though, was just how fast all the White baby dolls were adopted, and ultimately how few of the Black dolls were. Furthermore, once all of the White dolls sold out, the Asian dolls were adopted, and then the light brown ones (which were presumably Latina). When the campaign ended, the only dolls left in the nursery were the Black ones, along with a single damaged White doll, which ended up being adopted before the last of the Black dolls.

Not long after the FAO Schwarz story came out, CNN commissioned child psychologist Margaret Beale Spencer from the University of Chicago to conduct a pilot study assessing to what extent (if any) children's racial beliefs, attitudes, and preferences surrounding not just race but also skin color had evolved since the Clarks' pioneering research. Spencer's study, conducted in 2010, after the election of Barack Obama, included a sample of more than one hundred four-to-five-year-old White and African-American children, who were matched demographically and drawn from two schools, one in New York City and one in Georgia. Instead of just using Black versus White dolls, Spencer showed the children five different cartoon pictures featuring a child whose skin tone ranged from light to dark. The children were then asked to respond to a series of questions, such as which one of the five cartoons was a smart child, and who was the mean child. Perhaps not unexpectedly, the White participants more frequently selected the lighter-skinned cartoon figures in response to the smart-child question, and in response to the mean-child question, they chose the darker-skinned figures. But sadly, the African-American children also exhibited light-skin biases in their responses, although not as strongly as the White children did.

These studies clearly indicate that very young children are capable of picking up general associations about the value of lightness, and light skin, from the White normative culture, even while perhaps being too emotionally and cognitively immature to fully understand the larger implications of their preferences. Fortunately, African-American parents should be reassured that displays of light/White biases on the part of very young children do not indicate that they, the parents, are not doing enough to instill a positive racial identity in their children. In fact, research indicates very young children's beliefs about the value of Whiteness neither correlate with the views of parents, African American or otherwise, nor are predictive of future racial self-hatred. Thus light/White biases, while discomforting to witness, may only mean that by the time children enter nursery or elementary school, most of them have learned to recognize certain value-laden subtleties regarding race and color. This is especially true for young girls, who, according to psychologist Cornelia Porter, are twice as likely as boys by age six to be sensitive to the social importance of skin color. However, on a more encouraging note, Porter also reported in the 1991 published research that when the ninety-eight children in her sample were asked which skin tone they liked best, most selected a honey-brown color. A more recent study, conducted in 2001, also found that by the time African-American children were teenagers, a significant majority continued to endorse the view that a medium skin tone is most preferred.

Puberty is the next critical stage of development in the identity formation process. By the time African Americans hit the teen years, most have well-defined—if misinformed—notions regarding the value of certain skin-color tones. In general, most African-American teenagers come to the simplistic conclusion that light skin is feminine and dark skin is masculine. Unfortunately, this means that the very light-skinned boys and the very dark-skinned girls may find themselves out of step with a stereotyped mandate.

For young African-American teenage women living in a society saturated with visual media, it is hard not to notice that the love interests of African-American men on TV and in movies, or those women declared most attractive by fashion and beauty magazine editors, are almost exclusively light skinned. But it is the music videos that really drive home the message that Black guys only want light-skinned women. Although we have dedicated a whole chapter to colorism and images in the media, it is worth mentioning here the damaging influence that music videos can have on young Black women.

A group of African-American teenage friends—Trina, eigh-

teen; Tiny, seventeen; and Monique, seventeen and a half—
who all happened to have darker skin, shared with us how the
lyrics of rap songs and the prominence of light-skinned Black
women in music videos have affected how they see themselves.
"Black guys just ignore us," said Trina, the darkest of the three
friends, and she spoke about how sometimes she feels invisible
when she and her friends go out to parties. Her friend Monique
chimed in, using Black vernacular, "Yeah, Black guys our age
ain't trying to get with no dark-skinned girls. They're just hung
up on light-skinned chicks anyway." When asked why they
think that is true, they all answered, almost in unison: "Music
videos!" Then they begin to rattle off all of the songs and videos by young Black rappers that praise the "redbone" and virtually ignore, by mention or visibility, the darker-skinned Black
woman. "I listen to this stuff and it bothers me for real," says
the oldest girl, Trina. "No matter what my momma tells me
about how pretty I am and not to let anybody tell me anything
different—it still hurts when I hear songs like 'Boyfriend Girlfriend' by C-Side and Keyshia Cole, with lyrics that say they
'love a . . . redbone with long hair.'"

In an attempt to raise awareness of the psychological harm
light-skin preferences can inflict on young African-American
women, media personality, author, and businesswoman Tyra
Banks on her morning TV talk show once featured a segment
about African-American mothers who bleach their children's
skin. It drew a lot of response, including one comment from a
young African-American blogger, who identified herself simply
as Vixen. "I'm a sixteen-year-old girl and feel ugly because I'm
dark and all the boys want the light-skin girls," she wrote. "I
never used to feel this way until I started to notice that all the
girls in the media are light skinned and coz I want to be a video

girl, all the girls are light and I felt like I wasn't light. Many dark-skinned girls don't get very far."

But other dark-skinned African-American teenage women are empowered to resist colorism. At the age of only sixteen, Kiri Davis produced a documentary film called *A Girl Like Me* to help young dark-skinned African-American teenagers like herself see that they are not alone—and, more important, that they should reject negative feelings about their own beautiful dark skin. To first illustrate the pain of colorism, Davis's film opens with brief clips of women disclosing the agony and shame they have felt about their dark skin color. One featured female declares that "to be beautiful, you need light skin and long hair," while a second one claims she personally knew someone who poured a capful of bleach into her bathwater to get lighter. On the subject of dating, a teenager asserts that some African-American girls won't even date dark-skinned men because they don't want any more dark skin color in their "gene pool." And, sadly, one young African-American woman comments that when she tried wearing her hair in its natural state, her own mother told her to stop because she was "starting to look African." It is heartening to see young dark-skinned African-American women like Kiri Davis, who are proud of who they are, refuse to be oppressed by the prejudice of colorism, and are taking positive steps to raise consciousness about colorism.

A study published in 2010 suggests that African-American girls who are dark skinned may indeed have a harder time during adolescence, but with one important caveat. According to Tiffany Townsend and her colleagues, the teenage girls who endorse the light-skinned, long-hair ideal, but possibly do not live up to that ideal themselves, may be the ones who find this developmental period the hardest to negotiate. Girls who endorsed attitudes of colorism were more likely to engage in early intercourse and other high-risk sexual behaviors (e.g., intercourse with a partner who is not using a condom). In other words, it would appear that *having* dark skin color, per se, is not the problem as much as *feeling bad about the fact* that one doesn't possess light skin and long, straight hair. Furthermore, the researchers found that those teenage girls who actively rejected beauty standards consistent with colorism did better in school and thought themselves more intelligent.

A young dark-skinned woman named Brandi C. from Nashville is a positive example of someone who has found a way to resist internalizing societal messages that you must have light skin to be beautiful. Brandi says she has long had a positive self-image, and credits her mother and father for that, saying, "My parents taught us to love our beautiful chocolate selves. Black-hate was never allowed in our house."

Young Black women raised in positive Black identity-affirming households are generally better at maintaining high self-esteem when confronted with the often cruel things they hear from others about their dark skin color, especially during the trying teen years. But there also are those raised in identically positive home environments who nonetheless feel they must hunker down and endure adolescence with shame, before most eventually do come to feel good about themselves as adults.

We now turn to the challenges faced by young African-American men who feel their skin color falls short of the dark-skin masculine ideal. In coping with a belief that they don't measure up, some light-skinned Black males compensate by exaggerating their masculinity, acting overly tough and street-wise. In an article for *Essence,* author Itabari Njeri described the plight of her cousin Jeffrey, who looked like singer Ricky Nelson[6] but wanted to be "the baddest nigger on the block," and who, sadly, died young on the streets trying to prove he was neither White nor the enemy. Michel Marriott, who was once a reporter for *The New York Times* and is now a professor at Baruch College, recalled how he tried to compensate for his light skin when coming of age during the 1960s. He made sure his "black cool dictated [his] every rhythm," and that his Afro was large, his swagger bodacious, his knowledge of Black music and dance moves cutting edge. He could only hope that all these gestures would articulate what his light skin never could—that he was a "bro-ske."

Half a century later, these feelings of being insufficiently masculine still plague some African-American male teenagers, especially those derisively called "pretty boys." But just as femininity has nothing to do with skin color, neither does masculinity, and it is imperative that young Black men be taught this. Thankfully, adult life is not about the often-distorted beliefs and even narcissistic values of teenagers.

Coming into the next developmental phase of adulthood, attitudes about one's own skin color generally improve. Ron Holt, a brown-skinned corporate manager, has even observed that once light-skinned young men outgrow adolescence, many are quick to realize the enormous advantages their lighter skin color confers on them in the workplace. They seem to have better job prospects, appear less threatening to Whites, and suddenly find themselves more attractive to women, who now call them "pretty boys" teasingly. And as an added bonus, having

---

6.   Ricky Nelson was a popular singer-actor and is considered a prototype of the wholesome young White man.

fought so hard during the teen years to establish their Black identity, many of these same lighter-skinned African-American men now have a clear sense of who they are. Holt believes that it is the darker-skinned Black man, not his lighter-skinned brother, who is "Stepin Fetchit-ized" out of his masculinity.[7]

For the most part, as dark-skinned women reach their twenties and beyond, they, too, will come to realize that it is simply not true that all Black men prefer light-skinned women. There are plenty who love dark-skinned women, and a few who even actively reject lighter-skinned women because of prior bad experiences. This attitude is certainly reflected in the chorus of Del the Funky Homosapien's 1991 song "Dark Skin Girls":

> *Dark skin girls are better than light skin, light skin girls ain't better than dark skin. . . .*

In adulthood, light-skinned African-American women who coasted through adolescence with nary a thought about forming a sense of Black identity may discover that there is a price to pay for "light-skin privilege." Coauthor Russell interviewed Chelsea, a light-skinned African-American professor from a community college in the Midwest, who rejects the assumption that dark-skinned women are the ones most affected by colorism:

> *We live in a highly racialized color-conscious society and it cuts both ways. I've seen many studies on this issue and in my opinion they are all biased. I feel like all of these studies*

---

7. "Stepin Fetchit" was the stage name of an early Black film actor who always portrayed shuffling, laconic characters onscreen, although he fought hard for civil rights offscreen.

are skewed and the end result is always that the darker-skinned woman has it harder and this is just not the truth. I am always having to answer the "what are you?" question and being accused of thinking I'm better than other Black women because of my skin color. Recently I got in a heated discussion with a brother who told me that all light-skinned black women are stuck-up.

Yet Dee Dee, a dark-skinned African-American female hospital worker from Cleveland who now lives in Chicago, states she is tired of all the complaining from these "tragic-by-choice mulatto half-breeds." She challenges them to just once imagine what it is like to experience her dark-skinned universe, saying:

They have no reason to whine. All of the crying that someone is picking on them or is jealous of them or how they are so misunderstood. It's all BS. Try being a dark-skinned Black woman and have to not only deal with racism from Whites but also discrimination from your own people telling you that you ain't pretty enough. Bet they wouldn't trade places with me.

Adult light-skinned and dark-skinned African-American women may still sometimes squabble over who is more oppressed by colorism, but in a dominant White culture, it does not help either group to define themselves in opposition to their own people. Certainly, it's good to remember that while one person's struggle may not feel or look like another's, both people can experience emotional difficulties along the way to forming a strong Black identity.

Yet it is interesting to consider what underlies the negative attitudes and special name-calling reserved for African Americans who are deemed "too light skinned." Such attitudes appear unique to Black Americans. Throughout Latin America, for example, the expression of skin-color prejudice is more straightforward: being dark skinned is undesirable and being light skinned is good, and the lighter one is, the better. The no-holds-barred preference for light skin was reflected in a 2002 study conducted by Eric Uhlmann and his colleagues. They compared Hispanic Americans (i.e., Latinos living in the United States) and Chileans living in their home country, and found that when the two groups overall evaluated each other, a strong in-group preference emerged, but whether the participants were from one country or the other, they all ranked individuals with the lightest skin the most favorably. In other words, light skin always trumped nationality and there was no subculture ceiling effect operating on the Latinos that would lead them to view other Latinos with very light skin as anything but positive. One has to wonder if the pattern of color classism that emerged hundreds of years ago in Central and South America, versus the one-drop rule adopted by the early colonists in this country, is responsible for this curious difference in the rejection by some Blacks of other Blacks whose skin is very light. This is a topic we will revisit in chapter 6 on issues of colorism among family members.

Although generalizations are always full of exceptions, African Americans in the middle of the color spectrum tend to be most satisfied with their own skin color. As a result, they also tend to enjoy higher self-esteem and possess a stronger sense of self. Unlike their sisters and brothers on the extreme ends of the color spectrum, midrange African Americans typically do not have to go through the emotionally draining process of dealing with being either idealized or demonized because of the color of their skin. One medium-skinned Black woman named Jessica J., who proclaims her love for her "beautiful brown skin," said that self-esteem has never been an issue for her and that although she is well aware of intraracial skin-color discrimination among others, she personally hasn't had to deal with the issue in her immediate or even extended family. For that, she credits her grandmother—and perhaps the genetic good fortune of not being very dark skinned or very light skinned.

We now turn to the role that a birth name can play on an individual's journey to create a strong Black identity for himself or herself. Although a name is given at birth, it is usually not until adulthood that someone may start to question the perceived appropriateness of his or her given name, especially if it is one sometimes referred to as a "crazy Black name." These distinctive names can and do affect African Americans, especially those who feel a disconnect between an internal racial identity that is just emerging and the external impression their name may be conveying to others.

A thirtysomething African-American woman from Tennessee, whose original name was LeConetria, talked about how she had to change her birth name to be taken seriously in corporate America. "What possibly could my parents have been thinking?" she asks. "How can any parent name their child these ridiculous names? Then as you become an adult and go into the work world—employers don't take you seriously. I definitely felt that my name kept me from getting interviews. That's why I eventually changed it to Connie."

Connie's belief that in shedding the name LeConetria she would have more employment opportunities come her way is actually supported by research. In a 2003 workplace discrimination study, economists Marianne Bertrand and Send-hil Mullainathan found that resumes with "White-sounding" names—like Jay, Brad, Carrie, and Kristen—were 50 percent more likely than those with "Black-sounding" names to elicit a callback.

Even Bill Cosby, in the infamous speech for which he later was severely criticized, questioned the wisdom of burdening Black children with "crazy names." At a 2004 event celebrating the fiftieth anniversary of *Brown v. Board of Education* sponsored by the NAACP Legal Defense Fund, Cosby first accused economically disadvantaged African Americans of "not parenting" and "not holding up their end of this deal" (i.e., of the civil rights struggles and gains). "With names like Shaniqua, Taliqua, and Mohammed and all that crap," Cosby went on to say, these kids end up in jail or standing on a corner unable to speak proper English.

African American Theresa H. teaches at a major inner-city school district in the Northeast, and admits to agreeing with Cosby. She is appalled by the names of some of the students at her school:

> *A name says a lot about a person. Parents should think before saddling their children with these crazy names and consider moving toward more mainstream names. Call me a sellout if you want, but I work in the inner-city school system. I see the names that these students have to live with and I know the negative impact that these names will have on these students down the line. I'm not saying that you have to name your child Amy, but you surely don't need to name her Chatoxy, either.*

Yet in 2004, economist Roland G. Fryer and race scholar Steven D. Levitt found that after controlling for a child's circumstances at birth, there was no relationship between distinctive names and later life outcomes. Perhaps what is missing in this research is the variable of skin color and its perceived—even if not true—relationship to "crazy names" among economically disadvantaged African Americans. Given the documented income gap between light-skinned and dark-skinned African Americans, skin color would seem to be an important factor to consider.

Coauthor Wilson and two of her graduate students did just that and found a relationship between skin color and Black name distinctiveness. White and African-American participants were each shown twelve photographs of Black women of varying skin-tone shades. They were then provided with a list of twenty-four feminine names and asked to guess which name belonged to which woman. Half of the names on the list were traditionally western European sounding, like Laura, Susan, and Diane, while the other half were more stereotypically Black, like Lichelle, Sheronda, and Aretha. Results indicated that the darker the skin color of the African-American woman in the photographs, the more likely participants of both races were to guess that she possessed one of the stereotypically Black names.

The same African Americans who find Cosby less than fair in blaming the poor for their status are quite possibly the same ones who reject any notion that Black people should be the ones to have to end a popular tradition of naming just because White human resources personnel and White employers sometimes discriminate. As one African-American woman put it, no one would ever question why Puerto Rican parents would name their baby girl Guadalupe, or why an Italian-American mother might call her baby girl Giuseppina. "Then why," she asks, "should Black people be shamed into not naming their children unique Black names?" Although this individual raises an excellent point, the counterresponse would be that names like Guadalupe and Giuseppina are handed down through culture and ancestry, whereas the "crazy names" like Oronjello and Marqwasha that some African Americans are inclined to give their children are simply made up.

It is important to separate the issue of "crazy"-sounding Black names from those names that are simply atypical. When celebrities like Gwyneth Paltrow and Demi Moore name their daughters Apple and Rumer, respectively, it is doubtful anyone would mistake those "crazy names" for Black ones.

Or consider former secretary of state Condoleezza Rice. She has a fairly unusual first name, but there is something different about hers. If you didn't know already that she was African American and just saw her name in print, you wouldn't necessarily jump to the conclusion that she was Black. You might even think that the woman was Italian or Spanish. And yet it is somehow true that most of the highly unusual and made-up names that some African-American parents give their children are recognizable as belonging to someone who is Black. So, as unfair as racism is, a parent who graces (or burdens) his or her child with a highly unusual name may inadvertently make it harder for that son or daughter to later get ahead in life. But then again, if that child becomes the next Beyoncé or Shaquille, the name's uniqueness will enable it to become no less than a household brand, no surname necessary.

A radically different way to express one's Black identity through a name change is to reject a European-sounding name and replace it with one that is specifically African. The practice of claiming an African name began in the 1960s as an expression of Black pride. The Nation of Islam advocated replacing one's last name with an X to symbolize the renunciation of the "master's" name inherited from enslaved ancestors. Taking a Muslim name, though, is different from taking a specifically African name. According to one orthodox Muslim, Jaleel Abdul-Adil, the Muslim name suggests a religious conversion rather than a cultural reclamation. He says, "People bring a lot of assumptions to the table when they hear my name. Most think I'm a Black Nationalist, but Muslims embrace their culture within a spiritual context that affirms all races." Today, being given an African name at birth may be a great way to affirm one's Black identity, but such a name might also be used by others to make life difficult for the adult Black man or woman who doesn't necessarily want to project to others a strong racial message.

Another question to answer in forming a Black identity involves figuring out to what extent one wishes to embrace African-American culture. During the 1990s, psychologists William Cross and Janet Helms each studied the path along which African Americans may travel in reaching their own end point of racial identity and pride. While the two scholars propose slightly different models, both view the process in terms of successive stages that require attitudinal shifts regarding what it means to be Black. When one stage becomes fully integrated into a person's identity, he or she is then ready to move on to the next stage, although the individual may choose *not* to progress as well. Without going into the details of each stage, it is worth noting that in both models, readiness to move beyond the earliest stage of racial identity development requires a working through of anti-Black sentiment, lingering resentment about not having been born White, and deep feelings of alienation from one's African heritage and from other Blacks. A minority of African Americans never progress beyond this earliest stage. At the other end is the highest stage of racial identity development, and it is characterized by strong pride in the Black race, as well as a commitment to social activism that can include helping others regardless of race. While those of every skin color can be found at every stage of racial identity development, among the ones who never progress beyond the first stage there is a higher percentage with relatively lighter skin tones. Perhaps they are just light enough to feel it is not particularly important to embrace a positive Black identity.

Another reason for the slightly higher percentage of African Americans with lighter skin color at the first stage likely relates to the color gap in power and privilege. Compared to African Americans who are darker, light-skinned African Americans are more likely to live in predominantly White neighborhoods, work in predominantly White business environments, or attend predominantly White schools. Among these adults, some are clearly embarrassed by the behavior of "those other Blacks acting out negative stereotypes," and may additionally harbor resentment regarding any expectation that they are supposed to help "clean up the problems of the Black race." Among the children of such families, one can find kids who are serious minded about their educational goals, and who find it unpleasant to hang around the Black kids who enjoy mocking them for wanting to earn high grades. These good students may prefer associating with other high-achieving students, who may be White. Joi, a thirty-year-old, light-skinned, successful Black entrepreneur from Philadelphia, remembers being called an "Oreo" in high school. She still wonders why "Black people always wanna say you're trying to act like you're White just because you are trying to learn, especially if you are light skinned like me."

Probably the most famous African American who appeared to both reject and resent his own Blackness is the late Michael Jackson. Many people, especially African Americans, felt that with every plastic surgery operation and cosmetic procedure he underwent, Jackson was progressively abandoning his Black roots and culture. If an alien came down from Mars and had to identify what race Jackson was, it would surely not guess Black—and yet probably not White, either. To be fair, Michael's music never lost its hip urban crossover pop appeal, and whatever he was doing to himself on the surface may or may not have matched how he was feeling inside. But now we'll never know.

Even without surgery, sometimes an African American's naturally occurring physical appearance is such that he or she appears to be White. And if that same person is at the first stage of racial identity development, he or she may choose to take feelings of alienation one step further, and abandon Black identity altogether. Pretending to be White is called "passing," and it is a phenomenon hardly limited to African Americans. In Nazi Germany, Jews passed as Christian; in the workplace there are gay men and lesbians who pass as straight; and, from job applications to dating websites, there are many older people who try to pass themselves off as younger than they are. Historically, passing was an understandable strategy for African Americans seeking to escape slavery or Jim Crow segregation. But today, most African Americans view passing with high disdain and consider the act as tantamount to betrayal and a form of Black cultural genocide.

Yet there are African Americans who look White, or at least racially ambiguous, and are proud to be Black. For them, not being seen as Black by other African Americans is deeply frustrating, and sometimes gravely insulting and emotionally exhausting. These individuals are what sociologist F. James Davis calls "inadvertent passers." In his book *Who Is Black?* Davis identifies possible responses to finding oneself in this odd racial dilemma: one can (1) hate all Whites, (2) reclaim an African name or speak with a distinctly Black accent, (3) dedicate oneself to public service and the elimination of all forms of discrimination, (4) serve as a liaison between the White and Black communities, or (5) avoid issues of racial identity altogether, focusing instead on some other aspect of one's identity, such as that derived from work or a profession.

Author, educator, and inadvertent passer Kathleen Cross, the daughter of a White woman and a Black man, appears to have blended several of Davis's strategies. Cross often wears T-shirts emblazoned with racial slogans, such as "Before There Was Any History There Was Black History." She often speaks in a way that is suggestive of Black culture, and is happy to serve as a bridge to Whites. Interestingly, research on racial identity development indicates that it is not that unusual for very light-skinned African Americans to end up at a middle stage of racial identity development where Blackness is idealized and Whiteness is denigrated.

One reason inadvertent passers may become so anti-White is that they are on the front lines of hearing things said about Blacks that might otherwise be censored if the speaker knew there was someone Black in the room. A very light-skinned interviewee named Kai recalls arguing with the owner of a nail salon, after the berating comment was made that "Black women" don't tip as much as "White women." Kai shot back that maybe it was because so many Blacks have to listen to insulting remarks like hers. "It happens to me regularly," said Winston, another interviewee, "and unless you are grounded and have a high level of self-esteem, you can easily begin to hate the Black part of you and even 'pass' on an as-needed basis because you just start to feel as if you don't want to be associated with all the negativity associated with being Black." Kai admits that as a young girl she was not in love with the Black side of her. In fact, Kai goes on to say that as an adolescent, "sometimes I felt like the young Sarah Jane in *Imitation of Life*,[8] as I, too, didn't even want my mother driving me to school. I will always regret that." Kai is an example of someone whose Black identity early on in life was shaped by her light skin color but who later progressed to view her racial identity in a more positive, self-affirming way.

While passing as White is considered a shameful act today, multiracial activists accuse those of mixed heritage who claim solely to be African American of being the ones who are passing—as Black! They ask, "How is it that someone of mixed race—who may even be genetically more White than Black—can call himself or herself just African-American?" In a country where adherence to the one-drop rule is normative, and controversy about that is rising, those who are biracial or multiracial will likely experience, at least for some period during their development, confusion as to what their racial identity is or should be.

Critically acclaimed film and television actress (in, for example, *The Office*) Rashida Jones, who is also the daughter

---

8. *Imitation of Life*, originally produced in 1934 and remade in 1959, is considered the classic "tragic mulatto" film. In it, a light-skinned daughter rejects her dark-skinned mother and tries to pass as White.

of the iconic *Mod Squad* actress Peggy Lipton (who is White and Jewish) and music composer-producer Quincy Jones (who is Black), is one such individual. In a 2007 article for *American Jewish Life Magazine,* she described the challenge of establishing a self-identity that felt right and comfortable for her. When Jones was in high school, she identified as Black, but when she went off to college, she began exploring her religious heritage, in part because some of the African-American girls there didn't like her because she was light skinned, with long, light hair. Today she feels more comfortable identifying herself as a Jewish woman.

Once again the length of time it can take and the amount of fluidity in the process of establishing one's own racial or cultural/ethnic identity is evident. And as was the case for Jones, often those who are biracial or multicultural may need a bit longer to figure it all out.

The multiracial community continues its campaign to encourage those of mixed heritage to disclose and embrace the entirety of their racial background. But thorny questions do arise. Sandi K., an African-American teacher at a junior college, says she is fine with someone's choice to claim multiple racial identities, but also strongly feels if that is their decision, then they have no right to take advantage of scholarships and other affirmative action opportunities meant exclusively for African Americans. As Sandi puts it:

Many multiracial people reject being called Black. However, when I am at my school I see that many of them apply for grants and try to take advantage of scholarships that are targeted toward African Americans. You can't have it both ways. You can't run from your blackness but want to take

advantage of the benefits of being an African American.
That's racial prostitution.

Another point about the multiracial movement that bothers many African Americans is its lack of practicality. In America, when the rubber meets the road, racism will always trump biraciality or multiethnicity; if a light-skinned biracial male drives through a predominantly White neighborhood and is stopped by a cop, then, as Kenya, an African-American woman who manages a fast-food restaurant, sees it, "He is a Black man who has been stopped by a cop. Not a biracial man stopped by a cop. That's the reality."

The issue of how best to claim one's racial identity when born of racially mixed parents is only going to grow. In fact, results from the 2010 U.S. Census reveal that multiracial children are the fastest-growing population of young people in the United States. Census results also indicate that since 2000, the number of multiracial children born in this country has increased by nearly 50 percent, to 4.2 million. This figure includes, however, all combinations of racial makeup that do not necessarily involve someone of African descent. But in looking at just those who identified on their census form as both White and Black—which back in 2000 was the most common mixed-race classification—the change from 2000 to 2010 for Black-White biracial individuals was a staggering 134 percent, to 1.8 million people.

It is clear that the multiracial movement is not a passing fad. In 1996, clinical psychologist Maria P. P. Root, an advocate for the multiracial choice cause, wrote a powerful statement of empowerment to help those of mixed ethnic, cultural, and racial background to more fully claim with pride their own identity.

Bill of Rights for Racially Mixed People

I HAVE THE RIGHT . . .

Not to justify my existence in this world.

Not to keep the races separate within me.

Not to justify my ethnic legitimacy.

Not to be responsible for people's discomfort with my physical or ethnic ambiguity.

I HAVE THE RIGHT . . .

To identify myself differently than strangers expect me to identify.

To identify myself differently than how my parents identify me.

To identify myself differently than my brothers and sisters.

To identify myself differently in different situations.

I HAVE THE RIGHT . . .

To create a vocabulary to communicate about being multiracial or multiethnic.

To change my identity over my lifetime—and more than once.

To have loyalties and identification with more than one group of people.

To freely choose whom I befriend and love.

Chapter 5

Hair Stories: Politics of the Straight and Nappy

The history of Black hair styling has its roots in Africa. Ancient artworks from as early as 500 BC depict African women wearing their hair in twists, braids, and dreadlocks, and often accentuated with ornamentation. Such elaborate styles are made possible by the oval (as opposed to round) hair follicles, which allow hair to curl tightly (rather than lie flat) when it leaves the scalp. Because curls allow for scalp ventilation, this unique feature has kept heads cool for centuries. But when Africans were uprooted and shipped to the New World, all manner of traditions and practices, including language, culture, and hairstyles, were stripped from them. In the new land, the once magnificent and proudly celebrated hairstyles of African women became a source of shame. What emerged instead was a twisted weave of White, African, and native hair textures. This chapter will explore hair as a visible physical feature that, like skin color, came to signify status and assimilation. We will review the politics of letting hair go natural versus chemically processing it, and look at how children are influenced by larger cultural messages regarding certain hair types.

Following the Civil War, the mulatto elite, whose African blood was mixed with that of Europeans and sometimes Native Americans, tended to have tresses that varied from softly wavy to nearly straight. These society women did much to set the standard of beauty for all others of African descent in America. In an effort to emulate the mulattoes, Negro women with far less European ancestry (or none at all) sought various ways to make their tightly curly hair lie flatter against their scalp. Some used a "mammy-leg," or stocking cap, so called because it was cut from the leg of a woman's stocking, that they pulled over greased hair to make it go flat. Hours later, when the cap was removed, the hair would be flatter, but the cap worked only so well and for only so long. Humid weather, a common occurrence in the South, quickly returned the hair to its natural state.

Something more effective was called for, and salvation came from an African-American woman named Sarah Breedlove McWilliams Walker (aka Madam C. J. Walker). At the end of the 1800s, she claimed to have had a vision in which an old man revealed secret ingredients for a special formula that would make scalps and hair healthy. Whether that story was true or not, the secret formula seemed to work. In 1900, she established the "Walker System of Beauty Culture," and by 1910 Madam Walker was operating an impressive factory and laboratory in Indianapolis. She also adapted a European hot comb for use on Black hair. Walker then trained other Black women in how to straighten hair with the Walker Hair Care products and properly use her new hot comb. In fact, she marketed her merchandise so effectively throughout the United States, and also in Europe, that by 1910 *The Guinness Book of*

World Records had identified Walker as the first self-made millionairess in history. That the individual who became the first self-made millionairess would be someone who profited from revolutionizing hair care and cosmetics makes sense. As we know, people will pay good money to make their hair look good.

Walker was in some ways the Oprah of her day. Not in being a media mogul, certainly, but in how she came from humble beginnings and then reached, by sheer will and determination, and a little bit of luck, the very top echelons of wealth. In a country where for years few Black women had much of an opportunity to even make a decent wage, these two women's stories are truly remarkable.

Many have called Madam Walker "the hair-straightening queen," but she herself did not use the word "straightener" when discussing merchandise. Walker particularly resented accusations that her products were intended to make African-American women look White. According to her granddaughter A'Lelia P. Bundles, Walker stated in 1917:

> *Right here let me correct the erroneous impression held by some that I claim to straighten the hair. I want the great masses of my people to take a greater pride in their personal appearance and to give their hair proper attention.*

Like many others to this day who profit from selling beauty products that happen to trend a woman's appearance in a more Western direction, she defended the business on the grounds that the products sold were simply meeting a demand that they themselves did not create.

Fortunately, since the 1920s new and greatly improved chemical-based hair relaxers have been developed for African-

American women to use—or perhaps not so fortunately, as many of these products contain known carcinogens. Comedian Chris Rock dramatically illustrated this point in his 2009 documentary film *Good Hair* when he showed how a soda can could dissolve after coming into contact with a strong formula of the same corrosive chemicals used in hair-straightening products. And if they are not applied with precise timing, these same products can leave a woman bald, with third-degree burns on her scalp.

Between the 1920s and the 1950s, Black women continued to routinely straighten their hair. Some even took to wearing hairpieces and wigs to achieve the latest look. There were a few who left their hair natural, but probably more for reasons of cost than pride. All of the popular styles for "women in the know" during this period required diligent maintenance, which translated as regular straightening.

Fast-forward to the 1960s, when we entered a "more enlightened" era about Black features. This period marked a revolution in African Americans' attitudes about their hair. Up until that time most Black women, and some Black men, regularly straightened their hair. In fact, it was rare for a Black woman to appear in public with unprocessed hair; those who dared to do so risked ridicule and chastisement from family members, friends, and strangers alike. When the Afro became fashionable, it was considered radical in more ways than one. The style not only associated the wearer with the politics of the Black Power Movement, but, for women in particular, the choice to wear an Afro signified a clear rejection of the long-standing straight-hair preference in their community. Members of both sexes began letting their hair grow out naturally in an effort to look more like Angela Davis, who in the late 1960s and early

1970s became the icon of the Black Power Movement with her large Afro, or like Sly Stone, the famous musician. During the 1960s, other women, like the acclaimed Black actress Cicely Tyson, celebrated pride by styling her hair in cornrows or cutting it short. Most Whites didn't understand the hoopla about Black women letting their hair go natural; the Whites only knew they liked Black women's hair a lot better when it looked more like European-styled hair. Indicative of the negative attitudes toward natural hairstyles was the firing in 1971 of Melba Tolliver, a respected Black reporter, from an ABC affiliate in New York. The charge was that she dared to disrespectfully wear her hair in an Afro when assigned to cover the wedding of President Nixon's daughter Tricia. Ten years later, in 1981, African-American awarding-winning journalist Dorothy Reed from KGO-TV San Francisco was suspended for two weeks when she appeared on air with her hair styled in cornrows with beads. After much protest and negotiation, a compromise was reached: Reed could come back to work with braids but no beads in her hair.

Like any popular hairstyle, the 'fro eventually became unfashionable. During the late 1970s and into the '80s, Black women's attitudes about natural hair gradually "went back" to what they were before the '60s. The old tradition of calling hair that was straight or wavy "good" and hair that was tightly curled and nappy "bad" returned—or, as many would argue, it had never really gone away. Then, immediately following this time, beginning in about the mid-1980s, the Jheri curl exploded onto the scene. As one Black woman in her late forties puts it today, "The Jheri curl was for everyone who ever wanted to imitate having that 'good hair.'"

The 1990s proved to be an interesting time in Black hairstyles, as both ends of the hairstyle spectrum were represented.

At one end were Afrocentric styles like naturals, and at the other end were extensions, weaves, and processing. The decade began as the Neo-Soul era, so called because of the music popular at the time, which was a mixture of 1970s-style soul and contemporary R & B with elements of hip-hop. Like many cultural trends, Neo-Soul influenced how many young African-American women (and men) dressed and wore their hair. While some African-American women began to copy the more Afrocentric fashions and hairstyles of artists like Erykah Badu and the prolific singer-songwriter Angie Stone and singer-poet Jill Scott, other women embraced the wearing of long weaves and extensions. The latter style seemed to win out in the end. In summing up the 1990s, even *Essence* would declare, "Black Women Love Weaves." As the last decade of the millennium drew to a close, the "it girl" was Beyoncé, lead singer of the R & B group Destiny's Child, and it was her light-brown-long-tresses hairstyle that became the look all the girls wanted to imitate.

The new millennium is sometimes described as "post-PC," in reference to a time before that when political correctness dictated that stereotype-promoting comments were to be censored, out of concern about offending members of minority cultures. But in the post-PC era, the motto seemed to be "Anything goes," though always of course in the name of humor— that multipurpose escape hatch. Two recent events relating to Black hairstyles characterize the post-PC mentality.

On April 4, 2007, the day after the Rutgers women's basketball team played hard in the NCAA finals championship game only to lose to Tennessee, nationally syndicated MSNBC radio talk show host Don Imus, of *Imus in the Morning,* made a reference to the Rutgers team as "some nappy-headed hos." To many, Imus's comments were hurtful, distasteful, insensitive, and—to most African Americans in particular—outright racist and sexist. It was an affront not just to the Rutgers basketball team, but to all Black female athletes, and ultimately all Black women. That evening, Imus would eventually offer somewhat of an apology for what he had said, but the damage was done. On April 9, the controversial talk show host was fired. The Rutgers women's basketball team graciously accepted his apology, but as one Black female collegiate athlete said about Imus's comment, "How dare he? We take a lot of pride and put in a lot of effort to make sure our hair looks good. Any reference to black women's hair, especially using the word 'nappy,' is an insult."

On July 21, 2008, another media firestorm erupted when *The New Yorker* magazine ran a cartoon on its cover of Barack Obama, then a presidential candidate, wearing a Muslim-like turban and robe, giving his wife, Michelle Obama, a "fist bump." The future First Lady in the image was wearing a large Afro and packing an AK-47. Along with the many misleading stereotypes portrayed in this cartoon, the one that pegged Michelle Obama as some sort of Black revolutionary for having a large Afro, which she has never worn, was particularly offensive to women. Once again an African-American woman's hairstyle was defining her. Of this depiction of Michelle Obama, a writer named Shanna Miles, who blogs under the name "The Luscious Librarian," wrote:

> . . . *but what got me was not only the unfunny elitist satire that says, "If you don't get it you're just not sophisticated as we are," but the depiction of Michelle Obama with an afro that somehow makes her sinister and terroristic. . . . As a natural woman it is disheartening to still see the politics of hair played out on a national external scale. I under-*

stand that internally black folk have issues with straight and nappy (that's hundreds of years of psychosocial indoctrination), but we really have a long way to go if the entire nation still feels that way. . . . That cover says that with my natural hair I am not to be trusted, I am serious and pro-black, which means that I am anti-White and because of that I am anti-America and to be feared. I resent it and I have to say if you tell a joke and you're the only one laughing it's because it's not funny.

The New Yorker predictably defended itself on the grounds that the image was meant to be humorous. So, as it was with Imus, the sense of humor of those offended was called into question, which made those actions doubly insulting.

When children hear and see African-American women's hair being made fun of, it only reinforces attitudes already in the making. From an early age most Black girls come to understand all too well the meaning of "good" versus "bad" hair. And when a girl has naturally kinky hair and nappy "kitchens" (the hairline at the back of the neck), she may conclude that her hair needs to be "fixed," as if it were somehow broken. While probably a short hairstyle would work best for little girls with kinky hair, most of them reject outright such a suggestion, as it would make them appear too boylike. Surrounded by constant images of princesses, young girls nearly always want long hair to make clear their feminine identity. But for many African-American girls, long hair is unmanageable and simply unattainable in its natural state. Still, they want to grow it. Thus Black girls whose hair has a kinky texture gets braided and yanked, rubber-banded and barretted, into a presentable state. And when parents grow weary of taming their daughters' hair, many simply opt to treat it with chemical relaxers, or "kiddie perms." These hair relaxers, which are made from dangerous chemicals that can be absorbed through the skin, are sometimes used on girls as young as three or four years old. But one Black mother we interviewed said she was tired of fighting the comb, and defended her decision by saying, "I didn't have time to mess with that child's nappy head any longer, so I went and got it permed. It's been a lot easier on both of us since."

As adults, many African-American women look back with regret on getting a perm; some even wish their mothers had banned perms and simply let their hair be. A woman named Yvette longingly remembers what her hair was like when she was young. She says that many of her earliest memories feature her Afro-puffs (hair that is parted in the middle, rubber-banded, and "picked out" into two small Afros, one on each side) or her thousand braids with bows at the end. She also remembers how fascinated the White children at school were by the natural softness of her hair, and how they were always asking to touch it. "For me, my hair was a source of pride and uniqueness," she recalls. But as she neared adolescence her mother declared that she "was turning into a young lady" and that it was time for her first permanent relaxer. To this day, Yvette yearns for her natural hair, yet continues to get permanents regularly. "In order to reverse the process now, it would mean a lot of hair breakage and hair loss," she sighs. "At this point in my life, it's a lot less effort just to deal with it the way it is."

But for other African-American women, childhood memories of short, nappy locks bring forth feelings of shame, not sweet nostalgia. A dark-skinned woman named Caroline remembers other children's taunts of "Your hair's so short, you can smell yo' brains." Caroline was ecstatic when her mother marched her down to Sister Westbury's Beauty Nook for her first perm:

I had it doubly hard when I was in grade school. Not only was I dark-skinned but I also had short beady hair. I always got teased by the boys and laughed at by the girls because my hair was so nappy and always stuck up in the air. I hated my hair and cried many nights. I was so glad when I got my hair straightened. It changed my whole life.

It can be tough on a parent to hear a daughter express hatred of her hair, but also hard to know when to say no and when it might be better to let a child like Caroline have the perm. It did seem to change her life for the better—something every parent wants for his or her child. One mother expressed her frustration over her five-year-old daughter's feelings about her hair this way:

Raven's hair is really kinky. She takes after her father, who is from Ghana. Raven really hates her hair and cries when I comb it. She says she wishes she had pretty straight hair like her little White friend Emmie. That was so devastating for me to hear. I cried. I thought I was teaching her to be proud and to love herself.

Interestingly enough, men—who ironically as a group are often accused by African-American women of being the sole reason why they must absolutely keep their hair long and permed— are often the ones most upset when a daughter expresses hatred of her hair and a desire to get it permed. Perhaps mothers know better and understand the pressure a daughter is under. In 1992, essayist and cultural critic Gerald Early, who is currently the Merle Kling Professor of Modern Letters at Washington University in St. Louis, first published an article describing his intense disappointment the day his two daughters, then aged seven and ten, came home with their hair permed:

> *During that summer the girls abandoned their Afro hairstyles for good. When they burst through the door with their hair newly straightened, beaming, I was so taken aback in a kind of horror that I could only mutter in astonishment when they asked, "How do you like it?"*
>
> *It was as if my children were no longer mine, as if a culture that had convinced them they were ugly had taken them from me. The look I gave my wife brought this response from her: "They wanted their hair straightened, and they thought they were old enough for it. Besides, there is no virtue in wearing an Afro. I don't believe in politically correct hair."*

In 2009, when Chris Rock's film *Good Hair* premiered, Rock explained both during his promotional tour and in the film itself that his primary reason for making the documentary was to figure out what would make his daughter Lola want to ask why she didn't have "good" hair. Troubled by the question, Rock no doubt at the time said everything he could to convince his daughter that her hair was not just good but fabulously beautiful. But Lola's question and bad feelings motivated him to learn more about what lay behind this desire to have so-called good hair. How could such a yearning develop in a child so young? Rock drew on his considerable resources to make the film, and to his credit he made what is a very unfunny topic surprisingly humorous. And while the film itself may not have helped his daughter Lola or other little girls to love their kinky hair more, Rock did much to raise awareness and consciousness about Black women's hair among adults, many of whom were Whites learning about the issues for the first time.

Not long after the release of *Good Hair, Sesame Street*'s head writer and puppeteer Joey Mazzarino was similarly troubled when Segi, his four-year-old adopted daughter from Ethiopia, declared she hated her hair and wished that it was straight. Mazzarino and his wife, who are both White, were saddened by their daughter's comment, and felt they had to do something to help Segi, and other girls, too, feel that their hair is beautiful. Mazzarino developed a sketch and wrote an accompanying song called "I Love My Hair." In the sketch an adorable little brown-skinned girl Muppet with an Afro tosses her hair around, all the while singing a song with the opening line "Don't need a trip to the beauty shop, because I love what I got on top." The sketch debuted on *Sesame Street* on October 4, 2010, and the response to it has been nearly overwhelming. When the video clip was posted online, it immediately went viral. It is unlikely that Mazzarino knew just how deep the wounds go—not just in Black girls, but also African-American women—when it comes to shameful feelings about their hair. More than a few adult viewers admitted never having heard anything so positive and self-affirming about having kinky hair; they only wished they had seen something like that when they were little. And some Black parents wished that they had had it when their own daughters were young. Patricia, who is a fifty-year-old Black salesperson at a high-end department store in Chicago, lamented, "My girls hated their short hair and always said they wished they had some good hair. But it just wasn't in the genes."

Even with all the "happy to be nappy" attention, too many young girls still seem to be clamoring for their first kiddie perm—or, in some cases, are being subjected to one by their mothers. Perming not only has the potential to be physically harmful at the time that it is done, but also produces an unintended consequence. After getting their hair permed, young Black girls may no longer be allowed to go in the water for fear that their hair will "go back" if it gets wet. But what if they were to accidentally fall into a large body of water? The possibility of an accidental drowning from never learning how to swim must seem remote enough to be trumped by a decision to perm a child's hair and keep it dry and fresh. When Teresa, an African-American mother from the Bronx, was asked why she wouldn't let her daughter go swimming, she replied without hesitation, "I pay fifty dollars to get her hair done and it needs to last awhile. She will not get in a pool and get her hair wet after I have paid my hard-earned money to get her hair done." And Valerie D., now a fortysomething Black woman, remembers being made to get her first press-n-curl when she was nine years old, and afterward being told she could no longer do the one thing that she loved most, which was go swimming. Sadly, as a result of not ever learning to be comfortable in water as a child, many adult Black women have a deep fear of water—and perhaps rightfully so, because if they did fall in, they might drown.

As an aside, some in the Black community believe being discouraged from swimming is part of a larger reason why Black females are so underrepresented in recreational, professional, or amateur events like swimming and diving. But Valerie, mentioned above, who did eventually learn how to swim and even become a lifeguard at a community center, does not agree. She says that the issue of the lack of Black girls in water sports has less to do with vanity and more to do with segregation. "If more young black girls had access to swimming pools early in their lives, we would have more swimmers despite the hair issues." That would be nice, but it still doesn't "fix" the hair problem.

In short, for African-American women, hair is political. Although acceptance of naturals, processed hair, and weaves has grown over the years, no matter what choice a Black woman makes, there will be someone who will respond negatively to it. Such was the case many years ago for a Black woman who remembers being squawked at, teased, and harassed on the street for daring to have hair that was unprocessed. Another sister, with long brown "locs," now recalls, "When my hair was going through the 'wile chile' stage [the first phase of growing locs, in which the hair looks completely untamed], a brother actually stopped me on the street demanding to know 'when in the hell' was I going to 'do somethin' with my nappy-headed ass hair.'" The award-winning actress Whoopi Goldberg has had members of her own community tell her that her locs were disgusting and that she should "take those nappy braids out." During the 1960s, actress Cicely Tyson was even told by members of the Black community that while she might be a gifted actress, her short natural hairstyle was detrimental to the image of Black women.

The choice to go short actually regained ground when Halle Berry, the Black woman's poster child for the short hairdo, went short in the mid-1990s. Berry's iconic short hairstyle changed the way African-American women saw short hair, and everyone wanted to mimic her hairdo. Although celebrities can change their hairstyles for an upcoming part in a film or simply from personal preference, a short haircut today has become a staple—or at least a go-to style—for many

Black actresses and singers like Regina King, Tisha Campbell-Martin, Eva Marcille (née Pigford), Estelle, Keri Hilson, and Solange.

In the summer of 2009, Solange Knowles, a singer in her own right and the younger sister of the long-haired Beyoncé, did something that would forever distinguish her from her famous sibling. Solange sheared her lengthy tresses into an auburn buzz cut, and in so doing, reclaimed her hair's natural texture. On her Twitter page Solange stated that one of the reasons for shaving her head was "to be free from the bondage that black women sometimes put on themselves with hair." In response, the blogs went wild. At one point Solange was so enraged over all of the attention made of her short haircut that she tweeted, "I am #3 trending topic [on Twitter] before IRAN and some of you can't even locate it on a map. It's sad." At least one African-American woman got why Solange shaved her head and had this to say: "I love her short natural hair. Too often Black women hide behind long hair or weaves. Her short cut showed just how confident she really is." Of course, many African-American men said she should never have cut her hair, but others did praise her for having the courage to do it. Since then, Solange has grown her hair out longer, but not without criticism from those who think she should keep it short and natural forever.

Another illustration of the hot politics of hair occurred in May 2011 when a White fan of Grammy award-winning Barbadian chanteuse Rihanna questioned on Twitter why the singer's hair looked so nappy. The fan's comment was made following Rihanna's unveiling on Twitter of the cover artwork for her new single "Man Down." To many Black women, including Rihanna, who seems to change her hairstyle as much as her wardrobe, this White woman's use of the word "nappy" was as offensive as the "other N-word." The singer was quick to respond, "Cuz I'm black, bitch!!!!"

Other contemporary African-American actresses and singers, including Tracee Ellis Ross, Jill Scott, MeShell Ndege-Ocello, India Arie, and Dianne Reeves, have joined such longtime performers and writers as S. Epatha Merkerson, Cassandra Wilson, Chrisette Michele, Lauryn Hill, and Whoopi Goldberg in wearing their hair in a more natural style. But then, as celebrities, all of these women have greater artistic license to express themselves creatively—and more power to rebuff those who might be critical. Witness Rihanna's response. Yet even celebrities may find that the wearing of locs, which entails nothing more than letting one's curly hair grow out to the point where the separate strands begin to "loc" together, still carries lingering negative associations. Fortunately, the notion that only Black Nationalists or radical Rastafarians wear their hair in locs is fast fading as an ever-increasing number of musicians, artists, and athletes, as well as professors, journalists, and social workers—not exactly corporate types, but not members of a counterculture—now routinely loc their hair.

In many corporate environments, however, natural hairstyles like locs are simply not acceptable. Six Flags America amusement park in Largo, Maryland, was one of them. In 2006, two African-American women sued the corporation, claiming that they were discriminated against because of their locs. One woman said that as she was applying for a part-time job at Six Flags, she was told that her locs would disqualify her for employment there. The other Black woman, who also wore locs, had been called back for summer employment at Six Flags, but a supervisor told her that she first would have to get rid of that hairstyle if she wanted the job. Six Flags was following a standard conservative, corporate grooming policy that deems locs to be a "radical" hairstyle and therefore not acceptable. FedEx was also sued by several Black employees in New York who refused to cut their locs. The employees said they wore locs as part of their religion. Eventually, FedEx changed its policy to include locs being worn by employees, as long as they were for religious expression. These are but two examples of corporations that have been sued by Black employees who were asked to change their hairstyle or who felt discriminated against because of their hair. Blanche Williams, the founder of the National Black Women's Town Hall and former national radio talk show host of *Greatness By Design,* who also wears locs, says that examples like these are why a lot of women don't want to go natural. She had this to say:

> *There are many women who look at natural hair as a barrier to employment, advancement, and/or success. I take care of my locs like I take care of myself and my business. Everything is in order, appropriate and professional. Many women have come up to me and admitted they would love to wear their hair natural but they believed they would be fired because of that. This level of pseudo-fear is emblematic of the level of psychological damage our Black women internalize in every level of their life.*

It seems that a certain level of Black consciousness is necessary before a woman dares to go natural. The relationship between hairstyle and politics is far from straightforward, however. One African-American professional woman from Chicago told us that she could not imagine wearing her hair in any way but in locs, or perhaps cornrows, since everything she does emanates from an Afrocentric perspective. Yet she admits to knowing women as strongly Afrocentric as she who routinely process their hair, and others with no interest at all in fostering Black culture or politics who wear natural styles like cornrows.

Dark-skinned Black women who grow locs appear to have reached a point in their lives at which they no longer feel the need to compensate for the color of their skin or the texture of their hair. Breaking free of past conditioning about hair may be part of a larger spiritual awakening. Sandra B., who once managed an urban charity organization in Chicago, describes her locs in spiritual terms:

> I love my hair like this. I wouldn't trade it for straight hair any day. There is something so spiritual and in-touch about my hair. I feel connected with my roots. My hair gives me a sense of oneness with nature. You know how beautiful nature is when it's just left alone to grow naturally the way God intended? Well, that's how I look at my hair. Just growing naturally the way God intended.

Freelance writer Naadu Blankson, in an article for *Essence,* compared the locing of her hair with the unlocking of her inhibitions, and Alice Walker once wrote, in the same magazine, that the ability to loc may depend on the flow of one's natural energy not being blocked by "anger, hatred, or self-condemnation."

Black women with long hair, whether natural or processed, whether achieved by hair weaves or extensions, are acutely sensitive to accusations that they are trying to look White, or that they got a weave just to achieve length. In defense, some may cite ancient traditions from Africa, where hair weaving originated and is considered an art form. Thus, when asked about the mélange of long braids neatly twisted into a hair weave hanging down her back, Pamela, a Black graduate student in psychology, replies without missing a beat:

> I wear my hair like this for a reason. It's convenient and I feel very attractive. My ancestors from Egypt wore their hair long and straight or braided. Sometimes both. This is not about having long hair to try to be White; this is about being who I am as an African American. It has more to do with style and cosmetics than it has to do with being like some White woman. My hair is an accessory.

Hair texture, like skin tone, carries much social and historical baggage for Blacks. All things being equal, a Black woman whose hair grows naturally straight is usually thought to be from a "better" family than a woman whose hair is very nappy. Black women who wear natural styles, like braids, cut across socioeconomic lines, but a politically defiant style like locs is generally a middle-class expression of Black consciousness. Inner-city girls and women are probably the least likely to wear locs. Poor Black women with very kinky hair strive instead for straighter-looking hair, but because they cannot afford constant professional relaxation treatments (which can cost up to $85 a session), their hair often looks stiff and overly processed, in what is derisively called a "ghetto 'do." Still, hair is so important to Black women that, regrettably, some would rather be late paying their rent than miss getting their hair permed.

While some African Americans may assign varying degrees of political weight to hairstyle choice, most adult Black women, whether they process or not, respect and understand the choices of others. There is, after all, a reality factor to contend with in

White-dominated America. For example, a Black teacher from California who had been content with wearing her hair in a natural style decided to straighten it when she and her husband began to look for a house to buy.

While more and more Black women today are daring to go natural—by one estimate, during the period between 2009 and 2011 alone, the number of African-American women perming their hair dropped by 12 percent—they remain a distinct minority. Straightened hair is the standard for "respectable" African-American women—those with corporate careers as well as the wives of businessmen or Black politicians, such as Michelle Obama. It is estimated that about 75 percent of Black women have permed or relaxed their hair at some point.

In 2009, Tyra Banks aired a show on White women who wear weaves. The show was entitled "Fake Hair Academy," and in it Banks addressed the misconception that only Black women wear weaves. Tyra wanted to reveal the truth that White women wear fake hair, too. One of the show's guests was Meghan McCain, daughter of Arizona Senator John McCain. On air Meghan revealed to Tyra that not only does she wear extensions but the majority of her White friends do as well.

In all fairness, some African Americans do look better with long hair, in just the same way that some White women do. But many African-American women feel it is a double standard that White women can wear their hair any way they want with little public criticism from others, while Black women nearly always have to defend or even hide their choices, especially if they get a weave. As one African-American woman put it, "No one criticizes White women for wearing weaves. But Black women always get chastised for wearing fake hair."

Gabrielle, a black hairdresser who works in a mostly White

salon, commented about White women getting extensions: "I have been doing hair for fifteen years now and I have always worked in White salons. Believe me when I say White women have been getting extensions glued in and clipped onto their hair forever." Her warning to Black women: "Don't be fooled by all that long hair these White girls got. It ain't theirs either."

Neicy, an African-American woman we interviewed, believes that Black women are the ones who are always trying to hide their weaves. White women could care less if you know that their hair is not really their own. In fact, she said:

> I was in the Gap today and the young White girl behind the checkout counter began telling me how she had just gotten her new extensions put in. She asked me how I thought they looked. I told her they looked very natural. She said she had a hot date tonight and that she wanted to change it up. A Black woman would never tell you that. She would want everyone to believe that it is her hair.

Illustrating this point further, Neicy told us about an African-American colleague in the accounting department at her office who insists that the down-her-back Naomi Campbell–like weave is actually her own hair. "This woman is crazy. She told me and the other women in the office that she has been growing her hair for years to get it this long, when we can all clearly see the tracks on top of her head." Neicy continued, "We all used to go work out together but she said she could no longer go because she was 'sweating out her hair' and 'damaging her hair' because she had to keep getting it done again after her workouts. This is just the kind of woman that gives Black women who wear weaves a bad name!"

The fact that the work colleague refused to work out any longer because of the effect it would have on her hair is part of a larger problem in the African-American community. In a study conducted in November 2007 at Wake Forest Baptist Medical Center in Winston-Salem, North Carolina, 31 percent of the African-American women surveyed said the reason they don't exercise at all, or at least as much as they should, involves hair care concerns. This is particularly troubling at a time when the American Obesity Association, an advocacy group, reports that 78 percent of Black women are overweight, and, within that group, 50 percent can be considered obese. Even knowing the health risks, some African-American women still refuse to engage in a sweaty workout for fear of ruining their hairstyle. Even if they wear weaves—excessive sweat and water can damage these as well. As one Black woman put it, "It costs a lot of time and money for Black women to get their hair done. Sweating out our hair is not an option. Anyway, for me, my man will be pissed off if my hair ain't lookin' 'right.'"

Some African-American women point to Black men as the reason why they keep their hair long and straightened. A Black college student named Crystal says that when her boyfriend saw her getting her hair cut short, he walked out at the first snip and would not talk to her for two weeks. Then the very same type of man will tell his woman not to "wear that arsenal [rollers] to bed" or ask, "Why are you going to bed with that do-rag on?"—something African Americans with long hair often do at night to keep their hair looking smooth. Christine, a premed student at a major Black university in Chicago, says, "I wrap my hair every night and every night my boyfriend complains that I have my hair wrapped. He says I look like Aunt Jemima. I had to remind him that I ain't White and I can't go to bed and just wake up and shake my hair into place. It takes a lot of effort to get my hair to be presentable for the next morning." Christine went on to say that sometimes she just feels like cutting it all off but that she knows her boyfriend would "have a fit."

"Black men are not only obsessed with long hair," says Michelle, a twentysomething stylist living in Miami. "But they are obsessed with that good hair, too. You especially feel it living in Miami with all these gorgeous Cuban women who have long, dark, Rapunzel-like hair and olive skin. African-American men here don't even look at Black women—why should they? With Analena running around, they get the best of both worlds—ethnic and beautiful, with all that good hair."

Some African-American men do admit to using the texture and "grade" of a Black woman's hair to judge whether the quality of her hair and how she wears it will fit into their lifestyle. Music mogul and hip-hop impresario Andre Harrell says that some single men may feel it's important to consider whether an African-American woman can get into a sauna or go swimming without worrying about her hair, especially if these are the types of activities that he enjoys. And then there are men like rapper Yung Berg, who takes this concept to the extreme, as when he once famously spoke about what he termed "the pool test." "I love the pool test," explains Berg. "If a woman can jump in a pool exactly like [she is] and [she doesn't] come out looking better than [she] looked before going in the pool, then that is not a good look."

A Black man named Shamar said he doesn't dislike short hair on Black women, but admitted he prefers when hair is long because he finds it sexy and ultrafeminine. Another man, named Eric, added, "I like to grab my woman's hair during sex." Andre Harrell suggests this is not a good idea, especially if she has a weave. His advice is never to touch a Black woman's hair during sex: "Just keep your hands on another body part." African-American actress Nia Long would tend to agree, and has even talked about how awkward "weave sex" can be. Her advice: try to stay on top.

However, it is just not during sex that African-American women do not like or want anyone fingering their hair. Touching a Black woman's hair anytime by anyone, especially if it's a White individual, is a taboo and considered a sign of disrespect. Hair is a very sensitive issue for most African Americans and feelings about it are quite different from those most White women might have. Maleka, a thirtysomething Black woman from Atlanta, said she had to "go off" on a White woman, someone she did not know, who insisted on touching her long, bushy hair. "She obviously did not understand the extent of her racism when she decided she was going to touch my hair without my consent." Many African-American women believe that there are Whites who subconsciously feel a sense of privilege when it comes to a Black woman's body. Maleka would go on to say that "some Whites still feel they do not have to respect a Black woman's personal space." But others in the African-American community say that for most White people, the touching has less to do with racism and more to do with simply being arrogant. In fact, some in the Black community say that allowing someone of another race to inquire about, and even touch, what seems different or interesting to them should be used as an opportunity to teach. Regardless of how one may consider the action, as racist or inquisitive, no one should invade another person's space and touch that person without first gaining permission.

During the fifty-third annual Grammy Awards ceremony in

2011, teen crooner Justin Bieber committed the cardinal sin of touching a Black woman's hair when he "petted" the Afro of the Best New Artists winner, jazz bassist and singer Esperanza Spalding. During an Associated Press conference after Spalding's win, the interviewer asked the pair how they felt about each other. When it was his turn to answer, Bieber looked at Spalding, petted her Afro, and said, "I like your hair." Many in the Black community saw both race and gender dynamics play out in this exchange. Bieber should have asked Ms. Spalding if he could touch her hair. Those in the debate felt Bieber invaded Spalding's space and disrespected her by petting her hair like she was a "Chia Pet." Others, however, said that this should be used as a "teachable moment" and that Bieber should be given a pass as he was only sixteen. Also, since he is not from the United States, he may not understand how this type of action might be perceived from a racial perspective. One Black woman, angered at Bieber's "nerve," countered that "all White people need to understand that touching a Black woman's hair without her permission is like fondling a woman's breast or grabbing her ass. It is absolutely not acceptable."

Black men rarely have to deal with someone of another race walking up to them and touching their hair. This is not to say that Black men haven't had their own issues about hair, but hair in general is not as important to identity for them as it is for Black women.

Since 1920, Black men have been known to straighten their hair, whether it was for assimilation reasons or the rejection of an Afrocentric aesthetic. During the 1950s and '60s, Black entertainers, most notably Chuck Berry and Little Richard, donned the "city slicker" look by straightening their hair with chemicals and then slicking it down to their heads. Black men during this time were known to go to great lengths to get straighter hairstyles. Malcolm X famously wrote in his autobiography about the torture he endured to "conk" his hair. After going to the store and purchasing Red Devil lye and other ingredients, he would have his friend Shorty apply the conk (short for congolene). Shorty would warn Malcolm that the lye would burn real "bad" but that the longer he could withstand his scalp feeling as if it were in flames, the straighter the hair. Malcolm talked about how he felt at the sight of his freshly done "man perm." After enduring all of the pain of the lye burning his scalp, when he finally looked into the mirror his first thought was that it was all worth it. "My first view in the mirror blotted out the hurting," he wrote. "I'd seen some pretty conks, but when it's the first time, on your own head, the transformation, after the lifetime of kinks, is staggering." Later, Malcolm would come to regret his decision to conk his hair. About this he would say:

> *I had joined that multitude of Negro men and women in America who are brainwashed into believing that the black people are "inferior"—and White people "superior"—that they will even violate and mutilate their God-created bodies to try to look "pretty" by White standards.*

Although conking and straighter hairstyles fell out of vogue during the 1960s—when the Black Power Movement ushered in more natural styles like the large Afro, à la Sly Stone—the "man perm" could still be seen on some of the biggest Black entertainers, like James Brown, Jackie Wilson, and Little Richard, as well as on the religious leader turned activist Al Sharpton.

Leading out of the 1960s and continuing into the 1970s,

the man perm was epitomized by the long, flowing locks of Ron O'Neal, who starred in the 1972 smash "blaxploitation" movie *Superfly*. This movie transformed a culture, and everyone from pimps to the Black man on the street wanted to wear the long, wavy hair that would come to be known affectionately as the "Jesus perm."

In the 1980s, as noted earlier, the ubiquitous Jheri curl (aka "the Curl") and finger waves were the hairstyles of choice for many African Americans. Both styles gave the appearance of curly or wavy hair. During the height of its popularity, iconic male wearers of the Curl included everyone from Michael Jackson to Ice Cube. But the look didn't last very long, and by the 1990s, the Jheri curl was fading. In the Neo-Soul era of the late 1990s, Black men like the R & B superstar Maxwell turned to wearing more natural hairstyles.

Today, Black men can choose from a wider variety of hairstyles—from Afros to Caesar cuts, to shaving it off altogether. Yet there remains one style that is still viewed as a highly radical choice, and that is locs. In the same way that White businessmen must avoid wearing their hair very long if they want the establishment to take them seriously, few Black professionals would ever risk wearing their hair in locs. In general, Black men seem to have a more positive attitude toward their hair than most Black women do. Even when the men start to go bald, they can just shave it off and make a fashion statement.

On the other side of the globe, a very different fashion statement is curiously being made by youths in a Japanese subculture where the wearing of hair in braids, locs, twists, or the Afro is considered hip. As one Black women said after hearing about the new Asian hairstyle trend, "At least somebody's embracing the nappy."

Anguished concerns about hairstyles have hurt and held back far too many African-American women and a few Black men, too. It's best to remember that preferences are not necessarily prejudices and everyone has his or her own likes and dislikes. Instead of criticizing one another on hairstyle choices or spending large sums of money and time on hair care, it would be far more helpful to focus on issues of greater importance and relevance. Just ask sixteen-year-old Gabby Douglas who, shortly after making history as the first African American to win the All-Around Olympic gymnastics competition, was harshly criticized on the blogosphere for having an "unkempt ponytail." Sadly the cattiest comments posted on Twitter and Facebook came mostly from other African-American women who seemed to think Gabby had just competed in a beauty pageant and not the world's premier sporting event. Yet it was inspiring to see the young gymnast's class when she simply responded via Twitter, "I just made history. And you're gonna focus on my hair." Since Gabby's hair controversy erupted, other Black female athletes, most notably tennis stars Venus and Serena, have spoken up in the mainstream media about the ridiculous challenge of both sweating and maintaining a proper-looking Black woman's hairstyle. Even African-American television news reporter Nancy Giles of the CBS *Sunday Morning Show,* who wears her own hair in a short afro, did a feature on why there needs to be so much polarization around Black hairstyles. At least the issue is out of the closet as never before, so perhaps the sentiments of India Arie's natural hair anthem "I Am Not My Hair" (2006) will finally be heard and embraced.

Chapter 6

Families and Friends: Drawing the Color Lines

I n vitro fertilization (IVF) is a reproductive method, first carried out successfully in 1978, in which an egg is mixed with sperm for fertilization outside the body, and the resulting embryo is then implanted in a woman's uterus in order for a pregnancy to proceed. It has helped thousands of infertile couples have a child. Embryos obtained through IVF can also be screened, before implantation, for deadly genetic diseases, such as sickle cell anemia and cystic fibrosis. Increasingly, pre-implantation screening is also being used to increase the odds of having a baby of a desired sex. As long as there is a physical characteristic for which scientists can isolate the genetic markers, screening for it can take place. The assumption is that in some not-too-distant future, couples will be able to screen an embryo not just for disease or gender, but also for such physical traits as eye, hair, and skin color. In this future world where such choice is possible, could we witness a decline in African-American babies whose skin is not light in color? Will the desire to "lighten the line" spell the end of the line for dark-skinned babies?

In this chapter we will examine how the legacy of colorism continues to splinter families and emotionally injure those lacking a preferred or even necessary skin tone. Furthermore, we will explore how friendships from childhood and adolescence to adulthood are too often strained by skin-color differences or strictly maintained along lines of color.

When African-American families have a baby, relatives and friends can barely disguise their curiosity regarding the newborn's color. Following routine inquiries about its sex, weight, and health, the critical question will be asked: "What's he [or she] look like?"—a veiled request for information about skin color. What many of those in the family and outside it may not realize, though, is that a child's skin at birth, especially if it is premature, is far lighter than it eventually will be. During a baby's first year, comments may thus progress from "Look at that little yella thing" to "You better keep that child out of the sun."

A hospital preemie ward is an excellent place to overhear the many confused and often hopeful comments prompted by the sight of a very light-skinned African-American baby. One nurse recalls a mother shaking her head and sheepishly saying, "I don't know where he got that pretty color and hair from but he didn't get it from me or his daddy." Another mother was overheard to exclaim "Oooooh, she's so light!" before anxiously turning to the nearby nurse to inquire whether the baby would stay that color. After checking the infant's ears, genitals, and knuckles—the best indicator sites of eventual skin color—the nurse replied, pointing to the baby's ear, "She'll get a bit darker. Maybe about that color"—a tad darker than the new mother herself. The mother then frowned and sighed, "Oh Lord!"

Concern about a child's skin color is hardly limited to

African-American families. It is in fact common to many families of color, including those that are Latino and Asian American. In the book *Is Lighter Better?: Skin-Tone Discrimination among Asian Americans* by Joanne Rondilla and Paul Spickard, Charmaine Tuason, a young Filipino woman, first confessed to having her own color-complex issues to work through about having medium-dark skin, and then shared the following story:

> *When a dark baby cousin was born into my family a few months ago, I was constantly hearing remarks like "Oh no, he took after his father's side of the family" or "It's okay to be a boy and be dark. Thank goodness he's not a girl."*

Yet there are other family members who are relieved at the sight of a darker-skinned baby, and pleased by the darkening that occurs during the baby's first year. Misha, a light-skinned African-American woman, recalls hearing stories about how her West Indies–born, dark-skinned grandfather, already unhappy that his brown-skinned daughter had married a light-skinned Black man, reacted negatively when he first saw her, a pale-skinned granddaughter. But as the months passed and Misha began to darken, her grandfather would periodically issue the encouraging report "She's coming, she's coming." Unfortunately, this reaction is the exception and not the rule.

Fear about giving birth to a child of the "wrong" color can even drive those who are reproductively capable to instead adopt a baby whom they can ensure is light skinned. It is hard to imagine a couple making such a radical choice from skin-color prejudice alone, but according to Stephen Birmingham, author of *Certain People,* this is exactly what some wealthy Black families did in the past to keep family lines light.

When it comes to the adoption of African-American children, there is no denying that light-skinned babies go first. Zena Oglesby, founder and executive director of the Institute of Black Parenting, in Los Angeles, is among those disturbed by the pattern. He reports that about 40 percent of the African-American couples who come to his institute specifically request a child who is light skinned. Oglesby tries to combat their dark-skin prejudices and always encourages prospective parents to look at children of all skin tones, but too often he feels as though he is fighting a losing battle.

Selecting babies and adopting children by skin color is a long-standing practice, but is it also illegal? In 1990, the American Civil Liberties Union filed a report against the New York City Child Welfare Administration in which it charged the organization with a long list of violations in how foster home placements were made. Among the many complaints listed was that adoption placements were made on the basis of skin color. While evidence from case records did indicate that 72 percent of the children available for adoption or foster home placement were described not just by race but also by color, Sydney Duncan, the president of a child welfare agency in Detroit called Homes for Black Children, points out that skin-color information is not necessarily discriminatory; sometimes such descriptions are used simply to help African-American couples adopt a child who looks most like themselves. But others contend that darker-skinned, middle-class Black couples are known to pass on children who look more like them and instead prefer those with lighter skin and straight hair.

Interestingly, the same adoption biases are evident in China, a country known for its open-source international adoption policies. Since local Chinese couples, too, can suffer from infertility, these hopeful parents scoop up first male and then female babies with the lightest skin color. The darker-skinned babies, usually girls, are the ones left for international adoption, but fortunately most are placed in homes with loving parents more than happy to have a beautiful child to raise.

With the advent of reliable birth control and legalized abortion, the pool of available White babies for adoption started to shrink throughout the 1960s and '70s. Child welfare champions initially viewed this development as an opportunity to place needy Black children in the homes of childless White couples, many of whom might have preferred adopting a light-skinned child, but who also were happy accepting a dark-skinned one. As inquiries about transracial adoptions grew, agencies modified preexisting policies that restricted adoptions to parents of the same racial makeup. But as more and more White couples adopted Black children, African-American activists started questioning the wisdom of this practice. They began to ask, "How could White parents ever give Black children a positive sense of racial identity and prepare them to live in a racist world?" The situation so alarmed members of the National Association of Black Social Workers (NABSW) that in 1972 they passed a resolution to officially oppose the adoption of Black children, including those who were biracial, by Whites. In support of the policy, by 1987 thirty-five states had passed laws prohibiting the adoption of Black children by White families.

Opponents of these new anti-transracial adoption laws were quick to point out that White parents were better than no parents at all, which was too often the only other option for these kids. There simply were not enough African-American families to adopt the many Black children in need of placement. Furthermore, new research was indicating that Black children raised by White parents rarely suffered any long-term racial identity problems. Despite these arguments, the NABSW refused to budge from its hard-line position about the matter. But at the federal level, attitudes did change, and bans on transracial adoption were called into question. The Interethnic Adoption Provisions of 1996 (which amended the Multiethnic Placement Act, or MPA, of 1994) and the Adoption and Safe Families Act (ASFA) of 1997 were passed to allow agencies and states greater freedom in placing children for adoption. So that the Interethnic Placement Act (IEPA) of 1996 (a revision of the MPA) would have some enforcement teeth, the act included a provision that any public or private agency found not to be considering all races and cultures when placing children for adoption would lose its federal funding.

Many couples having trouble conceiving prefer not to adopt and instead use various assisted reproductive technologies (ART). If it is the husband who is infertile, then the couple can turn to a sperm bank, a relatively cheap and now fairly common route to pursue. But in the past, if it was the wife who was reproductively challenged, then the options were more invasive, costly, and less effective. Today, however, if a woman's infertility is specifically due to a lack of egg production or blocked tubes, there are egg donation clinics not unlike sperm banks to turn to for help. And for African Americans worried about the skin color of a future child, utilizing one of these clinics has the added advantage of hedging one's bets to produce a light-skinned child by preselecting sperm or eggs on the basis of donor criteria. Women's studies scholar Charis Thompson has found a curious but telling difference between how the reproductive centers run and market their wares. Thompson noticed that, compared to sperm banks, egg donor clinics are far more likely to employ skin color as a major categorical heading, not only in how eggs are inventoried but also in how they are advertised to prospective clients. This of course makes no sense; whether a donated egg or donated sperm is used to assist in production of an embryo, the sex gamete will never carry any more (or any less) than half of its total genetic makeup. But somehow the greater societal value placed on women having light skin has transmuted into a stronger desire on the part of prospective clients at these clinics to be more specific in requesting eggs, more so than in looking at sperm in terms of light-skin potential.

Regardless of whether a new addition to the family is conceived without medical assistance or by ART, when the biological parents are of very different skin tones, and especially when they are of different racial backgrounds, anticipation only grows regarding who the newborn will resemble. And as can happen, sometimes a child is born who looks far more like one parent than like the other. A difference in physical appearance can be so great as to even cause questions about paternity when a child is out with the "nonresembling" parent. Such was the case for one of coauthor Midge Wilson's graduate students, an African-American woman who is married to a White man. After giving birth to a beautiful boy, she brought the baby to work for everyone to see. As she was heading home, and was standing at the corner waiting for the light to change, a White woman peered into the baby blanket. Upon seeing a light-skinned infant, she asked the graduate student if she was the child's nanny. In the wealthy neighborhood where DePaul University is located, it is not uncommon to see women of color pushing strollers with White babies, but to be asked such a thing when the baby is in fact your own was upsetting. In response, the graduate student exclaimed, "This is MY baby!" As soon as the light changed, the woman scurried away.

When parents of very different skin tones (and sometimes even that surface difference is not necessary) have several children, the family will likely have a range of skin tones. Although issues of colorism are certainly not always a problem, when they do arise, a hornet's nest of simmering jealousies, seething resentments, and mean-spirited retaliations can result among the kids. A lone dark-skinned boy may internalize all of his siblings' vicious teasing and develop self-hatred, and a sole light-skinned daughter may vainly flaunt what she has been repeatedly told is prized, sparking anger and retaliation from her darker-skinned sisters.

A woman we'll call Rachel, who is the eldest—and by far the lightest—of four children of a very light-skinned mother and a dark-skinned father from Georgia, recalls the chaos color prejudice caused in her own family. Rachel was coddled by her parents because of her color. As a result, her younger siblings came to hate her, and one sister in particular acted out her resentment by slashing Rachel's clothes and, once, cutting off her long hair while she slept. Her parents made the situation worse by punishing the dark-skinned daughter and consoling the fair-skinned Rachel. Years later, the father left, and the mother invited a darker-skinned sister to live with the family. The children's aunt, who had always resented her own lighter-skinned sister, began to pick on Rachel, hissing, "Stop flipping your hair like a White girl—you've always wanted to be a White girl, you little bitch." Even after Rachel was well into her twenties, she still felt anxious and insecure whenever she happened to toss her hair back.

Rachel's story illustrates how families can be ripped apart by color complexes. Fortunately for Rachel, she was able to regain her confidence through seeing an African-American therapist who almost immediately zeroed in on her deep-seated complex about color—something that her previous therapist, who was White, had not explored.

Sociologist Elliot Liebow maintains that most African-American family members do not dwell obsessively on differences in color, but then again rarely is the subject neutral or left unmentioned. But we do wonder if the subject of colorism is *really* discussed in families. Most African-American parents prepare their children for a world full of racism, and the possibility that White kids may call them "nigger" or other bad names, but not as many explicitly teach their children how to handle hateful name-calling from their "own people." Black parents need to coach their children who are especially light skinned or dark skinned on how to handle color- and feature-related slurs. And of course African-American parents must also teach their children not to tease or judge others on the basis of skin color or features.

Interestingly, biracial families, with their potential to produce the widest variations in color and features among their children, seem less likely to experience these kinds of intense skin-color conflicts on the home front. Instead, in interview after interview we conducted with adult biracial children of Black-White marriages, all the interviewees maintained that their parents had been very much attuned to color issues. Perhaps because the parents had to more deliberately and carefully consider the consequences of race mixing, they often proved to be better equipped than even some African-American parents to handle skin-color-related differences and conflicts.

Even when biracial children's parents do engage in constructive discussion about color and race, outside that environment, taunts of neighborhood children and schoolmates are practically inevitable. "Light, bright, and damn near White, your daddy's Black and your mammy's White" is a common playground chant, along with "You're half-baked, your momma didn't cook you long enough." Bullying taunts about color appear to be a constant in the African-American child's repertoire of insults. But hopefully the biracial children return home to a safe space where loving parents are able to reassure them that they are not "half-baked."

Even when parents do carefully teach their children that skin color and hair texture have nothing to do with attractiveness, desirability, or Black identity, unsolicited comments from strangers may require quick action. One African-American mother recalls standing in a checkout line at the grocery store with her two daughters, one of whom was light skinned with long hair and the other several shades darker, when a woman walked up to the lighter-skinned daughter and sweetly remarked, "Isn't she beautiful?" Fed up with similar scenes, the mother grabbed the two girls and angrily retorted, "Don't you mean, isn't she light?" The woman took offense and backed off, while the mother quickly reassured her daughters that they were equally beautiful.

But clearly not all parents, biracial or otherwise, are supportive of their own children. A dark-skinned woman in her midthirties named Kelly recalls how her lighter-skinned mother made her feel less than special because of her appearance. Her mother repeatedly told Kelly that she would never get a man to marry her because she was too black. Haunted by her mother's warnings, Kelly confessed to marrying the first light-skinned man she could find, just to "get the black off" her. Sadly, like her mother, Kelly was shamed by her husband over her dark skin color. She eventually had a child to play out her own color prejudices:

> *I had a girl and I guess God punished me because she came out dark, and—as much as I said I would never do to my daughter what my mother did to me—I seem to be repeating the cycle of my youth by cautioning my own daughter to stay out of the sun and not to go out with any dark-skinned Black boys.*

Some girls may not even wait for marriage to try to correct the stigma of their dark skin. A program director at an urban clinic that provides social services to pregnant girls told us that she has witnessed teenage Black girls who intentionally got pregnant by a light-skinned boy in the hope that a light-skinned baby would finally bring them love—from their mothers as well as their babies. She has also observed that those girls who most intensely desire a light-skinned baby are nearly always the ones with lighter-skinned mothers. The director listens to their fantasies about having babies with light skin, light eyes, and "good" hair. And when things don't turn out as hoped, the girls end up devastated. A nurse who works with the clinic recalls the look of dismay on the face of one dark-skinned young teenager after the birth of the baby she had conceived with a Puerto Rican boyfriend. Like most newborns, the infant was fairly light skinned, but when the young mother inspected the baby's genitals, earlobes, and knuckles, where clues to a child's mature coloring can be found, she cried out, "Oh my God, my baby has been touched by the tar brush!" But when the baby does turn out light, the teenage mother proudly brings her child back to the clinic for the other pregnant girls to see and gush "oooh" and "aaah."

At the 2010 annual meeting of the American Sociological Association, JeffriAnne Wilder and Colleen Cain presented a paper entitled "Teaching and Learning Color Consciousness in Black Families: Exploring Family Processes and Women's Experiences with Colorism." The coauthors reported on what they found during a focus group conducted with twenty-six Black women on the topic of colorism. In analyzing the women's comments, Wilder and Cain came to the conclusion that even now, well into the new millennium, "Color differences are learned and reinforced and in some cases contested within families, ultimately shaping black women's perspectives and experiences with colorism."

African-American scholar Joy DeGruy Leary developed the term "post-traumatic slave syndrome" (PTSS) to describe the trauma of internalized racism and colorism that has affected so many African Americans. In her 2005 book *Post Traumatic Slave Syndrome*, Leary blames slavery for the intergenerational color prejudices that persist to this day. Typical of someone with PTSS is a thirtysomething dark-skinned Black woman named Stephanie W. from St. Louis, who described what she endured:

> My mother's side of the family hated my father's side of the family because my father's side of the family was all light-skinned. I have six brothers and sisters and we were split right down the middle as far as color was concerned. I was darker than most all of my siblings. The color issues ran so deep in our family that we even fought amongst ourselves about color. It made all of us kids hate each other and refer to each other in very derogatory terms: spooks and half-

breeds. It was ugly and I blame my parents for allowing such venom to spew and never trying to stop this. Even today as adults, there [are] still lingering unresolved color issues.

Black children suffering from PTSS may come to see one or the other parent as responsible for their "bad" color and features. And in an effort to absolve themselves, more than a few Black parents have encouraged such blaming. While applying chemical straighteners to her daughter's tight, kinky hair, one mother, interviewed by *Essence* for an article entitled "The Family Trap," commented, "Don't blame me, you got that head of hair from your father. Lord, child, you better not marry no nappy-headed man 'cause I can't deal with no Brillo-headed grandbabies."

When single-parent households join to create stepfamilies, light-skinned and dark-skinned Black children from the two parents can be forced to live together under one roof. This can be a recipe for disaster. Color-prejudiced stepparents may reject stepchildren not only for being too dark, but also for being too light. Singer and actress Eartha Kitt, whose stepfather spurned her for being half White, recalls him saying, "I won't have that little yellow gal in my house." Kitt's mother, forced to choose between her daughter and the man she loved, gave the child away, first farming her out to relatives but eventually placing her in a foster home.

Psychologist Nancy Boyd-Franklin identified the unique stresses associated with skin color in her book *Black Families in Therapy,* and emphasized that it is not always the darkest-skinned child in the family who suffers. Highly Afrocentric parents, for example, may view a child with very light skin as an ugly reminder of their slave heritage and even unconsciously blame the child for not looking Black enough. In his autobiography, Malcolm X describes how his light skin displeased his mother, since she was ashamed of having a White father.

Theresa H., a light-skinned Black woman working on the Strip in Las Vegas, told us, "So many people think that because I look the way I look I have had it easy. But it has been very difficult for me, especially as a young girl. I never had any friends because they all said I thought I was cute." Her story is similar to those of a lot of other light-skinned Black women we spoke to. As Theresa further observed, "Being light skinned does not make one immune to name-calling and insults. Because of the way I look, I would even find myself altering my personality to become overly nice, just to ward off confrontations that might lead to fights."

An African-American nurse from Knoxville, whom we'll call Marie, similarly experienced her near-White skin color as a curse on her childhood. She tried everything to make herself darker, including staying out in the sun all day, in the hope that her schoolmates would stop mocking her with names such as "School Bus," "Zebra," "Sunshine," "Yellow Submarine," and "Light Bright." (At the other end of the skin-color spectrum, very dark-skinned Blacks can be called "Shine," "Sambo," "Aunt Jemima," "Ink Spot," and "Blackie.") The name-calling never did cease, and neither did her classmates' routine of leaving Mello Yello soda cans on her lunchroom seat. To this day, Marie cannot stomach the taste or even the sight of Mello Yello.

Aren't verbal taunts just part of the inevitable cruelties of childhood? Why should mean remarks about skin color be any worse than calling a kid with glasses "Four Eyes" or an overweight child "Pork Chop"? Perhaps there is no difference experienced at the time of the insult, but unlike the wearing of glasses or being overweight, where at least there is an imagined future in which contact lenses or a diet will take care of the problem, one's skin color is not ever going to change. This is not to say that the majority of grown-ups who suffered through painful name-calling when children don't come to shrug off the comments later on. But the short-term effects of such teasing can be devastating, especially now with online social media. The taunting can take the form of posting images of "Mello Yello," for example, on Facebook next to someone's photo, for all the other kids to see and laugh at.

It should also be recognized that many taunts and jeers based on skin color are completely harmless, especially when hurled by siblings in families where skin color is a nonissue. After all, siblings use all sorts of weapons against each other, and skin color is but one of the many in their arsenal. In healthy families, such name-calling and sibling conflict may actually relieve pent-up feelings and make the whole skin-color issue seem less serious or threatening than it might otherwise be. Joni, a light-skinned woman, remembers how calling her even lighter-skinned sister a "green-eyed bitch" would inevitably send her into a frenzy of rage—which was great! And Lisa A., a thirtysomething light-skinned biracial woman, remembers experiencing the sting of her darker-skinned sister's ultimate taunt: "You think you White." At the time, there was nothing that pained Lisa more, but she outgrew the silly name-calling and now the two are close.

In some African-American families, skin-color concerns do not surface until the children are old enough to date. Then parents and relatives suddenly start expressing strong disapproval of certain boyfriends or girlfriends who are deemed too dark (or too light). As they hit their teen years, some young African

Americans are told in no uncertain terms that the best way to erase the stigma of dark skin is by dating and then marrying someone light, or even White. They must think about how the children will come out, and the way to "lighten the line" is to marry someone lighter than themselves. A middle-class, light-skinned woman named Susie recalls how her very proper aunt would slip into broken English to caution her about marrying someone "unsuitable," saying, "You don't know nothin' about combin' no nappy hair." A Black professional we'll call David, who is married to a White woman, has five siblings who also all married White. At the sixth sibling's wedding reception, David's light-skinned father gleefully gave the toast "Before long, there'll be no more black left in our family." In another family, a dark-skinned woman from Chicago recalls being told that as a "Black nappy-headed girl" she would probably never get married, especially not to anyone light skinned, so she had better get a good education instead. She now has a PhD and is divorced from the light-skinned man she married to please her family.

These same sentiments exist in many Latino families as well. In Mexico, for example, children may hear the dark-skin prejudice expressed through the colloquial phrase *"limpiar la raza,"* which means "to clean the race," or sometimes the phrase used is *"mejorar la raza,"* "to better the race." When a Mexican father was asked if he thought race mixing was a good or bad thing in his country, he replied:

> *Well, here in Mexico we do not consider it to be a bad thing because, as I told you before, my wife's color is cleaning the race a little bit, right? The children of my children will be White. They will not be my color.*

African-American families intent on "lightening the line" can be cruel in their treatment of in-laws who do not measure up on the color barometer. One such case the authors heard about involved a dark-skinned Black man who married a light-skinned woman from a colorstruck family in Mississippi. The in-laws eventually learned to accept him, but they continued to refuse to allow him in their house on New Year's Day—they adhered to an old superstition that having a dark-skinned Black in one's home on New Year's Day spelled bad luck for the rest of the year.

A woman from the South named Jade, whose light-skinned family always boasted that they came from generations of good looks, talked about how her family was so color obsessed that they would pick apart her boyfriends feature by feature:

> My *uncle was the worst. He would argue with my mother every time I brought a guy home that he thought was not light enough. He would initially start with his skin color. Was he light enough? If he wasn't quite light enough, then did he at least have good hair, because they figured our strong Creole genes would help lighten the line. Then they would look at his nose and his lips and they would make a determination as to whether he was acceptable for me to bear his child. My uncle always said, "Make sure you marry light now—even if he ain't that good looking, remember the old Japanese proverb that White makes up for seven defects."*

Jade finally went away to college, so she didn't have to go on hearing all of the negativity about dark-skinned people. But she confessed that her uncle's beliefs were so ingrained in her psyche that she found herself having a hard time seeing dark-skinned Black men as attractive.

Of course, not all Black parents want their children to marry someone as light as or lighter than themselves. Most of the time they don't care one way or the other, as long as their child is happy. And in still other cases, there is a strong preference for a son- or daughter-in-law who is *not* light. One dark-skinned professional woman with hair in locs, divorced from a White Englishman, was worried to distraction that her son would marry the Asian woman he had been dating for several years. The mother was determined that he marry someone at least as dark as she was, and even admitted that if she could, she would arrange a marriage to someone suitably dark, just to prevent him from running off with someone light.

Predictably, pressure from Black parents to "lighten the line" or "darken the line" can lead some children to rebel. Light-skinned teenagers, in particular, may intentionally date Blacks who are darker. One such African American, who today is a prominent businessman, recalls his youthful ways:

> There was a time in the sixties when I would actively seek out only tar-black women to date. No puke-yellow Black women or snow queens for me. Dark-skinned women were not only a way for me to confirm my Blackness but also a way for me to rebel against my parents and their bourgeois ways.

Eventually, though, his marital choice was more conventional.

We now turn to the pernicious effects color prejudices can have on friendships between individuals of the same sex. Young children are oblivious to the significance of race or color and will readily make friends with anyone who is fun to play with. But as the children get older and gain awareness of the status and stigma of having certain features, their pledges of being

BFF[9] give way to new rules of engagement. Light-skinned adolescents may discover that their social value is on the rise, and conclude that continued friendships with dark-skinned chums is not wise. The color lines are drawn.

Whether the friendships are real or virtual, adolescence is the time when skin color becomes more closely tied to popularity and self-worth, especially for girls. Research has demonstrated that those who are physically attractive are more likely to be friends with each other, and given the connection between skin color and perceived attractiveness among African Americans, it is not surprising that the lighter-skinned teenage girls gravitate toward each other. Many darker-skinned Black girls find it nearly impossible to penetrate the top-tier cliques. "The most popular girls in the school are nearly always light skinned," one Black high school girl told us. "If a dark-skinned girl is allowed to 'hang with them,' it is either because she has a car or is from a wealthy family. Otherwise, she isn't going to cut it."

Fortunately, not all dark-skinned girls are passively resigned to the new order. For a school project, Kiri Davis decided to challenge the color-coded social milieu of high school by making a film on the topic. In 2007, Davis released what is a brutally honest and sometimes disturbing documentary on the deep-seated feelings of inferiority and shame experienced by many young African-American girls regarding their own and others' skin color and features. Her film, *A Girl Like Me,* is divided into two parts. In the first, Davis interviews several high school girls who openly acknowledge believing that in order to be beautiful you need to have long hair and light skin. Davis had also persuaded the girls to open up about their use of skin-

---

9. Text shorthand for "best friends forever."

bleaching creams and what they knew of other girls who would never date a dark-skinned guy because they didn't want to risk having any dark-skinned babies themselves. For the second part of the documentary, Davis replicated Kenneth and Mamie Clark's research, whose findings were presented at the *Brown v. Board of Education* Supreme Court case (1954) that resulted in desegregating public schools. As discussed in chapter 4 on identity, the Clarks found that when African-American pre-school children were given a choice between playing with a Black doll and playing with a White doll, most chose the White doll. Fifty years later, in Davis's documentary, we still witness fifteen out of twenty-one African-American preschool children preferring the White doll over the Black doll when presented with the same choice.

Black teenage boys also have to struggle with colorism, although perhaps because boys are more likely to compete on the playing field or in other arenas beyond looks, issues of color are not as central to their sense of self-worth. In 1993, public television aired a documentary called *A Question of Color* that also tackled the topic of intraracial color discrimination. Among the many people whom director Kathe Sandler interviewed for the project were two Black male friends named Keyonn and Keith (nicknamed "Shay"). The two of them discuss how skin color has affected their relationship:

Keyonn: Shay is always the cute one. He's the cute one 'cause he's the one with the light skin and the nice hair. And it's like, he smiles and gives everybody that low, adorable look, and it's like, Shay is always the cute one. And that has even gone as far as to the point where I be trying to talk to somebody and they be like, "Yah, you're cute 'n' all, but . . .

but, who's the light-skinned one?" And that's like . . . that's rough!

Keith: He may feel at the time real rejected, just a little rejection. But yet, he and I are above that. We know that I'm light skinned and he knows that my hair is a better texture, or ya know, a different texture. It's no better, it's just a different texture . . . and, that being in America, people like White. People like light.

Keyonn: We don't even discuss it between the two of us and we're best friends. I mean, I know why I don't bring it up. I don't bring it up because I wouldn't want to cause an argument over something like that. Cause we're not friends over the color of our skin. We're friends over the people that we are.

Although Keyonn and Keith seem to have a healthy attitude, it took a filmmaker asking them some very pointed questions for the two boys to really open up about their true feelings and for first time talk to each other about the subject.

Not only in high school but also on college campuses, African Americans of similar skin color seem to hang out together. On historically Black college campuses such as Howard University, in Washington, DC, membership in some of the most exclusive sororities and fraternities was long known to hinge on an applicant's skin color and hair texture. While many "Greeks" dispute this charge, others will confess that the more elite the fraternity or sorority, the lighter skinned its members seem to be. Alpha Kappa Alpha sorority and Kappa Alpha Psi fraternity continue to have reputations—whether true or not—for being partial toward those with light skin and "good" hair.

Color considerations enter into the selection of college

beauty queens as well, although the trends observed today have modified from what they once were. Historically, homecoming queens at Black colleges and universities were nearly always light skinned, but since the 1970s, perhaps as a show of Black pride, darker-skinned women are now routinely crowned. On predominantly White campuses, when an African-American woman is elected homecoming queen, she is still invariably light skinned.

One might hope that in adulthood, compared to the peer-obsessed years of youth, divisive issues surrounding the color of skin would be shed. For men, this is generally the case; as they work to maintain old friendships and start to form new ones, the basis tends to be occupational success, athletic activities, night-clubbing, or some other shared interest. Sadly, though, color and features still have the power to undermine relationships among adult women, no doubt because most women, regardless of racial background, are still more often judged, especially by men, on how they look. Given the current shortage of marriageable Black men, a topic discussed more fully in the next chapter, it remains hard for some dark-skinned African-American women not to feel as though they're competing in a buyers' market.

A letter written by a twenty-seven-year-old light-skinned Black woman to "The Ebony Advisor," an advice column in *Ebony*, illustrates how ugly color tensions can be between women who were once friends. The letter writer began by describing how she had gone to a club one evening with a darker-skinned girlfriend. The writer had been approached several times by African-American athletes and businessmen, while her friend was approached only once. The writer claimed that when she commented on all this attention, her dark-skinned friend suddenly turned defensive, saying, "The guys were blind to pass over a beautiful cocoa-brown chick for a pale yellow girl." In anger, the writer retorted, among other things, that "lighter-skinned women were born to dominate chocolate-brown ones" and "the only black men . . . brown women get are the leftovers we don't want." The darker-skinned friend had not spoken to her since, and the writer was seeking advice about what she could say to make her dark-skinned friend forgive her. "The Ebony Advisor" had this stern reply: "You owe an apology to millions of Black people—including, undoubtedly, many of your own past and present relatives—who happen to be a few shades darker than you are."

Happily, we can end this chapter on a more positive note. Perhaps because there are more women of all races in all kinds of workplace environments today, many of them are forming friendships with each other more as men do, on the basis of shared interests and activities. The rule that friendships between women of widely varying skin color can't survive may finally be lifting. A very light-skinned African-American nurse in her late twenties who worked at a hospital in upstate New York is but one example of a more hopeful trend. She describes what happened when she was first transferred to a new department headed by a dark-skinned female supervisor:

On the first day of work, I thought to myself, "I better start looking now for a new job because this dark-skinned woman is gonna hate me; they always do." I stuck it out, though, and then one night my boss and I both had to work late. We got to talking and discovered we had something in common—being fed up with the skin-color issue. We shared our respective pain about being too dark and too light, and for the first time we were both able to laugh about all this "color crap." We have been best friends ever since. Still, when we go out together, we often get these weird looks. Strangers even come up to us to ask, "What in the world do you two have in common?"

To their credit, these two women have not let the rudeness of strangers interfere with their growing closeness. For too long the color fault line divided families and polarized friends, but as these two women and many others like them demonstrate, it doesn't have to be like that.

— Chapter 7 —

The Match Game: Colorism and Courtship

To spot the next big trend in beauty, one only need look to the "it girls" from the worlds of fashion and entertainment. Long gone are the once-popular girl-next-door looks of a brunette Cindy Crawford, the willowy paleness of a Kate Moss, or the blond sexiness of a Britney Spears. In the new millennium, the "it girls" are Jennifer Lopez and Beyoncé, named the World's Most Beautiful Woman by *People* magazine in 2011 and 2012, respectively. Then there are such renowned beauties as Giselle Bündchen, the Brazilian supermodel; Sophia Vergara, the Colombian actress; and Rihanna, the Barbadian recording artist. These women have voluptuous figures, full lips, and skin that is darker than the "White" gold standard. A seismic shift is happening in the Western world's concept of ideal beauty, as facial features and skin color traditionally associated with African Americans and Latinos are now being embraced, envied, and emulated by White women and women of color alike. This new mixed-race trend in looks has caught the attention not just of modeling agencies, fashion designers, talent agents, and casting directors, but even of social scientists who study attractiveness. Findings from one recent study indicate that a woman who appears racially mixed is now evaluated as more attractive than a clearly identifiable White female figure. For women of color, this sounds like something to celebrate, until one considers the fact that the vaunted racially mixed woman was also evaluated as more attractive than a traditional-looking Black female figure. Is this latest appreciation of the mixed-race woman just another example of how the more things change, the more they stay the same?

"Gendered colorism" is the term adopted by social scientists to describe how skin color uniquely influences impressions of women versus men. The effect is most salient in comparing judgments about the perceived attractiveness of someone as a function of his or her skin color. Researcher Mark Hill reanalyzed data from the 1979–1980 National Survey of Black Americans and found that when African-American field researchers assigned a rating of perceived attractiveness to each survey respondent, its number correlated with the rated skin color of women but not of the men. In short, the lighter-skin-toned a woman was in reality, the prettier she was *judged* to be by the surveyors. Of course, it is false to say that dark-skinned women *are* less attractive than light-skinned women. But social constructs, especially for a subjective attribute like beauty, are powerful forces to combat.

Given the enormous role that beauty plays in the world of dating and mating, it is reasonable to assert that there is no other life experience in which skin color plays a greater role—and no one knows this better than the dark-skinned African-American woman. In the twenty years since we wrote, in our first edition, "Go to any Black nightclub and observe how fast

Black men's heads turn when a light-skinned Black woman crosses the room," not much has changed. The heads of African-American men (and more than a few women) still turn to gaze. Those women *not* light skinned themselves may even detect subliminally how male attention redirects away from them and toward the light skinned woman entering some domain. Yet most African-American men will still deny that color prejudice is that big a deal in the Black community. This assertion can be challenged, especially when it comes to prominent African-American men.

Since the 1920s, when anthropologist Melville Herskovits first set out to answer the question of whether powerful Black men tend to marry lighter-skinned women, the empirical evidence that they do has mounted. Herskovits studied successful Harlem couples and found that more than half (56.5 percent) of wives were lighter than their spouses, while less than one-third (29 percent) of wives were darker than their husbands. Of the remaining couples, 14.5 percent were judged to be about the same color. In 1984, sociologists Elizabeth Mullins and Paul Sites similarly found that eminent Black men were significantly more likely to have light-skinned spouses. As recently as 1997, when African-American males at two historically Black institutions were sampled, more than one-third (35 percent) said they hoped to date or marry a woman with a light complexion. And in 2002, researcher Margaret Hunter hypothesized that light skin operates as a kind of social capital for women that advantages them not just professionally, but also in the interpersonal marketplace. Her analysis of empirical survey data indicated that for African-American women, light skin was directly related to marrying an African-American man of higher status. One need only look at the wives and partners of some of the Black community's highest-profile athletes and entertainers, couples such as hip-hop artist Jay-Z and Beyoncé (she's light), R & B singer John Legend and Chrissy Teigen (light), actor-director-producer Spike Lee and Tonya Lewis Lee (light), actor Don Cheadle and Bridgid Coulter (light), Miami Heat NBA player Chris Bosh and Adrienne Williams-Bosh (light), and New York Knicks NBA player Carmelo Anthony and LaLa Vasquez (Latina/light), to confirm the finding.

Several explanations have been put forth as to the origins of this inclination on the part of so many African-American men for a light-skinned woman. One conjecture is that the preference emerged as yet another harmful consequence of our country's slave past. During the antebellum period, southern White slave owners began to breed for profit racially mixed light-skinned female slaves, some of whom were the offspring of the owners themselves, and others who were the offspring resulting from the rapes that owners forcibly caused to take place between their light-skinned male and female slaves. These light-skinned women were called "fancy girls," and many were indeed strikingly attractive, so much so that wealthy White men were willing to pay huge sums for the prettiest of the pretty in order to possess such a woman as a mistress or concubine. Over the years, these racially mixed beauties became a mainstay in the fantasies of southern White men. The hypothesis is that in witnessing all the adulation for the light-skinned racially mixed women, Black men simply came to do the same.

But another historically based explanation asserts that African-American men's attraction to light-skinned women did not develop until after Emancipation. As discussed elsewhere, during Reconstruction the previously free mulatto elite did everything they could to segregate themselves from the newly freed, generally darker-skinned Blacks. One way for these racially mixed families to preserve their fragile status was to make sure that their children only married someone else as light or lighter than themselves. The repudiation of the dark-skinned woman as suitable wife-and-mother material became ingrained in the psyches of Black men across the socioeconomic spectrum. Thus, even today, more than a few African-American men mindlessly date and marry light-skinned women just to produce lighter-skinned children.

Filmmaker Spike Lee offers yet another reason for the light-skin preference. As someone who works in a visual medium, Lee is perhaps more attuned to the role of media in promoting the desirability of the light-skinned woman. He touches on that theme in an article for *Essence* by Jill Nelson, in which he is quoted as saying:

> *Whether Black men admit it or not, they feel light-skinned women are more attractive than dark-skinned, and they'd rather see long hair than a short Afro, because that's closer to White women. That comes from being inundated with media from the time you're born that constantly fed you the White woman as the image of beauty. That's both conscious and unconscious. . . . But on the whole, talking to my friends and knowing men, I see that a premium is put on light-skinned sisters with long hair.*

A more sociologically based possibility has to do with the hundreds of years of European dominance, both in the Americas and in many countries elsewhere, that has forged a seemingly unbreakable link between color and status. In short, light skin both signifies and grants power by association. Like men everywhere, African-American men know that others will judge them on the attractiveness of the woman they are with.[10] So, for the dark-skinned Black man in particular, having a beautiful light-skinned woman by his side is an effective way to broadcast to others that he is someone who has "made it."

Evolutionary psychologists provide yet another take on what drives the light-skin preference: they credit biology. For over thirty years, social scientists have been conducting studies to support a theory—challenged by many—that certain features, including facial symmetry, skin color, skin quality, and bodily proportions, are universal markers of beauty that dictate our unconscious mating preferences. In particular, they speculate that tens of thousands of years ago, feminine indicators of youth, attractiveness, and fertility arose to be selected and retained by humans as indicators of a woman's potential health and fertility. They further reason that since skin darkens (and beauty lessens) with age, the lighter skin color of a young woman signifies her greater youth and fertility. Thus the evolutionary psychologists believe that humans attract one another primarily on the basis of their looks, much as birds of a feather find their perfect mate through the splendor of song.

Arguably, there is simply too much historical, societal, and cultural baggage in the Black community to reduce the desire for light-skinned women to something as fundamental as biology. And besides, since cultures worldwide socially construct their own unique markers of beauty, why shouldn't skin color function in a culturally specific way as well? For hundreds of

---

10. Empirical research confirms that men of all races and ethnicities are judged more favorably when paired with a beautiful woman, as opposed to a plain one, a phenomenon known as "the radiating effect."

years, small feet were believed essential for erotic appeal in a Chinese woman, but once foot binding was outlawed, the intense preference for a small-footed woman gradually faded away. Theoretically, the preference for light skin color could "lighten up" as well.

In looking through the above discussion of what might have originally produced the attraction for light-skinned African-American women, some might question why the preference even needs any deep analysis. In other words, how is an African-American man's liking for a woman with light skin and long hair any different from a shared preference on the part of many White men for a woman with blond hair and blue eyes? The short answer is that within the African-American community, skin color is not just personal, it's political. Were African Americans to date one another across the skin-color spectrum without discernable pattern, then indeed there would be no grounds for analysis. But when a singular feature preference such as skin color becomes so persistently evident in the dating choices of men (and some women) of African descent, a red flag has to be raised.

To further elaborate the point, when African-American men (of varying skin tones) date only light-skinned women, it helps to know exactly what is their motive in not dating dark-skinned women. There are multiple possibilities, some more innocuous than others. If a man is very dark-skinned himself and exclusively dates light-skinned women, he may be trying to compensate for his own color complex, and hoping to lighten the skin of future children. But if a man is himself light skinned, is he one of those Black bourgeois types under pressure to keep the line light? Conversely, if an African-American man of whatever skin color never dates light-skinned women and only goes out with very dark-skinned women, are his actions an expression of rebellion against color-conscious parents? Is there some sort of dark-skin fetish involved, or does he somehow feel he can't do any "better"? If such a man is very light skinned and only dates dark-skinned women, someone might question whether he is just trying get back to his "roots" and hoping such a woman will bear him children who look unmistakably Black.

When one considers the nearly endless barrage of questions facing the African-American man with an exclusive dating preference, one can't help but realize there is a big difference between a Black man with a fixed skin-color preference and a White man choosing to date only Nordic-featured women (or Aryan-featured, to use a term that is more fraught). For one, a White man would never be called on the carpet for his exclusive preference (although if he were a White Jewish man, he just might be). More likely, other Whites, if they even notice this man's Nordic preference, would either not say anything or say nothing more than "Oh, right, he likes his women to have blond hair and blue eyes." End of discussion.

A more serious reason why an exclusive skin-color preference should not be dismissed has to do with the harmful consequences that can occur when a dark-skinned man becomes fixated on light-skinned women because of his own troubling insecurities. If such a man does end up marrying the light-skinned woman of his dreams, and his neurotic anxieties are not allayed, problems can erupt. He may start to question whether she could ever love a man like him, which in turn will only fuel worries regarding whether or when she will leave him. This kind of painful self-doubt is evident in the comments of one dark-skinned man married to a lighter-skinned woman, as quoted in Calvin Hernton's *Sex and Racism in America*:

I see her sometimes looking at me when I am naked or just milling around the house—I see the resentment in her well-guarded eyes. Whenever I do something she doesn't like, she always calls me a black bastard. If she catches me in a lie, I'm not a lying bastard, I'm a black bastard. If I cheat on her, I'm not a cheating bastard, I'm a black bastard. No matter what it is she's mad at me about, I'm a black bastard.

Other darker-skinned husbands give vent to their insecurities violently. One light-skinned woman who was formerly married to a prominent black-skinned businessman from Los Angeles recalls how her ex-husband would parade her in front of others, praising her "fine" bloodline and proudly predicting that their children were going to be "high yella." Yet in private he would punish her for being lighter than he, slapping her around, calling her a "half-breed bitch," and angrily accusing her of thinking she was "too good" for him. She tearfully describes what usually happened after one of their frequent fights:

He would beat me as we made love. He wanted to hear me whimper. Whimper was all I dared do. Never did I dare cry out. Then after we made love he would turn on the lights and look at my pale, bruised body and smile. Then he would say how beautiful the love marks looked against my "white" skin. Wiping the tears from my eyes, he would proclaim, "You love it when I'm in command, don't you? You're a real woman."

The abuse of a light-skinned woman at the hands of a dark-skinned partner is depicted in Zora Neale Hurston's critically acclaimed novel *Their Eyes Were Watching God*. Only when the dark-skinned Tea Cake whips his light-skinned girlfriend Janie is he able to conquer his fear that he is not good enough for her. Tea Cake discovers that beating Janie garners him respect from other Black men, too, including one named Sop-de-Bottom:

> *"Tea Cake, you sho is a lucky man," Sop-de-Bottom told him. "Uh person can see every place you hit her. Ah bet she never raised her hand tuh hit yuh back, neither. Take some un dese ol' rusty black women and dey would fight yuh all night long and next day nobody couldn't tell you ever hit 'em. Dat's de reason Ah done quit beatin' mah woman. You can't make no mark on 'em at all. Lawd! wouldn't Ah love tuh whip un tender woman lak Janie! Ah bet she don't even holler. She jus' cries, eh Tea Cake?"*

At the end of the novel, Janie kills Tea Cake in self-defense. In an *Essence* essay entitled "Embracing the Dark and the Light," novelist Alice Walker speculates that by including this scene Hurston was attempting to challenge beliefs that light-skinned Black women are more fragile and easily subdued than women who are darker skinned. Walker adds that any light-skinned Black woman who sells herself as a prize to a successful dark-skinned Black man is ultimately more to be pitied than blamed.

As always, the exception must be acknowledged. There are many African-American men who marry a lighter-skinned woman for reasons completely unrelated to her color or his own. A successful Black engineer with a beautiful light-skinned African-American wife defends his relationship this way: "Not all Black men who have a light-skinned woman or wife pur-posely chose her for that reason. It may just be that they've found the woman they love and that she simply happens to be light skinned." But even when an African-American man is truly innocent of color prejudice, it would seem that in this country it is still necessary for him to defend his marital choice.

As will be discussed more fully in the next chapter, where the role that skin color can play in politics will be addressed, it is worth noting here that many folks in the African-American community believe the best thing President Barack Obama ever did for his career was to marry the dark-brown-skinned Michelle Robinson. In the words of William, a Black middle-aged man from Nashville, "If President Obama was married to a light-skinned Black woman, she would be acting all 'hoity-toity' like she was too good for the common folk. That would not have been good for the president." Instead, he concludes, Mrs. Obama appears to be a down-to-earth woman who loves her family.

Like William, other African-American men may prefer darker-skinned women because they perceive them being less "stuck on themselves." More than a few men have discovered that dating a high-maintenance type of light-skinned woman was exhausting, and finding a darker-skinned woman to date was a relief. And if that same darker-skinned woman has a painful history of being rejected by colorstruck men, and then finally meets a good man who loves her for herself, she can indeed be a most loving partner.

African-American women can have their own skin-color preferences and prejudices driving their dating choices, although the patterns observed among women are slightly different from those of men. African-American women are equally likely to reject a man for being too light skinned as for being too dark skinned. In fact, the percentage of women who exclusively date light-skinned partners is about half the rate it is for men (15 percent versus 30 percent), according to survey research conducted in 1980 by Kenneth and Mamie Clark. Although somewhat dated, these percentages likely still hold true today, given that approximately 16 percent of African-American women express a specific preference to date or marry a light-skinned man.

African-American women who do exclusively prefer light-skinned men will sometimes confess that their preference is bound up in their hopes and fears for future children. For the dark-skinned woman in particular, her underlying motive in dating a light-skinned partner may be rooted in a desire to spare some future daughter the insults she had to endure from being dark skinned. As an aside, it is interesting to note that when light-skinned African-American women are pursued by men for reasons of "lightening the line," the women seem to understand and accept their vessel-like role in the relationship, but when light-skinned African-American men get any hint of the same reason driving a dark-skinned woman's interest in dating them, they often bolt. It would seem that light-skinned men are vigilant against the possibility that a dark-skinned woman is motivated to take a dip in their pale gene pool. A blogger has this to say:

> It's no secret that dark-skinned black Americans have had a rather strong affinity for dating and marrying light-skinned black Americans, to the point of identifiably and selectively inbreeding to ensure that their future generations don't suffer the bias, prejudice and other negatives that come with having darker complexions in a white/light-skinned-driven American society.

The factor that most drives African-American women's dating choices has less to do with skin color per se than with related issues of sexual attraction—or lack thereof. One college student claimed she would never date a dark-skinned Black man because she was turned off by the contrast of "pink lips on black skin." But a waitress professed to having a strong dislike for light-skinned Black men because, in her opinion, they lacked certain "soul brother" credentials. A dark-skinned professional woman expressing her preference for a "soul brother" put it this way: "When I see these Africanized Black brothers looking the way my ancestors may have looked, I get turned on." One African-American woman, a secretary, finds the darker the man's skin, the less inhibited and more animalistic, exotically erotic, and masculine he is.

When all is said and done, most African Americans, male or female, may simply gravitate toward others whose skin color is approximately the same as their own. Yet even when that is the case, different coupling patterns can still be seen. African Americans in the medium-brown range, by far the vast majority on the bell-shaped curve of skin-color distribution, are typically the least concerned about skin color. Being in the middle, they have been less scarred by color prejudices and thus tend to prefer others who are equally unbothered by the dynamics of colorism. Very light-skinned African Americans also primarily date and marry other African Americans who are light skinned, but may do so for specific reasons. Some may simply feel more comfortable with another person who is similarly light skinned, while others, as discussed elsewhere, come from haute bourgeois families who still place a lot of emphasis on preserving social status through color. Finally, very dark-skinned African Americans tend to date darker-skinned African Americans, but also are most likely to sample partners across the full color spectrum. In some cases, if they are financially secure, they may prefer to date only similarly economically positioned dark-skinned African Americans as a way of making a political statement regarding their freedom to make a conscious and personal choice. But if the man is dark skinned, financially secure, and socially ambitious, he may want to pursue a light-skinned woman, as noted earlier, to broadcast his success and his ability to do so. But for the dark-skinned man who is economically disadvantaged, choices may be limited to other women in the same socioeconomic bracket, many of whom may also be dark skinned. In part, this is because a light-skinned woman who is poor may spend her lightness capital to trade up and out of the "hood."

We now turn to the role of skin color in relationships that cross racial boundaries. In the new millennium, race mixing has become so common that the sight of a mixed-race couple hardly raises an eyebrow anymore, especially in large urban areas like New York City, Chicago, and Los Angeles. In fact, one might even ask, at this moment in our nation's history, if it still makes much sense to discuss interracial marriage as though it were only a coupling between individuals from two separate racial groupings. Given that the vast majority of African Americans are of mixed blood, marrying a White American is technically at some level an intraracial affair. Then there are the offspring of racially mixed couples who came before and will come after them to consider. How would we describe their dating and mating choices? And let's not forget the growing number of African Americans (and Whites) who marry Latinos and Asian Americans. When you add up the figures, you end up with a lot of Americans today marrying someone who is ethnically/racially somewhat different from and/or partially similar to themselves.

Statistics support the observation that interracial marriage is becoming increasingly common in the United States. Consider that when the soon-to-be parents of Barack Obama got married in 1961, less than 1 percent of all new marriages were interracial, and less than one-tenth of that percentage were of the profile of a Black man marrying a White woman. By 1980, the general rate of interracial marriage had jumped to 6.7 percent, and by 2010, the percentage had more than doubled again to 15 percent of all marriages. Of that total, the percent of African Americans who marry outside their race (i.e., to Whites, Asians, Hispanics, etc.) is fairly low, with only 14.4 percent involving a Black man and as few as 6.5 percent involving a Black woman. In further breaking down the 2010 census data to Black-White marriages only, we find that 64 percent of those involved African-American men marrying White women, a decrease from 1990 when it was 71 percent, and 36 percent involve African-American women marrying White men, a figure up from 1990 when it was 29 percent.

Approval of interracial marriage has increased dramatically as well, especially among young people. In 1958, only 4 percent of Americans said they would be accepting of an interracial marriage, but today, 60 percent say that they not only accept interracial marriage in principle, but also would be fine with a family member marrying someone of another race or ethnic group.

Suffice it to say we've come a long way since 1958, when a White man named Richard Loving married in Washington, DC, a woman named Mildred Jeter, who was of African and Native American descent, and then was arrested for having done so when he brought her back to his hometown in Virginia. In the

District of Columbia, interracial marriage was legal, but in Virginia there was still an antimiscegenation statute on the books. Accused of violating state law, Loving faced a prison sentence of up to five years, which was later suspended on the condition that he and his wife not set foot in Virginia for the next twenty-five years. Since the Lovings did not believe they had done anything criminally wrong, they sued. The case went all the way to the U.S. Supreme Court, and in 1967 the court's decision in *Loving v. Virginia* overturned not only the antimiscegenation law in Virginia but all such laws still on the books in fifteen other states.

Beyond challenging the law of the land, the Lovings, at that point in our nation's history and in that region of the country, were courageous simply to be seen in public together. Before the 1960s few Black men risked pursuing a White woman. After all, it was not that many years before that, in 1955, that Emmett Till was lynched for allegedly flirting with a White woman in Mississippi. But during the rebellious 1960s, social mores loosened, and Black men and White women came together sexually with greater frequency. The African-American historian Paula Giddings believes that this rise in interracial romance began after liberal northern Whites went south to work in the Civil Rights Movement. When southern Black men expressed interest in the White women who joined the freedom riders, the women were only too happy to oblige. In their minds, sleeping with a Black man was a show of solidarity for the "cause." As for the motives of the Black men, the White woman had long been forbidden fruit and it was surely a "power trip" to finally possess the so-called ideal beauty: now he was the master and she the slave. These extracurricular activities may have been meeting the needs of Black men and White women, but they enraged a number of Black women. Tensions grew in the civil rights camps, and Black women ordered the White women to pack up and leave.

In a what's-good-for-the-goose-is-good-for-the-gander vein, one might ask why the Black women didn't simply do the same with White men. But in looking back through the lens of history, it is easy to see why that wasn't going to happen. What might have been forbidden fruit for the Black man in sleeping with a White woman was rotten fruit for the Black woman, in knowing that her ancestresses had been raped and abused by White men during slavery. For many, the sight of a Black man with a White woman induced rage because the union represented an egregious violation of solidarity. Back in the day when plantation owners put White women on a "pedestal" while they overworked Black women, Black men stood with their women against the racist White man. And during the Civil Rights Era, Black men and women together braved the violence of guns, hoses, and police dogs from southern back roads to city boulevards until those northern White women arrived.

It is also the case that it is much easier for African-American women to blame White women for stealing "their men" than to consider why African-American males might be drawn to these women of another race. The African-American women's anger about the Black man–White woman unions may have also masked a fear that Black men didn't find them, women of the men's own race, pretty enough. It's a vague anxiety that persists among some today. As the late novelist BeBe Moore Campbell wrote in 1992, it's "like being passed over at the prom by the boy we consider our steady date. For sisters, the message that we don't measure up is the nightmare side of integration." More recently, Grammy Award–winning singer-songwriter Jill

Scott described her feelings about interracial relationships in an article written for *Essence*:

> My new friend is a handsome African American, intelligent and seemingly wealthy. He is an athlete, loves his momma and is happily married to a White woman. I admit when I saw his wedding ring I privately hoped. But something in me knew he didn't marry a sister. Although my guess hit the mark, when my friend told me his wife was indeed Caucasian I felt my spirit . . . wince. I didn't immediately understand it. My face read happy for you. My body showed no reaction to my inner pinch but the sting was there, quiet like a mosquito under a summer dress.

The "wince" is something many other African-American women know all too well, as they, too, have experienced its physical twinge. When Nahla, a dark-skinned African-American woman from the South Side of Chicago, was asked about the "wince," she thoughtfully replied:

> We are not monolithic, so I can only speak for myself. But what that wince is or that pain that goes real deep down in my gut when I see a brother and a White girl together is not about being a hater. That I am not. What it is for me is that I know, because of that union, there will be one less young Black girl or young Black boy that will be able to call a successful Black man "Daddy." That's what makes me wince. It's like a dagger in my heart.

Perhaps the "wince" occurs most strongly when the Black community's most successful African-American men marry interracially. Historically, the list includes artist Archibald Motley Jr. (1891–1981), former NAACP leader Walter White (1893–1955), author Richard Wright (1908–1960), and playwright August Wilson (1945–2005). And there is no letup in the trend today, as evidenced by the interracial marriages (some since ended) of composer and music producer Quincy Jones, musicians Seal and Ice-T; actors Sidney Poitier, James Earl Jones, Cuba Gooding Jr., and Taye Diggs; Supreme Court Justice Clarence Thomas; and athletes Tiger Woods and O. J. Simpson, to name just a few. Perhaps it is just reality that powerful people are attracted to each other, and in the stratosphere of high-profile African-American men, there are fewer opportunities for them to find equally high-status African-American women to marry. But another, less benign explanation would be that once an African-American man reaches a certain level of success, he may come to believe that even brighter lights will shine on him if he is married to a White woman. As was the case with O. J. Simpson, this pattern of wedding a White woman, and a blond one at that, is particularly irksome when the man's first spouse was an African-American woman.

While many more African-American men marry outside the race than do African American-women, as noted above, it is also true that the number of African-American women choosing to marry White men has edged higher over the past twenty years. One reason driving the increase in the number of Black women willing to date or even marry White men is the very real shortage of eligible Black males. African-American women, even those who are light skinned, are finding it increasingly difficult to find good matches. Contributing factors include high unemployment among Black males, and the sad statistic that one in four Black males between the ages of twenty and twenty-nine is in prison (and usually serving a longer sentence than a White man convicted for the same crime). Even more tragic are rates of Black-on-Black violence, which has reduced the number of African-American men in the inner city and shortened average life expectancies. One study found that in some urban areas there are as many as eight marriageable Black women for every marriageable Black man.

Marriage rates alone do not tell the whole story. Over the past few decades, the choice to cohabit instead of actually marry has become more acceptable among all Americans, but it is especially common among African Americans. Their rate of marriage fell by a whopping 34 percent between 2001 and 2010. Another way to look at the situation is to consider that in 2008 among all African-American households a married couple resided in only 45 percent of them, compared to a rate of 80 percent for Whites and 70 percent for Hispanics. U.S. Census data further indicate that in 2001, 43.3 percent of Black men and 41.9 percent of Black women in America had never married. In comparison, 27.4 percent of White women and 20.7 percent of White men had never been wed. In short, according to Howard University relationship therapist Audrey Chapman, African Americans are the most uncoupled people in the country.

The provocatively titled book *Is Marriage for White People?: How the African-American Marriage Decline Affects Everyone* that was published in 2011 argues that the lack of African Americans getting married hurts the larger society. The advice of author Ralph Richard Banks, a Stanford law professor, is that more African-American women should "marry out." This rather glib suggestion has angered more than a few African-American women who see his advice as akin to someone telling them to give up on their own people.

An interracial match is clearly not the answer for every African-American woman looking for a husband, as the cultural differences can be too big to overcome. Some women report that their Black features, which feel comfortable and right in the presence of other Blacks, become mortifying in the presence of Whites. For example, one African-American woman became obsessed with the idea that her pubic hair was too "bristly," and shaved herself every day so that she wouldn't "scratch" her White lover. (Fortunately, the current popularity of the Brazilian bikini wax makes that practice seem rather routine.) One extremely light-skinned Black woman with gray eyes and high cheekbones had plastic surgery on her nose, the only feature she believed might reveal to the White men she was interested in that she was Black. Yet another African-American woman washed, blow-dried, straightened, and curled her hair so much, it fell out—all because she was too embarrassed to wear rollers at night, knowing that her boyfriend's former White girlfriends had "simply flipped their hair into place" every morning.

Dana, a dark-skinned thirtysomething single who mainly dates White men, does so because she believes most African-American men are simply not interested in how she looks. She commented:

> It is a shame that White men love my blackness—my nappy hair, my dark skin, and my full lips—more than my own brothers. I stopped dating Black men because I got tired of feeling that I wasn't quite beautiful enough to be by their side.

It is indeed curious how some White men seem to be more accepting of African-American women's more natural looks than some Black men are. We interviewed Eric T., a White educator who mainly dates ethnic women, particularly African-American women. When asked what type of Black women he is attracted to, he was quick to point out that light-skinned Black women just don't "do it" for him. He said that he finds Halle Berry attractive, but if he wanted to date a White woman, he would just date one:

> In my mind, Halle Berry is just a dark-skinned White woman. That just doesn't interest me. What interests me about "truly" ethnic women is their connection with their inner beauty, since the world has told them that they are not attractive on the outside. That really builds an individuality that I find attractive. I don't get this from blond, blue-eyed White women. They live in a world that worships them.

There also are White men who pursue African-American women to satisfy a deep-seated psychological urge. One handsome White man, the manager of a famous rock band, claims that he likes African-American women because of their warmth and their kind, motherly ways. It happens that he grew up in a wealthy, racist household and was raised by a Black nanny. He has memories of being rocked to sleep in this woman's arms. As he grew older and heard his parents spout racist ideology, he became confused. How could they despise Black people when it was a Black woman who had first offered him love? Much to his family's dismay, he took to dating African-American women, a phenomenon the African-American community calls "the Black-nanny syndrome."

Stephanie K., who runs a beauty shop on Chicago's West

Side, is suspicious of the motives of White men who date Black. She is not so quick to sing the praises of these White men "loving our blackness," and offers the following words of caution:

> Be careful thinking that these White men are so liberal and loving Black women so much. These Black women may look all Afrocentric and whatnot. But listen to them talk. Most of them talk and act White. These White men only gonna take this "black love" thing so far. They ain't gonna bring home Shenequa!

Then again, why should every White man be expected to bring home a Shenequa? Who else would be held to a standard of having to like everyone in a particular group in order to be sincere about a few? As an analogy, would it mean someone was not gay or lesbian if there was a same-sex person out there that the person didn't find attractive?

It is true of course that some White men do prefer more educated African-American women who speak properly and have light skin and wavy hair. Perhaps they just feel more comfortable with looks and mannerisms that are relatively similar to their own. Even so, many White men, if they are honest, do sometimes struggle to wholly accept a lover's Blackness. In an *Essence* article entitled "Guess Who's Coming to Dinner Now?" by Dorothy Tucker, a White politician from Detroit shared his feelings about being in an interracial relationship:

> I seldom think of my girlfriend, Kathy, as Black as long as we are out at a restaurant, a cocktail party or playing tennis. [But] I remember once when we woke up in the morning I was staring at her and she looked awfully Black right then. A lot of times I look at her and it's as if she is

White; there's no real difference. But every now and then, it depends on what she is wearing and what we're doing, she looks very ethnic and very Black. It bothers me. I don't like it. I prefer it when she's a regular, normal, everyday kind of person.

A question to ask Black men is how they feel when they see "their women" with White men. Ironically, some of them experience, albeit for slightly different reasons, similar feelings of insecurity and territoriality that Black women report when they see one of "their men" with a White woman. With men, though, the fear of not being pretty enough is replaced by a fear of not being successful enough. The insecurities may turn into accusations that the Black women are nothing more than "gold diggers" and the White men have a case of "jungle fever." Some African-American men refuse to believe that a White man could ever truly love a Black woman, and then there are those who can't believe that a Black woman could ever forget the years of rape and humiliation White men inflicted on her female ancestors. In their defense, African-American women say they have not forgotten their legacy of exploitation, but, as someone who is currently dating a White man put it, "Why should we deprive ourselves of each other because of the history that neither one of us had anything to do with?"

We now turn to the gay community, where we find many of its African-American members are similarly affected by complexes and attitudes about skin color. A light-skinned Black gay professional man told us:

There are basically three types of people who signal their attraction to me: straight [Black] women who don't know I'm gay, Black men, and White men. With the women, I often feel the main reason they want to go out with me is because I'm light, but with the Black men I have never really felt that my coloring was that much of a factor. As for the White men I've dated, my color is important only to the extent that it is part of a larger package that makes me safe for them—I'm educated, with a prestigious job, and I happen to be a Black with fairly light color. Of course, there are some White men who date Blacks like me because they are dinge queens [White men who date Black men because of the eroticism of black on white skin].

A very dark-skinned Black gay actor named Michael, who has been accused of being a "snow queen" (i.e., a Black man who "gets off" in being with someone White), denies the charge and insists that his attraction to White men has more to do with class than with color. He claims that, to his chagrin, he has been unable to find another gay African-American man in his own socioeconomic bracket. Yet he adds, "It makes all the difference in the world to walk into a restaurant with a White man, as opposed to another Black man. We are treated much better because they assume we have money." Another Black gay actor, Eric F., who is very light skinned himself, also prefers having a White boyfriend. He recalls how in high school he was constantly teased not only about his light skin tone but also about his proper speech and even his popularity with girls. As Eric put it, "being harassed by [his] own people about skin color" only added to feelings of isolation, especially at a time when he began to explore his alternative sexuality. Eric is disturbed by the constant references to color he hears in the Black gay community, and believes the same color issues that affect the straight community can be found in the gay community.

"All this dinge queen and snow queen stuff is a bunch of crap, and only perpetuates a form of racism in the homosexual community," he says.

Skin color can infect African-American lesbian relationships as well. As one woman succinctly put it, "There are as many lesbians as 'breeders' who are colorstruck." Another African-American lesbian, Mary Morten, who is the founder of an organization dedicated to creating social change through public policy and advocacy, observed that both White and light-skinned Black lesbians sometimes assign special erotic value to a dark-skinned Black woman, whom they will call "an African goddess." Still, being in the camp of dark-skinned lesbians does not exempt such women from feeling bad about themselves. Morten recalls one woman who, even on vacation, avoided going out in the sunshine because "she didn't want to get any darker than she already was." Morten also remembers the time that an African-American woman she did not know called her on the telephone hoping to get a date. The woman began describing herself as "a green-eyed, light-skinned stud who was so light she could pass"—as if that was supposed to impress Morten. It did not. "A lot of work still needs to be done in terms of making women feel it doesn't matter what color skin they have," she concluded.

We agree. For someone of any sex or race, straight or gay, substantive characteristics, such as trustworthiness, intelligence, ability to love, and reliability, should weigh more heavily in deciding whom to date and with whom to share one's life than the literally surface quality of skin color. Yet at a time of ever-increasing popularity of online dating, it is more—not less—likely that decisions regarding dating choice will come down to the more basic attributes, such as race, religion, height, weight, and skin color. Niche sites in particular, such as those for individuals interested in interracial dating, are even more likely to use skin color as a categorical filter for identifying potential matches. But we would add a word of caution: skin-color fantasies do not necessarily come true.

Chapter 8

The (In)Justice of Color:
Politics, Policies, and Perceptions

In the months preceding the 2008 presidential election, accusations began to fly that the conservative Fox News network was altering stock photos of then presidential candidate Barack Obama to make him appear darker than he actually is. Whether the accusations were true, the outrage stemmed from a fear on the part of Obama supporters that if he started appearing darker, he would start becoming less electable. A similar charge of foul play was made in 1994, when *Time* magazine ran on its cover an obviously darkened photo of O. J. Simpson. The criticism surrounding that incident was that in darkening his picture, the magazine would activate stereotypes of criminal intent, thereby increasing the perception that Simpson was guilty of murder. But surely such a concern was not the case when it came to Barack Obama. Why then would even a slightly darkened photograph of candidate Obama cause such an uproar? Beginning with the against-all-odds victory of Obama, in this chapter we will explore how skin-color prejudices continue to exert influence in the arenas of politics, employment, and earnings. We will also take a look at some of the growing number of Title VII cases having to do with charges of colorism that have been filed during the thirtysome years since the first such case involving the category of color was heard in 1981.

As we all now know, on November 4, 2008, Barack Obama was elected the forty-fourth president of the United States. How the son of a White mother and an African father could achieve such stratospheric success still astonishes. Particularly impressive was how Obama managed to negotiate not only his racial identity but also his light skin color so as to appeal to a broad base of not just White voters, but Black voters, too. No other event in America could better encapsulate the politics of color than what happened on that day.

In his book *Dreams from My Father,* Obama describes how by the age of twelve or thirteen, after his return from Indonesia to live with his White maternal grandparents in Hawaii, he stopped mentioning his mother's race when asked about his racial identity. He realized that by insistently saying he was half White he was unintentionally giving the impression of trying to ingratiate himself with Whites. Obama soon developed feelings of racial solidarity with other Blacks. But he was also acutely aware that his lighter skin color and straighter features were allowing him to cross racial boundaries that other Blacks seemed unable to cross—not an uncommon realization experienced by those who are biracial and/or light skinned.

At some point Obama began to identify himself specifically as "African-American," a label that wasn't much in use until the 1990s. For years, most African Americans resisted the new term, instead preferring to stick with the word "Black." Perhaps this was done in remembrance of the struggle for civil rights in the 1960s, when "Black and Proud" replaced "Negro" as the proper way to refer to one's race. Arguments for replacing "Black" with the new term eventually won out; not only was saying "African-American" more in keeping with how other ethnic groups identified themselves, but it also put the emphasis on culture and geography instead of skin color. But when Obama started referring to himself as African-American, many questioned his right to do so. "African American" was a label meant for Black Americans who had historical roots going back to slavery. Yet, ironically, given that Obama was the offspring of a native-born African and a native-born American, one could argue that the "African-American" descriptor could not be more authentic and fitting.

Eventually, Obama, by declaring himself African-American, began to alienate the multiracial community. Members of that community were actively campaigning to expand categories of racial identification so that those of mixed heritage could celebrate all their racial and cultural identities, and not just the "one-drop" part of them. And they've had some successes. Multiracial activists are often credited for revisions first made in the 2000 U.S. Census form that enable respondents to select from a greater number of mixed-race categories. Yet they have more work to do. The multiracial community continues to challenge the passive acceptance of the arguably racist one-drop rule, and questions why those born of Black-White unions, or some other combination with a Black parent, must solely claim a "Black" identity. Thus it was very disappointing and frustrating for the multiracial activists when Obama denied his biraciality, dismissed his White ancestry, and further reinforced the legitimacy of the one-drop rule.

At the 2004 Democratic National Convention, Obama

first gained national attention when he delivered a speech that knocked it out of the ballpark. One of the most memorable and quoted lines from that address was this:

> *There is not a Black America and a White America and Latino America and Asian America—there's the United States of America.*

The sentiment was appealing to White people, many of whom preferred the notion of a color-blind society. But the words generally didn't sit well with "race folk," who believed Obama had just suggested Blacks should "whitewash" their identity and ignore important and celebrated cultural differences.

It was inevitable that some in the African-American community would accuse Obama of not being Black enough. Early in the campaign many African Americans had thrown their support behind Hillary Clinton, in part because her husband, former president Bill Clinton, is fondly recalled by many African Americans as "the first Black president." In 1998, esteemed African-American author Toni Morrison, winner of both a Nobel Prize and a Pulitzer Prize, summed up the views of many in the Black community this way:

> *. . . white skin notwithstanding, Clinton displayed almost every trope of blackness: single-parent household, born poor, working-class, saxophone-playing, McDonald's-and-junk-food-loving boy from Arkansas.*

Among the most stinging criticisms during the early days of the primaries came from the Reverend Jesse Jackson, who on CNN accused Obama of "talking down to Black people"—this remark made specifically in response to another of Obama's speeches, one in which he emphasized a theme of personal responsibility and family values. When Obama later failed to more publically and vigorously defend a group of six Black teenagers in Jena, Louisiana, who had been charged with attempted murder in a free-for-all that involved both Black and White high school students, Jackson again criticized Obama for "acting like he's White." Jackson did later apologize for both remarks and eventually became an enthusiastic Obama supporter. On election night, he could be spotted up front, close to the action with Oprah and other prominent African Americans.

No one doubted Obama's commitment to Black culture, however, when it came to the African-American woman he fell in love with and married. Most African-American men, and especially those who are Black-White biracial and highly successful, tend to select wives who are not just light skinned but also often lighter than themselves. Not only was Michelle Robinson darker than Barack Obama, but her "Black credentials," in being the daughter of working-class parents from Chicago's South Side, were beyond question. As far as many Blacks were concerned, Michelle was Obama's saving grace, and once she hit the campaign trail full-time, any qualms about his not being Black-enough looking or Black-enough acting began to recede.

Historically, individuals of mixed-race ancestry and light skin have long been the political mainstay of the Black community. Walter White, NAACP executive secretary from 1931 to 1955, was so light skinned that he was often mistaken for a White man, and close to all of the early Black leaders were light-skinned mulattoes (e.g., Frederick Douglass, John Mercer Langston, and Booker T. Washington). The trend continues. A recent survey found that lighter-skinned African Americans are overrepresented by a margin of nearly two to one in Congress.

In our discussion of the politics of color thus far, we have touched on only those issues raised within the Black community. But there was also a lot going on among Whites in response to the first African American with a real chance of being elected president. On the one hand, there were many young and older White grassroots supporters who did much to get out the vote for Obama. On the other hand, there was no shortage of prejudiced White individuals willing to turn Obama's image into bigoted caricature, or to make him a constant target of subtle and not-so-subtle racist jabs. Beyond the darkening of Obama's photo on Fox News, there were such incidents as the ridiculous uproar about the so-called ganglike power-fist gesture between the Obamas after a big primary win, the mock-horror reaction to Michelle's comment about for the first time "really being proud of America," and the portrayal of Barack and Michelle Obama as radicals on the cover of *The New Yorker*. That Obama was able to endure all the attacks and keep his eyes on the prize long enough to actually win the election still amazes many of us.

We now turn to social science research to better understand colorism's role in the electoral process. Scholars Eugene Caruso, Nicole Mead, and Emily Balcetis conducted a cleverly designed study to demonstrate that skin color can affect, on a seemingly subconscious level, perceptions of a political candidate, in this case Obama. During the early stages of the presidential campaign, the researchers invited a group of mostly White participants to first self-identify their own political ideology. Then they gave the participants three photos of Barack Obama to look at and asked them to identify the one that was most representative of Obama himself. In the first photo, Obama's appearance was unaltered, but in the second and third photos, respectively, he was lightened and darkened. Caruso and his colleagues found that liberal participants thought the lightened version of Obama most resembled him, while conservative participants thought the darkened version of Obama was most representative. In short, political partisanship can lead not just to a desire to portray Obama as darker than he really is, but to actually *see* him as darker.

In a related study conducted during the two to three months preceding the election, coauthor Midge Wilson and two of her graduate students looked at the effects of Obama's skin color on his perceived suitability for high office. White and non-White participants for the research were recruited online. Because by then the majority of Americans had already made up their minds for whom they were going to vote, the participants were instructed to pretend they were among the small pool of undecided. Their task was to look at a poster of Obama for the purpose of evaluating his suitability for the presidency along a number of traits (perceived toughness, patriotism, etc.). The participants also were asked to what extent they thought race and color were factors in the election. There were two versions of the poster, one in which Obama's photo was altered so that he appeared lighter than he really is, and one in which he appeared darker. The researchers hypothesized that those participants who viewed the light-skinned version of the poster would more favorably evaluate Obama than those who saw the dark-skinned version. However, no such difference emerged from the analysis. Given that emotions ran high during the campaign, it was probably almost impossible for participants to imagine being undecided. But Wilson and her students did find a significant difference between the White and non-White participants' perceptions about the role of race and skin color in the presidential campaign. Non-White participants believed race and color were much more negative influences than did the White participants.

In 1993, Nayda Terkildsen conducted one of the first empirical studies on the perceived electability of candidates as a function of their race and skin color. Her participants were recruited from a list of Kentucky potential jurors, who were first asked to complete an inventory on racial prejudice. Then the participants were randomly assigned to read one of three fictional accounts of a candidate running for public office. Each account was exactly the same except that in the first version the candidate was described as a White male; in the second, as a dark-skinned African-American male; and in the third, as a light-skinned African-American male. As predicted, the participants, who were mainly White, expressed greater liking for the White candidate over the two Black candidates. Contrary to expectations, however, Terkildsen found that the White participants who scored highest on measures of racial prejudice particularly disliked the *lighter-skinned* African-American candidate. She reasoned that among these individuals, the sight of darker skin may have cued a greater need to racially monitor their reactions, which could have led them to respond with an eye toward political correctness.

History, surveys, and empirical research all point to the existence of a politically charged racial gap in how life is perceived in America. The outcome of the October 1995 O. J. Simpson trial is probably the most dramatic event in our nation's recent past to lay bare the schism. According to an ABC News–*Washington Post* survey taken shortly after the verdict was read, 70 percent of Whites thought Simpson was guilty and the verdict wrong, while 74 percent of Blacks were satisfied with the jury's verdict.[11] Sixty-four percent of African Americans also cited a possible "police conspiracy" to frame Simpson. Fast-forward eleven years to a 2006 CNN poll which found that randomly selected samples of African Americans and (non-Hispanic) Whites still filter the world through different lenses. Eighty-four percent of African Americans believe that racism continues to be a "somewhat serious" or "very serious" problem in this country, while only 66 percent of Whites do.

For a study published in 2006, Richard Eibach and Joyce Ehrlinger conducted research that sought to understand the underlying cognitive reasons for the differing perceptions about race. First the researchers confirmed through a questionnaire that perceptions about "progress toward racial equality" differed significantly between two populations of Whites and Blacks. As expected, Whites tended to see significantly more progress than Blacks did. Eibach and Ehrlinger then asked the participants what they were thinking while answering the question regarding their perceptions about racial progress in our country. It turns out that when Whites answered the question, they were comparing the status and treatment of Blacks today with what it was like before the Civil Rights Movement. But when African Americans answered it, they tended to compare the status and treatment of Blacks today with a hoped-for future when true racial equality would exist. Interestingly, these race differences

---

11. For many African Americans, the issue with O.J. was more nuanced: he might well have been guilty, but they felt it was good for once to see a wealthy Black man beat the system, not unlike other White men with celebrity and a lot of money who walked free from murder charges (e.g., socialite Claus von Bülow and actor Robert Blake).

could be minimized or eliminated altogether with prequestionnaire instructions instructing participants to adopt one or the other of the two perspectives when responding to items.

This difference in point of reference likely explains the findings of Wilson's study as well. When White participants were asked about the roles of race and color in the Obama campaign, they were probably reflecting on the unlikely possibility that an African American was not just running for president but also had a good chance of winning. What a great place America is! In comparison, African Americans, along with other non-White participants, no doubt recognized and appreciated the historical significance of the election, but also were more cognizant of the slew of uniquely racist attacks on Obama's character during the long campaign. As a result, they saw race and color as having a large impact in Obama's run for the presidency.

Elections in which the Black candidates have won similarly elicit race-based differences in what the outcomes mean. For example, in the early 1990s two prominent African-American men (both of whom are light skinned) were elected to high office: David Dinkins as mayor of New York City and Doug Wilder as governor of Virginia. When a sample of Americans were asked what, if anything, these elections signified, Whites tended to view the outcomes as proof that race was no longer a factor in American political campaigns. African Americans were far less sanguine about our nation's sudden "color blindness" in the voting booth (Terkildsen, 1993).

Not just elections but high-level government appointments of African Americans, such as former secretaries of state Colin Powell and Condoleezza Rice, U.S. Attorney General Eric Holder, and Supreme Court Justice Clarence Thomas, similarly produce varying views. When Whites see individuals of color reach the highest pinnacles of success in their fields, many tend to view these accomplishments as further evidence that America is a meritocracy where anything is possible, as long as someone is willing to work hard. This belief rests on the fundamentally flawed assumption that all Americans start off life on a level playing field. Whites, especially those from professional middle-to-upper-class backgrounds, are typically oblivious to the gentle backwind pushing them along on the road to success. For many, it blows just strongly enough that even with minimal effort it is still possible to reach lofty levels of success. Former president George W. Bush is Exhibit A in this regard. In contrast, economically disadvantaged Americans of all races and ethnicities must confront powerful headwinds, with the result that only the most persistent and strong can stay the course. In the face of such struggle, most individuals, regardless of race, will eventually stop trying.

Nonetheless, in the wake of Obama's election, many Whites took to saying we now live in a postrace era in which color and race no longer matter. Given this country's long racist history, such a declaration was a bit premature—naïve at best and ignorant at worst. As long as privileged Whites believe that all it takes for those living in deep poverty to achieve the American dream is some greater effort on their part, not only will necessary structural and institutional-level changes not take place, but funding for existing programs and policies like Head Start and Affirmative Action will cease to exist.

As we segue into the role of skin color in the workplace, it's worth noting that an election campaign is in a sense like a job interview, and in the case of a presidential election, a very, very long one that lasts nearly two years. During these increasingly extended campaign periods, voters have the opportunity to get to know applicants well, certainly beyond a first impression. Changes of heart and attitude can and do occur with greater exposure to someone, as evidenced by upward shifts in Obama's favorability ratings over the course of the campaign and increasing negatives for Sarah Palin after her hugely popular start. But for the rest of us, the old expression "You never get a second chance to make a first impression" still applies.

An implied assumption in this platitude is that applicants can exercise a certain degree of control during a job interview. And that may well be true for some. When a White employer is interviewing White job applicants, things like their choice of clothing, hairstyle, hair color, grammar, and posture may indeed make the difference in the hiring decision. But when White employers interview a Black individual, the first thing that they will notice is the applicant's race and skin color, and these are attributes over which the applicant has no control.

Unfortunately, White employers, even those who genuinely believe themselves free of prejudice, can still be influenced by the insidious effects of racism and colorism. According to implicit race theory, today's—or what is termed "modern"—racism assumes a more subtle form, and may operate subconsciously. A computer-based measure known as the Implicit Association Test (IAT) was developed to demonstrate how subtle racism can occur. In the standard paradigm, participants are asked to rapidly categorize two target concepts through the assignment of different associations, such as "good" or "bad" or various traits such as "lazy" or "intelligent." In study after study, Whites unconsciously associate and pair the more negative words with the sight of a Black individual.

For individuals who appear racially ambiguous, skin color alone can cue negative associations. This was demonstrated in a study in which research participants were invited to sit on a mock jury. Their assigned role was to view "evidence slides" portraying either a dark-skinned or (this time with another group of participants) a light-skinned male as a perpetrator doing something possibly criminal. The researchers found that in comparison to participants whose "evidence slides" showed a light-skinned potential perpetrator, those who saw a dark-skinned man were inclined to weigh subsequent information more heavily as pointing to evidence of the man's guilt.

In recent years the IAT has been challenged on its external validity, or whether findings collected in a lab when participants are required to make extremely rapid association choices can generalize to situations in the real world where there is more time to consider all the incoming data. It is safe to assume that, unlike police officers or military personnel in the throes of gun battles, individuals such as White employers interviewing Black applicants have much more time to reflect on the whole package. Still, something powerful is being cued by skin color, even when there is ample time to render an evaluation and make a decision.

A recent study indicates that a job applicant's skin color can actually trump qualifications. Shilpa Banerji and her doctoral student asked participants to engage in a mock-hiring task in which they would be asked to indicate their preferences for hiring applicants who varied by manipulated criteria. The design of the study was such that there were two different resumes, one in which the job candidate's credentials were quite strong, and the other in which they were minimal. Attached to each of the two resumes was one of six possible photographs of an African-American man who was either light skinned or dark skinned. The most startling finding was that, out of all the possible combinations of skin color and resume strength, a lighter-skinned applicant was preferred over a darker-skinned applicant who had more managerial experience and was more highly educated with an MBA degree.

Once a job is landed, an employee's skin color continues to shape the trajectory of occupational success. Several studies support this contention, even when preexisting differences tied to socioeconomic background (i.e., wealthier families spawn children who earn higher salaries) are held constant. In 1990, scholars Michael Hughes and Bradley Hertel reanalyzed raw data from the 1980 National Survey of Black Americans (NSBA) and found that the difference in earnings between light-skinned and dark-skinned Blacks was proportional to that between Whites and Blacks. Using the same data set, in 1991 researchers Verna Keith and Cedric Herring established that the overall income of very light-skinned African-American families was about 50 percent higher than that of very dark-skinned African-American families. And in 2007, Arthur H. Goldsmith, Darrick Hamilton, and William Darity Jr. used data from the 1992 Multi City Study of Urban Inequality survey to find that the income gap, whether between light- and dark-skinned African Americans or between Whites and African Americans, widened as skin color darkened. Remarkably, according to findings from the 2003 *New Immigrant Survey,* the first nationally representative survey of immigrants and their children ever conducted in this country, a similar pattern emerged among recent immigrants to this country. When a multitude of factors, such as educational level, English-language proficiency, occupation in source country, family background, ethnicity, race, and country of birth were controlled for, those with the lightest skin color earned an average of 17 percent more than comparable immigrants with the darkest skin color. A better life indeed, if one happens to have light skin.

Another significant skin-color correlate is occupational prestige, which has to do with how much a particular job is held in esteem by others. In only reporting average income differences between light- and dark-skinned African Americans, how much a particular career is respected and valued can be obscured. For example, there are some jobs, like pastor or professor, that don't necessarily yield soaring salaries but do offer very high levels of prestige. Other forms of employment, most notoriously drug dealing, may bring in lots of cash, but they sit on the lowest rung of occupational prestige. Historically, the observed correlation between skin color and occupational prestige was assumed to be a legacy of color classism in which generations of mulatto-elite families perpetuated their prestige through offspring. Sociologist Mark Hill, however, challenged this assumption. He discovered that when it comes to social status, skin tone in itself may trump family background. Hill creatively linked archival childhood census forms from the 1920s that indicated whether a newborn was "mulatto" to death certificates from the 1980s, and then again correlated the information with the person's career and social success. In taking a longitudinal approach, Hill was able to call into question the oft-made assertion that the benefits of being light skinned were simply remnants of a bygone era. He concluded that light skin color acts as a separate force on individuals, gently pushing along those who possess it to greater occupational prestige and higher life outcomes.

Given the relationship between skin color and career success, it is not surprising that employment settings are hot zones of simmering resentment, jealousy, and loathing. We now look at how unfair treatment stemming from skin-color prejudices and privileges has played out legally in the workplace.

Nearly fifty years have passed since the landmark 1964 Civil Rights Act (CRA) was signed into law. Although the bill contained many "titles," or sections, and a multitude of provisions prohibiting various forms of discrimination, ranging from voter registration to public access, it was and remains the case that Title VII, which prohibits workplace discrimination, is the most commonly known and cited piece of that law. To enforce the new legislation, Title VII mandated the creation of a new government agency called the Equal Employment Opportunity Commission (EEOC), which has had a reputation for uneven enforcement. While the vast majority of the hundreds of thousands of cases heard by the EEOC have to do with racial discrimination, in this chapter we look at the smaller number of Title VII cases stemming from charges of colorism.

"Color," along with race, religion, sex, and national origin, has always been included as a category of protection under Title VII, but it was 1981 before the EEOC was willing to hear its first case based solely on that attribute—one that was between two Latinas, to be discussed later. But it took nine more years before the EEOC agreed to formally consider a charge of color discrimination between two African Americans. The plaintiff was a light-skinned African-American woman named Tracy Walker (who is now known as Tracy Morrow and will be referred to as such). In the late 1980s, Morrow worked as a clerk typist in the Internal Revenue Service's Atlanta office. The defendant was Morrow's supervisor, a darker-skinned African-American woman named Ruby Lewis. Not long after Lewis became Morrow's supervisor, a strained relationship developed between the two women. Morrow attributed this to the fact that Lewis, as a dark-skinned woman, was jealous of Morrow's lighter skin color. To support this assertion, she alleged that Lewis made multiple derogatory comments specifically referencing the color of Morrow's skin. Tensions reached the point where Morrow felt it necessary to schedule a meeting with the local Equal Employment officer to complain about the situation, although, at the time, Morrow wasn't sure what could be done, since both parties were of the same race. When Lewis got wind of Morrow's meeting and what was discussed, she terminated Morrow's employment, either because of that knowledge or not (this became another issue in the case). In her defense, Lewis stated that her reasons for the firing were Morrow's constant tardiness, laziness, incompetence, and poor attitude. Lewis also accused Morrow of fabricating stories about Lewis's suffering from skin-color jealousy. The EEOC decided to accept the case under the rarely considered protected category of color, with the result that in 1991 *Walker v. IRS* went to a bench trial.

Coauthors Hall and Wilson testified as expert witnesses on behalf of the plaintiff. Their primary responsibility, since neither knew Morrow personally, was to educate and explain to the elderly White southern judge assigned to the case exactly what colorism was, its history, and the evidence of its existence today. Like most White people, especially those of his advanced age, the judge had not a clue about why two Blacks would not get along because of their skin color.[12] In the end, Morrow lost the case, in large part because her record of work performance

---

12. One comical moment came when Walker was testifying how Lewis used to say things to her like "You think you're so bad with your light skin," which led to a whole other discussion with the judge about how the word "bad" can sometimes mean "good" in the African-American community.

was not all that strong. Nonetheless, *Walker v. IRS*, which was the first federal case of colorism involving two Blacks and also took place in Atlanta, where CNN was based, generated a lot of media coverage. It was probably the first time the subject of skin-color prejudice was even discussed on CNN as a news story. And there were no doubt many Whites who, like the judge, learned for the first time in their lives something about this taboo topic, hitherto confined to the African-American community.

The next notable case of skin-color discrimination was *Porter v. Illinois Department of Children and Family Services* in 1998. Thomas Porter, a light-skinned African-American male who was the plaintiff, had worked at the Illinois Department of Children and Family Services. Marcia Williams, a dark-skinned woman, was his supervisor. Porter contended that Williams informed him at one of their first meetings that she did not care for light-skinned men and that it was her goal to fire him before the end of his probationary period. Defendant Williams denied ever saying such a thing to Porter, although she did acknowledge that it was true that she preferred dark-skinned African-American men as boyfriends. She further admitted that she had had conversations about this preference of hers with friends at work, but said she did not recall ever sharing such personal information with Porter. In her defense, Williams questioned what difference it would make even if she did tell him about the preference, as there was no causal link between what she liked in boyfriends and Porter's dismissal. The court agreed; there was not enough evidence to indicate that Porter's termination had anything to do with Williams's preference for lighter skin color.

In 2003, another color-discrimination case involving two African Americans was settled by consent, suggesting admission of colorism. The case was *EEOC v. Applebee's* and the plaintiff was Dwight Burch, a dark-skinned African American who worked at an Applebee's restaurant in Georgia. His manager was a light-skinned African-American man who, according to Burch, repeatedly made derogatory and humiliating comments about his dark skin color. Tired of the verbal abuse, Burch told the manager that if he didn't stop, Burch would report the harassing behavior to someone at the Applebee's corporate office. Upon hearing the threat, the manager promptly fired Burch, who then headed to the EEOC office to file a Title VII complaint of color discrimination. Burch was awarded a $40,000 settlement, based on charges not just of color discrimination but also of retaliation in being fired after complaining. Applebee's was further ordered to amend its harassment and discrimination policies to include color as a protected class. The restaurant franchise denies any wrongdoing.

African Americans have not been the only ethnic or racial group to look to Title VII for help in resolving workplace color discrimination; Latinos, too, have been using the law. This makes sense, as Latinos generally come from countries with evident color-caste hierarchies but no rigid race lines. Thus, if one comes from a country that purports to have no racism, then color would almost have to be the category of protection under which charges of workplace discrimination would be filed, especially if the case involved two self-identified Latinos. Yet since "Latino" is not a racial designation per se, but instead a cultural grouping, there are Latinos who identify as "White," "Black," or "Native American / Indian / Indigenous," or by other ethnicities such as "Hispanic" or "Chicano." Other self-labels are indirectly related to skin color. Mexicans are most likely to choose as their race the category of "Other," while Cubans are most likely to choose "White." And because "White," or *"blanco,"* is valued above all other skin tones, Cubans are quick to correct anyone who might misidentify them as Mexican. Another interesting skin-color-related reality about Cuba is that during the Castro revolution, an estimated 85 percent of those who emigrated to the United States were White, while 90 percent of those who stayed behind were dark skinned.

We now turn to studies on Latino immigrants that document American colorism. In 2003, researchers at the Lewis Mumford Center for Comparative Urban and Regional Research investigated the effects of skin color on the lives and incomes of Latinos in the United States. They found that Latinos who identified themselves as White earned about $5,000 more per year than Latinos who identified themselves as Black. Yet when Latinos identified themselves as "some other race," the gap between those individuals and White Latinos narrowed to $2,500. Another study indicated a clear color gap in earnings among Mexican Americans alone such that even when differences in family background, occupation, and educational levels are adjusted and controlled for, the color-class pattern still emerges. In 2002, Rodolfo Espino and Michael Franz similarly discovered that when they compared the employment experiences of Mexicans, Puerto Ricans, and Cubans once they arrived in the United States, it was the lighter-skinned immigrants who came to enjoy the greatest occupational prestige. In fact, even when job performance was held constant, darker-skinned counterparts did not fare as well in terms of income. In summary, the lighter the skin color of an immigrant, the better the chance to achieve the American dream.

According to the EEOC, *Felix v. Marquez* (1981) was the first case on record to draw on Title VII to file a complaint of color discrimination. The claim involved two Latinas. The plaintiff, Felix, was a dark medium-skinned female employee of the Office of the Commonwealth of Puerto Rico in Washington, DC (OCPRW), and the defendant, Marquez, was her lighter-skinned supervisor. Felix believed that Marquez had failed to promote her due to color prejudice. In her testimony, Felix claimed there was a clear pattern of light-skin-color preference by Marquez, as evidenced by the fact that among Felix's twenty-eight (former) colleagues employed at the OCPRW, only two were as dark as she or darker. The two darker-skinned employees referenced by Felix were invited to testify, and although they described themselves as Puerto Rican, they noted that in the United States they were often assumed to be African-American. Two other employees whom Felix had designated as being lighter than herself also testified, but they appeared to be of the same skin tone as Felix. Their testimony thus contradicted Felix's assertion that there was a rigid color line between herself and her fellow employees. The court ruled against Felix, finding there was a justifiable reason unrelated to colorism for her not being promoted.

The outcome was different in the 2009 case of *EEOC v. Koper Furniture*. The plaintiff was a dark-complexioned Puerto Rican sales associate who alleged that his lighter-skinned manager at the furniture store where they both worked frequently harassed him about his dark skin, taunting him with questions regarding *why* he was "so black." When the sales associate complained to the manager about this, and asked him to stop, he was fired. The EEOC took the case on behalf of the darker-skinned man and won an undisclosed voluntary settlement. Although some Puerto Ricans later mocked the plaintiff for complaining about something as trivial as skin color, the EEOC's Miami regional attorney disagreed:

Harassment based on skin color can be just as humiliating and degrading as other forms of discrimination. Employers must treat colorism complaints seriously and punish the perpetrators—not the victims.

Most cases of color discrimination today actually also involve racism, with both protected categories identified as reasons for bringing charges of discrimination. However, the EEOC website lists five significant cases won between 2003 and 2009 under the single category of color. Two of those have been discussed (i.e., the Applebee's employee and the furniture sales associate), and two of the remaining three are interesting in that they involved Asian Americans. In *EEOC v. Blockbuster* (2008), a Bangladeshi female employee at a Blockbuster video store was assigned to be store manager at a Staten Island location, but was subsequently told by the district supervisor that she should change her dark skin color if she wanted to work there. He went on say that she should have been assigned to work in Harlem. Some liability must have been acknowledged, as the case was settled out of court for $80,000. The second Asian-American case is *Chellen et al. & EEOC v. John Pickle Company* (2006), and it is perhaps the EEOC's biggest color-discrimination case. It was filed on behalf of fifty-two skilled male workers from India who were recruited by the John Pickle Company, an oil-industry-parts-manufacturing business from Tulsa that is out of business today. The workers were segregated on the basis of their dark skin color and then subjected to widespread abuse, intimidation, and exploitation. The charges were upheld and the John Pickle Company was ordered to pay $1.3 million in damages to the victims. It needs to be noted, however, that the settlement amount included the far more serious charge of human trafficking, so it is impossible to tell how much compensation came from color discrimination alone.

The last of the three cases, *EEOC v. Family Dollar,* was between two African Americans. In December 2007, the EEOC sued Family Dollar Stores after a light-skinned Black female manager subjected darker-skinned African-American employees to a hostile and abusive work environment because of their color. The lawsuit alleged that the manager told one employee she looked as "black as charcoal" and repeatedly called her "Charcoal" until she quit. The EEOC settled the case with Family Dollar in 2009.

Despite the growing numbers of workplace colorism cases, involving not just African Americans but also Latinos, Asian Americans, and people of other ethnicities, there is no doubt that many more instances of color discrimination take place but go unchallenged. However, in the last three decades, the EEOC has made significant progress in its recognition of color discrimination as a Title VII violation. As the number of racially mixed persons continues to grow in this country, there will surely be more colorism cases filed in the future. But meanwhile we can hope that as more people become conscious of colorism as a form of prejudice, and realize that color discrimination is illegal and can have costly consequences for employers and businesses alike, there will be fewer, not more, Title VII color-discrimination cases.

Chapter 9

The Narrative of Skin Color: Stories in Black and Light

A narrative is a story that may find expression in literature, poetry, theater, or film. In nearly every narrative, there are images, symbols, and stock characters deployed to represent something larger than surface appearance. In the film noir genre, for example, a woman's blond hair is typically used to forecast her treacherous nature. Generally we hear no complaints about this commonly deployed stereotype, perhaps because blondes are somewhat privileged people in our society. But when images of those from underrepresented groups are repeatedly used to symbolize something negative about a character, then anything from grumblings of criticism to outright cries of protest will eventually follow.

For example, in the early 1990s, gay activists were alarmed by the portrayal of members of their community as deviant and potentially dangerous when two back-to-back blockbuster movies, *Silence of the Lambs* (1991) and *Basic Instinct* (1992), featured psychotic killers who were gay or bisexual. Similarly, throughout the history of American film, especially before the

Civil Rights Movement, African Americans frequently had to speak up about the unflattering and one-dimensional images by which they were constantly being portrayed on the silver screen. If male, they were cast as either a brute or "coon," and if female, as a mammy or a "tragic mulatto." Blatant stereotypes of this sort are no longer tolerated. Thanks in no small part to the growing cadre of African Americans who are now film directors, producers, and screenwriters, the roles of African Americans in films today are far more nuanced, complex, and multidimensional.

And yet what seems to have changed little over the years is the way in which skin color is encoded to represent something larger in regard to an African American's character. When a woman is light skinned, we can expect she will be desirable and kind, and when a man is very dark skinned, we can bet he will be either criminally dangerous or sexually potent. And when there is a dark-skinned woman in the story, we can assume she will be some combination of undesirable, eccentric, or impoverished. This sort of color coding of characters was evident in *Precious* (2009), one of the most critically acclaimed African-American-directed-and-produced films in recent years. Because of this film's enormous success, and the controversy it aroused within the Black community, it will be discussed more fully later in the chapter. We begin with the role skin color has played in Black literature, poetry, theater, and film.

Scholars of African-American studies continue to unearth early Black writings. Today a woman named Lucy Terry (1730?–1821) is widely recognized as author of the oldest literary work by a Black American. It was a ballad called "Bars Fight," first written in 1746, although not published until 1755. Remarkably, Terry was born in Africa, enslaved with her mother, and sold to a Massachusetts Christian, who baptized her at the age of five. Her ballad tells the story of an attack on Whites by Native Americans, which suggests Terry knew a little something about what Whites would find acceptable to publish.

Phillis Wheatley (1753?–1784) was another early literary figure, also born in Africa, enslaved, and purchased by a Massachusetts man who early on recognized her brilliance. Like Terry, Wheatley appears to have been savvy enough to know which topics would lead to publication and which would not. In fact, one of her poems honored George Washington, who personally thanked her for it. Predictably, there were other Whites in the country who refused to believe that someone from Africa could have written anything so refined. To defend her authorship, Wheatley was summoned to appear in court. Perhaps because she had to experience such a racist episode, in 1778 Jupiter Hammon (1711–1806?), another early African-American literary figure, penned an ode to Wheatley in honor of her great talent.

Two Black men, Victor Séjour (1817–1874) and William Wells Brown (1814?–1884), are credited with writing some of the earliest stories whose narratives centered on skin color and how that feature shaped the course a fictional female character's life would take—a genre that would later become known as "the tragic mulatto." Séjour was born in New Orleans but at the age of nineteen moved to France, where in 1837 he published his first short story, "Le Mulâtre." Brown, too, was born in America but was able to flee to Europe, where in England he published his first novel in 1853. It was entitled *Clotel: or, The President's Daughter: A Narrative of Slave Life in the United States*. Brown's book tells the story of three mulatto women, a mother and the two daughters she had by a White man who later abandons the family. It ends tragically with a gang of Whites chasing one of the daughters, Clotel, into the Potomac River, where she dies—and, as a nice touch, within sight of Thomas Jefferson's White House.

Skin color remained a crucial element of female fictional characters in popular nineteenth-century literature. Typical of the plotline was a biracial heroine who was light skinned, beautiful, and passive, and the love interest of either a Black or a White man. Unable to fit into either Black or White society, the heroine tries to pass for White or sometimes some other ethnicity. The stories were filled with coincidences and ironic twists of fate, but the central light-skinned female character nearly always suffered a dramatic downfall in the end.

Narratives about tragic mulattoes were equally popular themes in the early work of both Black and White nineteenth-century authors, albeit for different reasons. For Whites, in writing about mulattoes, whose numbers were rapidly growing in America, vices could be attributed to a racially mixed character's Black blood, and achievements to his or her White background. In reality, the mulatto symbolized the vanguard of a fully integrated society, and culture critics believe that stories about their tragic downfall may have helped soothe Whites' anxieties about unchecked race mixing. The tragic downfall of female characters in particular may have helped mitigate the jealousy of White women who knew all too well why mulattoes on the plantations bore an uncanny resemblance to their own children. Also, as true now as it was then, White women were the primary consumers of the novels, and authors knew how to cater to their target audience.

For early Black American writers, however, there were likely very different reasons for writing tragic-mulatto stories. First, the authors themselves were usually mulatto, and writers generally write about what they know best. Second, mulattoes provided a convenient illustration of the injustices of slave rape and racism. Third, portraying mulattoes who were light enough to pass gave the writer an opportunity to explore the question of allegiance to the Black race. And finally, like White authors, Black fiction writers were trying to make a living and thus were inclined to give White publishers stories that would sell. If the mulatto heroine had to die tragically in the end, then so be it.

Among the first to depart from the tragic-mulatto formula was African-American writer Harriet Wilson (1825–1900), whose book *Our Nig* was first published in Boston in 1859. While other Black women before her may have published ballads, odes, and poems, she is recognized as the first female African-American novelist to actually get a book published in this country. Perhaps because she was not writing for a White audience but for Blacks (*Our Nig,* in fact, opens with an appeal for the patronage of her "colored brethren"), Wilson's mulatto heroine, Frado, is neither tragic nor apologetic. Frado's relations with White men are more pragmatic than romantic, and her oppressor, a White woman, suffers a slow and agonizing death. A Black man named Jim, moreover, becomes an equal partner in a marriage to a White woman. Wilson's refusal to conform to the conventional literary treatment of Black characters may have been one reason why her remarkable novel was not better received. When it was first released, it was not even reviewed. Seemingly destined for obscurity, the book was rediscovered and reissued in 1983, with an introduction by African-American studies scholar Henry Louis Gates Jr.

We now fast-forward to the 1920s, when Black artists and intellectuals gathered in large numbers in New York to produce a virtual explosion and celebration of Afro-centered music, art, and literature. This was the era of the Harlem Renaissance, energized by an economic boom, social activism, and the "Great Migration" of southern Blacks to the North. While thousands of books, plays, and poems were written during the Harlem Renaissance, it was still the case that Black authors needed the patronage of Whites to get their works published and reviewed. Since melodramatic stories about tragic mulattoes remained a tried-and-true formula, many of the Harlem Renaissance writers conformed, but there were also a growing number who began to break out of the mold.

The books of Nella Larsen (1891–1965), *Quicksand* (1928) and *Passing* (1929), both depicted beautiful mulatto heroines struggling with racial identity and their place in society. But unlike traditional tragic-mulatto stories, hers focused more on the subjective experiences of racially mixed women. Like Larsen herself, the central characters were educated and solidly middle-class in their values. She clearly drew from her own life, as evidenced by the fact that in *Quicksand* the protagonist Helga had a father who was Black and a mother who was Danish—the same racial makeup as that of Larsen's parents.

Novelist Jessie Redmon Fauset (1884–1961) similarly wrote about complex mulatto characters in her two books, *Plum Bun* (1928) and *There Is Confusion* (1924). And like many other artists from the Harlem Renaissance, Fauset herself was light skinned. She also was well educated, having earned an MA from Cornell University and studied at the Sorbonne in Paris. The fascination with mulatto characters for Fauset, as for Larsen, undoubtedly stemmed from personal social experience.

It was also during the Harlem Renaissance that Black male writers began to critically address color prejudice within the

"Negro" community. For example, George Schulyer (1895–1977) felt creatively free enough to undertake the delicate topic in a satirical manner. In 1931, he published *Black No More,* a novel whose title alone implies a ridiculing of skin color. And Wallace Thurman (1902–1934), in his novel *The Blacker the Berry* (1929), portrays a Black female protagonist as miserably unhappy because of her skin color. In response, a male character named Truman (whose name is rather similar to the author's own) challenges her and others to abandon their ignorant views about race and color discrimination. In one scene set as a gathering of Harlem intellectuals, the novelist has Truman declare:

> *"Then consider that the mulatto is much nearer White than he is black, and is therefore more liable to act like a White man than like a black one, although I cannot say that I see a great deal of difference in any of their actions. They are human beings first and only White or black incidentally."*

The critically acclaimed poet, novelist, playwright, and social activist Langston Hughes (1902–1967) was another artist from that time who openly explored the psychology of color from a Black perspective in his writings. In a play he wrote called *Mulatto,* which enjoyed a successful run on Broadway from 1935 to 1937, illicit relationships in the South were tackled through a narrative centering on the conflict between a mulatto son and his White father.[13] And Hughes's poem "Cross," arguably his most notable piece of writing on the topic of race mixing, served as the epigraph to Nella Larsen's 1928 novel *Quicksand*:

---

13.   An opera based on *Mulatto,* titled *The Barrier,* premiered in 1950.

My old man died in a fine big house.
My ma died in a shack.
I wonder where I'm going to die,
Being neither white nor black?

By the end of the Black Renaissance, there was no questioning anymore that Black authors were writing for Black audiences without worrying whether White readers would understand or approve the topics. Perhaps the most striking illustration of this new attitude can be found in two 1930s novels of Zora Neale Hurston (1891–1960), both of which are conspicuously free of White characters. *Jonah's Gourd Vine* (1934) tells the story of a mulatto preacher whose illicit love affairs lead to his self-destruction, and *Their Eyes Were Watching God* (1937) describes the trials and tribulations of a mulatto named Janie in an all-Black community in Florida.

And finally, from what might be referred to as a post–Harlem Renaissance era, we have American Pulitzer Prize–winner and celebrated poet Gwendolyn Brooks (1917–2000). She, too, was unafraid to directly confront the sting of intraracial discrimination. "The Ballad of Chocolate Mabbie" (1944) relates the tale of dark-skinned Mabbie, who discovers that her boyfriend, Willie, prefers a girl who is lighter. The first verse goes:

It was Mabbie without the grammar school gates.
And Mabbie was all of seven.
And Mabbie was cut from a chocolate bar.
And Mabbie thought life was heaven.

Later, we feel sorry for the joyous Mabbie when she spies her young beau holding hands with her long-haired rival:

Out came the saucily bold Willie Boone.
It was woe for our Mabbie now.
He wore like a jewel a lemon-hued lynx
With sand-waves loving her brow.

In the literary arena at least, Black Americans had found their own voice, finally free enough to exercise creative control. We now turn to other types of narrative expression that played on issues of skin color.

During the early part of the twentieth century, Harlem set the world to dancing, and the Black musical emerged as a new theatrical form. Negro singing and dancing were suddenly in great demand, by White and Black audiences alike. Yet the casting of women in chorus lines and the like continued to cater to fantasies of "exotic octoroon girls"—as the White-looking Black dancers were often billed.

Among the greatest and most widely known of Harlem entertainers was Josephine Baker. Skin played a huge role in her life, although not in the usual or predictable way. While sometimes described as light skinned, Baker actually was deemed not "quite light enough" when she auditioned for Noble Sissle and Eubie Blake's Black musical *Shuffle Along* (1921). The director ruled that her "dark skin" would not fit in with that of the "high yella" girls. Yet he must have liked something about her, as he offered Baker the job of dresser instead. On a fateful evening, one of the regular chorus girls did not appear and Baker, who had memorized the steps from watching the show backstage, persuaded the director to let her go on. To the other girl's dismay, the crowd adored the newcomer, and Baker became a permanent cast member of *Shuffle Along*, one of the most successful Negro musicals ever to run in New York. Riding high from that success, Baker traveled to Europe, where she mesmerized audiences in Paris and elsewhere with her beauty, charm, humor, and flirtatious sensuality. She became known as "the girl who put Harlem on the map of Europe." Ironically, the attribute that had initially held Baker back in her own country—her medium-brown skin color—contributed to her enormous success abroad.

Regardless of Baker's obvious appeal, the belief that dark-skinned girls would offend middle-class White and Black patrons alike persisted. Directors of subsequent Black-American musicals, including *Hot Chocolates* (1929) and *The Chocolate Dandies* (1924), continued to hire only those girls with White or near-White skin to appear in their chorus lines.

Despite such obvious color prejudice, these musicals represented a vast expansion of opportunities for work by Black stage performers. Only two decades before, popular minstrel shows seemed only able to feature Negro actors in blackface portraying shiftless drunks addicted to watermelon and chicken, usually stolen.

With the rise of the new art form of film, the stereotypic depictions of Black characters were largely imitated and extended. According to African-American film scholar Donald Bogle, during Hollywood's early years especially, White directors seemed only able to cast Black actors and actresses (or Whites in blackface) into five basic roles, several of which we have already made mention of in this chapter: the Tom, the coon, the buck or brute, the mammy, and, of course, the tragic mulatto.

The African-American men who played these stereotyped roles were mostly medium-brown skinned, and if a director considered them not dark enough, they were simply smeared with blackface. For women, however, skin color was an even more limiting factor in casting. Since a medium-skinned woman couldn't be lightened, only light-skinned Black actresses were cast to play the tragic, sympathetic, or sexually charged roles. Dark-skinned actresses were left playing mammies.

During this early silent film era, one of the first blockbuster-type movies to exploit the two Black female prototypes was D. W. Griffith's controversial *Birth of a Nation* (1915). The NAACP found the film so offensive that its members picketed the New York premiere, and riots broke out when the film opened in Boston and Chicago. Eventually, the film was banned in five states and nineteen cities. Typical of the discrimination against Black actors at that time, it was White actresses in blackface who were cast in the roles of the sensual tragic mulatto, Lydia, and of the dark-skinned, overweight mammy.

Playing on racist fears about the uncontrollable sexuality of Black men, *Birth of a Nation* furthermore perpetuated the buck, or brute, stereotype. In one episode a very dark-skinned Black man (again, a White actor in blackface) attempts to defile a White southern woman, whose rescue by the KKK is sympathetically depicted. Seven years later, in a film called *One Exciting Night* (1922), Griffith seized on yet another offensive stereotypic role of the Black man, that of the cowardly but funny Negro frightened to death by his own shadow. Again a White man in blackface played the part, but throughout most of the 1920s and '30s, it was actually a Black actor, with the stage name Stepin Fetchit, who came to epitomize this sexless, buffoonish type of character in the roles he played. (Unlike the shuffling, laconic character he often played on-screen, Fetchit was a social activist who worked hard offscreen to eliminate segregation in the film industry.)

In 1915, a group of Black actors and investors set out to counter such demeaning stereotypes by forming their own film company, the Lincoln Motion Picture Company, which, curiously, was located in Omaha, Nebraska, one of the Whitest cities in America. This little-known company produced a number of important silent films, such as *The Realization of a Negro's Ambition* and *The Trooper of Company K,* that were for and about Blacks. Reflecting the lifestyles and close associates of the Black bourgeois backers, however, the company's first president was the light-skinned actor Noble Johnson, and casting was still essentially restricted to light-skinned Blacks, usually in middle-class roles. In fact, some of the actors who appeared in these early black-and-white films were so light skinned that it was difficult to tell they were Black. By 1923 the Lincoln Motion Picture Company had gone under, a victim of poor distribution and perhaps of obstacles faced by those who attempt to challenge stereotypes.

Black production companies seemed to fare better if they stuck to traditional melodrama and the narrative of the tragic mulatto. Such was the case with a silent film called *The Scar of Shame* (1927), produced by the Colored Players Film Corporation (which, although White owned, was formed to make films specifically about Blacks). The plot centers on a lower-class mulatto named Louise Howard, who escapes from her brute father by marrying an aspiring middle-class Black composer named Alvin. Louise's gambler father arranges for a man named Eddie to kidnap her and bring her back, but the plan goes awry; she is accidentally wounded in the neck in a pistol fight between Eddie and Alvin, who is trying to save her. With her beauty marred (the scar of shame) and Alvin in prison, Louise turns to prostitution. After Alvin's release, Louise tries to win back his love, but when that fails she commits suicide, leaving Alvin free to marry a woman of his own social standing. The film, produced with the financial backing of the Black bourgeoisie, offers a stern warning about marrying outside one's social caste. Film scholar Jane Gaines explored the subversive message about color in *The Scar of Shame*:

> The Scar of Shame *is not able to speak about its own subtle racism or about the racism in the Black film industry in the 1920s. On the screen the actors playing Louise, Alvin, Alice, and the baser element, Eddie, appear exactly the same degree of light brown. The actor playing Spike, Louise's father, seems darker than the other actors (with the exceptions of the inhabitants of the local bar).*

Gaines goes on to note that much of the color-code casting in early White films tended to be the reverse of color biases operating in Black films:

> *That is, light-skinned African Americans could not find work in White motion pictures. Black-and-white film stock registered too much truth—on the screen racially mixed actors looked White. Conversely, the dark-skinned Blacks preferred by White producers were unacceptable in star roles in race films. They were not idealized (i.e., White) enough.*

Oscar Micheaux (1884–1951) was the best-known early Black filmmaker. Like others of the era, he cast exclusively light-skinned Black actors and actresses in the more than twenty silent and sound movies he made. Micheaux's first film, *The*

Homesteader (1919), was adapted from his semiautobiographical novel of the same name. Before his career ended, Micheaux had covered the entire cinematic spectrum, from his 1927 film adaption of Charles Waddell Chesnutt's book *The House Behind the Cedars* (1900), which created a positive portrait of a racially mixed Black man passing as White, to examples of the less critically acclaimed genre known as "ghetto films." No longer silent, the new films, which flooded the market from the 1930s through the 1950s, were cheaply made, usually directed by Blacks, and featured light-skinned Blacks in ridiculous Western and gangster roles. While these grade-B films gave some Black actors their start, most such actors longed to appear in the bigger and more respectable Hollywood releases. Apart from playing the usual stock characters, however, few Black actors or actresses were able to land decent parts.

By the 1930s the Black mammy character had emerged as a staple in White commercial films. Most people today probably think of Hattie McDaniel as the definitive mammy for her Oscar-winning performance in *Gone with the Wind* (1939), but the brown-skinned Louise Beavers had personified the role well before then. Beavers received critical acclaim for her mammy character in the melodramatic *Imitation of Life* (1934), in which the White-skinned Black actress Fredi Washington played the part of Beavers's tormented light-skinned daughter. In this classic tragic-mulatto narrative, a light-skinned girl grows up in a White household and is the best friend of the White daughter of the woman for whom her mother works. In one tearful scene after another, the mulatto daughter denies and abandons her dark-skinned mother so that others will think she is White, like her childhood friend.

Black moviegoers had varying reactions to this film; some

enjoyed it but most thought that it only reinforced tired old stereotypes of Black women as either tragic or passive. Despite its commercial success, the film did not much help the career of either Beavers or Washington. While Beavers went on to star in other films, her salary never increased, nor did she get very far beyond maid roles. And White directors considered Washington too light except for parts requiring someone light enough to pass (yet not romantically involved with anyone White).

Passing was a popular theme of several Hollywood releases of the 1940s and '50s. *Lost Boundaries* (1949) was based on a true story about a doctor and his family who pass as White during the Depression. All goes well until the doctor attempts to volunteer for the navy, just before Pearl Harbor, and is exposed as Black. The film is fairly sympathetic in its treatment of the doctor and his family—the scene in which he reveals to his children that they are not White is especially moving—and Black audiences generally approved of it. In contrast, *Pinky* (1949) resorted to the usual simplistic stereotypes. A tragic mulatto (actually played by a White woman) falls in love with a White doctor and flees in confusion when he proposes marriage. She returns to the home of her dark-skinned mammy-like grandmother, who urges her to become the private nurse of a rich, elderly White woman. When the old woman dies, the dutiful light-skinned granddaughter inherits all her money. Society's and Hollywood's obsession with the tragic mulatto was again reflected in a 1959 remake of *Imitation of Life*.

The frequent casting of White rather than Black actresses in the tragic-mulatto roles reflected Hollywood's discomfort with interracial romance. In fact, the Code of the Motion Picture Industry, a rigid and often ridiculous instrument of self-censorship, prohibited any on-screen sexual (i.e., romantic) contact between a White and a Black actor and actress. This left very light-skinned actresses, like Fredi Washington and Lena Horne, with hardly any available parts. The code was not relaxed until the late 1950s.

When the late Lena Horne signed with MGM in the early 1940s, studio executives were not sure what to do with her. Since she had already achieved fame as a singer, she was able to have her contract stipulate that she was not to be cast as a maid or a jungle type. Yet on her first screen test the casting directors thought that she looked too White, and as a result, Hollywood never could figure out how to type her. Horne ended up playing herself, a lounge singer, in her first two films, *Cabin in the Sky* (1943) and *Stormy Weather* (1943).

Finally, with *Island in the Sun* (1957), Hollywood lifted its ban on interracial love affairs, allowing the portrayal of two such relationships: one with Black actress Dorothy Dandridge playing the love interest of a White man, and the other, even more scandalous, featuring a Black man, Harry Belafonte, in love with a rich White woman, Joan Fontaine. Still, no kissing was shown; there was one quick embrace between Dandridge and her White boyfriend but virtually no physical contact between Belafonte and Fontaine.

During the 1950s and '60s, Hollywood began offering Black actors and actresses somewhat more complex and varied roles, but if dark skinned, Black men continued to be cast as brutes, and if light skinned, like Sidney Poitier, they were sympathetically portrayed and "desexed." Poitier achieved fame in a string of hit films, including *The Blackboard Jungle* (1955), *Raisin in the Sun* (1961), *Lilies of the Field* (1963), *To Sir with Love* (1967), and *Guess Who's Coming to Dinner* (1967). Poitier's parts varied tremendously from film to film, but his characters were often impossibly virtuous and hardly Black. Even in *Guess Who's Coming to Dinner,* a film about interracial love, Poitier's character was so deracinated that one angry Black writer called him a "warmed-over White shirt."

The 1970s marked the appearance of the genre that would later be called "blaxploitation"—films that portrayed Black males as inner-city thugs who made a living pimping women or selling drugs. The best-known films of this genre were *Super Fly* and *Shaft.* Although blaxploitation films gave Black men more interesting and dynamic roles than had previously been open to them, the films tended to revive the old association between dark-skinned men and violence. The exception was the light-skinned actor Ron O'Neal, who played *Super Fly.* Yet even the popular O'Neal would later complain about his difficulties landing film parts because directors felt he came across as too racially ambiguous on the silver screen.

If O'Neal were alive as a young man today, he would likely have been cast in one of the latest Black film style types, a genre known as "mixploitation." Historian Gregory T. Carter coined the term to capture action films that thrive on presenting racially ambiguous male leads. Two films, *The Fast and the Furious* (2001), starring Vin Diesel, and *The Scorpion King* (2002), starring Dwayne Johnson, epitomize the mixploitation trend. Interestingly, these films share the action genre of the blaxploitation films of the 1970s, but in a departure from that formula, the racially ambiguous male lead character serves as a commodity to attract a younger and increasingly diverse audience of filmgoers.

During the late 1970s and the 1980s, Black actors Richard Pryor and Eddie Murphy became major box-office attractions. In spite of being relatively dark skinned, they did not have to play the kind of morally superior roles that Poitier did in order to gain respectability. Instead, it was their humor that made these actors unthreatening and acceptable to the general White public.

In the late 1980s, we see the emergence of the first young Black directors, most notably Spike Lee, who wrote, directed, and produced some of the best Black films made up to that point. *She's Gotta Have It* (1986), *School Daze* (1988), and *Do the Right Thing* (1989) received numerous accolades; the last of these earned Lee an Academy Award nomination for Best Original Screenplay. The young director also gave little-known African-American actors and actresses a lot of work, and provided them with a chance to perform in leading roles. Although *School Daze* included a narrative about skin color, it was the first in which the topic was satirized at the skilled hands of a Black director. And for many White audience members, it was the first time they learned about the issue of colorism in the Black community.

Apart from their being able to play the love interest in a Black-directed film, African-American women, especially those who were dark skinned, did not find the 1980s to be a great time to be a working actress. There were limited roles in mainstream movies, and they tended to be given to lighter-skinned and racially mixed Black actresses like Jennifer Beals, Irene Cara, and Rae Dawn Chong. A notable exception during that decade was the darker-skinned actress Alfre Woodard, who was nominated for an Academy Award for Best Supporting Actress for her performance in the 1983 film *Cross Creek*. *The Color Purple* (1985), which was based on Alice Walker's Pulitzer Prize–winning novel of the same name published in 1982, also represented a big exception to trends of that era. *The Color Pur-*

ple featured an all-star Black cast that included Oprah Winfrey, Whoopi Goldberg, and Danny Glover, among others. It took a White director—Steven Spielberg—with enough clout in Hollywood to persuade producers that the film would attract enough White viewers to be commercially successful. And that it was; with box-office receipts of over $142 million, it earned eleven Academy Award and five Golden Globe nominations. Although some in the Black community criticized having a White man direct the all-Black cast in a film based on a novel by an African-American woman, most were pleased with the outcome. And they give Spielberg credit for not casting a light-skinned woman to play Shug, the sexiest, most desirable female character in the narrative. Instead, the medium-skinned Margaret Avery played the part unforgettably. Today, *The Color Purple* lives on as a musical, giving yet another generation of African-American actors new opportunities to make their big break.

During the 1990s, the number of important movies made by African Americans exploded on the silver screen. Spike Lee continued to direct and produce some of his best work, including *Jungle Fever* (1991), the film that first brought Halle Berry notice. African-American filmmakers Reginald Hudlin, Mario Van Peebles, and John Singleton, director of the critically acclaimed *Boyz n the Hood* (1991), all emerged as major talents. Other films from Black directors during that decade included *House Party* (1990), *New Jack City* (1991), *Boomerang* (1992), *Poetic Justice* (1993), *Losing Isaiah* (1995), *A Thin Line between Love and Hate* (1996), and HBO's *Introducing Dorothy Dandridge* (1999), for which Halle Berry was awarded both a Golden Globe and an Emmy for her portrayal of Dandridge.

However, it is fair to say that the 1990s continued to favor the light-skinned African-American woman as the standard bearer of what a Black leading lady should look like. In addition to Berry, other light-skinned female actresses like Vanessa Williams, Tisha Campbell-Martin, Lynn Whitfield, Lonette McKee, Vivica A. Fox, Lela Rochon, and Robin Givens continued to be cast, while few darker-skinned Black women seemed to be featured at all in commercial films, especially as a love interest. The exceptions of relatively darker-skinned actresses still finding work during this decade were Oscar winner Whoopi Goldberg, who played a psychic in *Ghost* (1990) and a hooker in *Sister Act* (1992), the kind of alternative characters best cast with a dark-skinned actress; Angela Bassett, who played Tina Turner in the biopic *What's Love Got to Do with It* (1993), with a performance that earned her a Best Actress Oscar nomination; and Regina King, in *How Stella Got Her Groove Back* (1998), which also starred Bassett and Goldberg, and, like *The Color Purple,* was a commercially successful film that centered on the lives of African Americans.

Today, American actresses of African descent like Zoe Saldana, Paula Patton, Thandie Newton, Kerry Washington, Jennifer Hudson, Jada Pinkett Smith, Halle Berry, Queen Latifah, Regina King, and Mo'Nique are recognized as some of the best performers, Black or otherwise, in the business. Yet it's hard not to notice that many, albeit certainly not all, of these illustrious women are on the lighter side of light on the skin-tone continuum.

It is encouraging to see that there are more opportunities for African Americans to find work in the film industry, and that they have many and more varied roles offered to them. However, what has not changed to some extent is how skin color is often coded to foretell the narrative. This was evident in the acclaimed film *Precious: Based on the Novel "Push" by Sapphire*

(2009), usually shortened to just *Precious,* directed by African-American filmmaker Lee Daniels, with Tyler Perry and Oprah Winfrey serving as executive producers. The symbolic representation of color in the film seemed designed to evoke reaction and spark discussion. It didn't disappoint.

Precious is named for its title character, Precious Jones, whose life is anything but precious. She is an overweight, illiterate, lonely, invisible, dark-skinned, Black sixteen-year-old girl, who has been sexually abused by her AIDS-infected father. Impregnated by her father's rape, she is the mother of two children, one of whom has Down syndrome. And then there is Precious's mother, who is also physically, emotionally, and even sexually abusive to her. By the end of the film, the initially ironically named Precious manages to discover, with support from a gifted teacher, her own self-worth and to find that she is indeed a precious person.

In the book *Push*, Precious is described as dark skinned and overweight, and thus it is no surprise that a dark-skinned overweight woman would be cast to play the part. If Daniels had not selected someone fitting that profile, he would have been heavily criticized for not being true to the book, or even perhaps for trying to make a film that would appeal more to White audiences. But that didn't happen. After a long search to find just the right young woman to be Precious, Daniels selected newcomer Gabourey Sidibe. To everyone's surprise, he also cast stand-up comedian turned actress Mo'Nique to play the cruel mother. Both would be Oscar nominated for their convincing performances, with the unknown Sidibe as Best Actress, and Mo'Nique as Best Supporting Actress, the award she subsequently won. Clearly Daniels's instincts were spot-on in the casting of these two unlikely women. But if you look closely at who else was cast to play roles in the film, you start to see skin color as a signifier. All of the characters who want to help Precious are light skinned, including her teacher, played by Paula Patton; her social worker, played by Mariah Carey; and her nurse, played by Lenny Kravitz. They are the ones who are loving, caring, and benevolent. And all the characters who hurt Precious are comparatively dark skinned, and are portrayed as violent, abusive, and exploitive. Other than Precious, with her resilience and spirit, none of the dark-skinned characters in the film has any redeeming qualities. *Precious* may have been critically acclaimed and showered with accolades, but to many, Daniels took the Black community a step backward in the stereotypic images of how dark-skinned and light-skinned African Americans are portrayed on-screen.

Lee Daniels himself is dark skinned, and he has been open about how color affected his own life. In an article appearing in *The New York Times Magazine,* he is quoted as describing how when he was younger, at the church he attended, the lighter you were, the "closer you sat to the altar." Raised in such an environment, Daniels understandably developed prejudices against those who were darker than himself. But Daniels went on to say that making *Precious* has changed his heart and thinking about heavier people, whom he used to regard as dirty and unintelligent. Daniels claims that now he will "never look at a fat girl walking down the street the same way again."

Lee Daniels is not the only Black producer-director of late who has had a finger pointed at him for skin-color-code assumptions about the nature of Black characters. African-American filmmaker Tyler Perry, one of *Precious*'s executive producers, similarly has been accused of portraying dark-skinned Black males as aggressors and lighter-skinned males as saviors. In his films *Diary of a Mad Black Woman* (2005) and *Madea's Family*

Reunion (2006), predictable stereotypes of dark-skinned and light-skinned characters are played for laughs.

On the television screen, Black actors and actresses have come a long way from the days of *Amos 'n' Andy* (1951–1966), when dark-skinned characters embodied the traditional buffoonish stereotypes. Today, among African-American actresses who grace the small screen, we find a diversity of skin color in women such as Rashida Jones in *Parks and Recreation*, Vanessa L. Williams in *Ugly Betty* and *Desperate Housewives*, Jada Pinkett Smith in *Hawthorne* (she was also the show's executive producer), Gabourey Sidibe in *The Big C*, and Lisa Gay Hamilton, who even sports a 'fro, in *Men of a Certain Age*. And African-American actors, including Blair Underwood, Omar Epps, and Malcolm Jamal Warner, are increasingly featured on network shows in a variety of roles not solely defined by their skin color.

In this chapter we've looked at the persistent role of skin color across various storytelling forms, from books to musicals, films, and television. Clearly there has been progress from the days when skin color was central to the trajectory of a narrative plot, or even later, when those of particular skin tones were limited to playing specific character types. We would seem to be at a tipping point of either actively rejecting or lazily relying upon the predictive and signifying role of skin color. The question is what needs to come first, the elimination, or at least the minimization, of societal color prejudices, or the encoding of skin color in stories to represent something larger. In our media-driven culture, visual imagery inevitably mirrors and maintains the same color prejudices found in the larger culture. That is a topic for further discussion in the next chapter.

Chapter 10

#TeamLightskinned: Color and the Media

On November 30, 2010, the fifteenth annual prime-time broadcast of the Victoria's Secret Fashion Show aired on CBS. Over 9 million viewers, the largest audience yet, tuned in to watch thirty-four female models, six of whom were women of color, parade around in lingerie and little else. The display of wares was organized around six differently themed sets, and in each, even the country-themed one featuring a barn and blond wigs, the subset of "girls" participating was racially integrated—with one notable exception. The single themed presentation in which the producers saw fit to showcase only the six models of color was the segment entitled "Wild Thing." The setting was a jungle and the models entered wearing nothing more than African wraps on bodies covered in tribal body paint. From the African-American community could be heard a collective moan: "Seriously? Again, you put us back in the jungle?"

Since before the Civil War, the dominant White culture has abused and manipulated images of African Americans, usually for purposes of fear, humor (i.e., what Whites thought was amusing), and marketing. The classic example of the latter was the dark-skinned mammy-like figure on the box of Aunt Jemima pancake mix, apparently the perfect image to sell real down-home cooking. Far worse were the editorial cartoons and post-cards popular in the South that featured typically dark-skinned caricatures of pickaninnies, coons, and little Black boys being chased by alligators or eating watermelon. And this inclination to portray Blacks as exotic, primitive, and wild, as recently put on display in the Victoria's Secret show, remains a standard image practice.

Fortunately, most of the patently offensive racist imagery has been laid to rest, at least in the mainstream media. But ugly racial imagery seems to be resurrected whenever prejudiced Whites feel threatened by racial change, the latest examples being the unbelievably hateful caricatures of President Obama that started appearing during his first presidential campaign and have endured ever since among certain segments of the population. Even excluding the extremists, it remains true that images of African Americans are constantly being manufactured, pro-jected, accepted, and occasionally rejected in our media-driven culture. This chapter will explore the role that skin color has played and continues to play in portrayals of Blacks.

We begin with the modeling industry, a business that traffics in image making. The first notion that occurs to most people when they are asked to picture a model tends to be an ultrathin woman who walks fashion runways and appears on the covers of glossy magazines. In reality, only a tiny fraction of models do this kind of high-end work. Instead, the majority make a living in catalog work, and by appearing in ads and commercials selling everything from canned soup to souped-up cars. Traditionally, advertising agencies hired only the most mainstream-looking models, which meant only Whites need apply. Yet as media studies scholar Marilyn Kern-Foxworth reported in her 1994 book *Aunt Jemima, Uncle Ben, and Rastus: Blacks in Advertising, Yesterday, Today, and Tomorrow,* since the late 1960s, no deleterious effect in sales, across a variety of multiple print and electronic media forms, from using African-American models to sell products to predominantly White consumers has ever been demonstrated. It has taken about forty years, but the message seems to have finally gotten through. For anyone who regularly reads magazines or watches television, there is a visible increase over the past decade in the number of African-American models being hired for this kind of bread-and-butter work. We now even see on the TV screen attractive Black couples in commercials for Viagra; this would have been unheard of not that long ago, as it would have raised the notion that Blacks have sex just like Whites do.

It is encouraging to see so many more African-American models being hired to do commercial work, but not so great is the hard-to-miss fact that most, especially the women, are so light skinned and Caucasian featured that they could be just about any race. And when it comes to African-American women in print ads, they can always be made even lighter with postproduction software like Photoshop.

The touching-up of people in pictures has been around since the dawn of portrait painting, but the utterly routine way in which the skin of the African-American woman is "brightened" in virtually every printed image of her reveals the true depths of colorism. Even when an African-American woman is already considered light skinned to begin with, she seems never to be quite light enough. This inclination to lighten and brighten was evident in a 2008 ad campaign for a L'Oréal hair-coloring product. The ad, which ran in *Elle* and other fashion magazines and set off an eruption of controversy, portrayed the very light-skinned superstar Beyoncé Knowles even lighter still. The cosmetic giant denied that it had lightened Beyoncé's skin, but it was obvious that somebody had. Of further annoyance was the fact that Beyoncé's long hair was "Photoshopped" to look perfectly straight and dark blond—in other words, to make her look overall more racially ambiguous and mainstream.

Not only was L'Oréal criticized for the ad, but so was Beyoncé. Under the dubious assumption that her consent was required for the ad to run, Beyoncé was accused of "cultural and racial treason." But even if she didn't approve the ad beforehand, many of her fans, including Kendra, a thirtysomething Black bartender from Chicago whom we interviewed, thought Beyoncé had a responsibility to her fans to make sure her image was true and not manipulated. As Kendra put it, "If anyone had enough celebrity and influence to call L'Oréal on the carpet for the touching-up of her image, Beyoncé did." The talented singer and actress was not the first African-American female celebrity to be criticized for the "Westernization" of her looks. Supermodel Naomi Campbell also was accused of "compromising" her heritage by the wearing of "platinum and honey-blond wigs," which Campbell maintains are nothing more than accessories.

Two years later, in 2010, *Elle* had another skin-lightening controversy on its hands. This time it involved a cover shot of the dark-skinned and full-figured Gabourey Sidibe, star of the critically acclaimed film *Precious*. Beside her were three other actresses, Lauren Conrad, Amanda Seyfried, and Megan Fox, all of whom were chosen to appear on *Elle*'s special twenty-fifth-anniversary-issue cover celebrating women in their twenties. Although Sidibe is far from the blond, size-zero White women who usually grace the covers of *Elle,* she did look stunning alongside the other three women. And it was great that she was selected. But the image of Sidibe nonetheless came under fire for two reasons: first, Sidibe's skin tone was manipulated a few shades lighter, and second, unlike Conrad, Seyfried, and Fox, whose entire bodies were portrayed, Sidibe was shown in a shot that zoomed in on her face only. Many questioned whether *Elle* was trying to minimize Sidibe's plus-sized figure and darker skin color. *Elle* of course denied both charges, offering the weak explanation that Sidibe's cover photo was "not retouched any more or less than the others."

The recent hiring of darker-skinned women as models by internationally renowned fashion designers should be evidence enough that no skin-lightening touch-ups are necessary. But then again the world of fashion is not attempting to appeal to the mainstream, as would, say, those selling household cleaning products. Instead, designers want their models to look "exotic," not exactly the most preferred term to use for many women of African descent. The first member of this new category of "Other" women to make it big in the fashion world was Alek Wek. During the mid-1990s, the Sudanese-born Wek, from the Dinka tribe, was discovered in London when she was eighteen. At the time, Wek was an extreme anomaly in the business. She was a dark-skinned African woman in a world that would normally have rejected her looks. Yet Wek defied all odds. In 1997, she passed a milestone when she appeared on the cover of *Elle*'s November issue. The fashion giant took a risk in putting her on the cover, because at the time it was commonly believed that a dark-skinned woman would hurt magazine sales. But Wek and the *Elle* cover garnered rave reviews. *Elle* also received an abundance of letters to the editor thanking the magazine for its bold choice and praising it for redefining beauty.

Media mogul Oprah Winfrey invited Wek to appear on her talk show and confessed that she wished someone like Wek had graced a beauty magazine when she was growing up. Oprah lamented that had that been the case, she probably would have developed a different concept of who she was. Another Wek fan is New York–based fashion photographer Steven Meisel, also known for taking the photographs for Madonna's book *Sex*. Meisel gushed in regard to Wek, "I haven't seen anybody that interesting, that black and that beautiful in a long time."

Wek sells magazines, makeup, clothing, and fragrances, and unlike some of the other Black supermodels, she is not simply a "White girl dipped in chocolate." She and other medium-to-darker-hued "other type models," such as the brown-skinned Latina Sessilee Lopez, the Ethiopian-born stunner and Estée Lauder spokesperson Liya Kebede, and Victoria's Secret models Selita Ebanks and Chanel Iman, are increasingly featured in high-fashion magazines such as *Vogue, Harper's Bazaar, Mademoiselle,* and *Elle,* as well as on the runways during Fashion Week.

Some suggest that the problem today is less about the complete exclusion of models of African descent, or even the general preference for lighter-skinned African-American models, than it is about how African-American models are portrayed. The "Wild Thing" segment on the Victoria's Secret television show was but one demeaning example of the fashion industry's tendency to paint these women, especially those who are darker skinned, as exotic.

The representation of the Black woman as fetish can be traced at least as far back as Sarah Bartmann. Captured in

Africa and enslaved, she was brought to England in 1810 and put on display and taken around Europe, not unlike a savage beast captured in Africa might have been. Bartmann was renamed "the Hottentot Venus" to emphasize her exotic nature and extreme sexuality. Around the same time in New Orleans, White plantation owners were bringing to market their carefully bred octoroon female slaves. These women, too, were invariably described as "exotic," a term meant to be a big selling point. In fact, so frequently paired were the words "octoroon" and "exotic" that eventually these women became known simply as "exotic octoroons."

Black feminist scholars have critiqued and interpreted this urge on the part of Whites to represent the Black body as exotic. From a psychoanalytic perspective, one school of thought posits that by placing Blacks in a dehumanized category of "exotic" or "Other," Whites are better able to project onto Black bodies, both male and female, their own complex feelings of repulsion, attraction, and anxiety.

In the world of modeling, the image of dark-skinned Blacks as savage-like and wild is hardly limited to females. This portrayal of Black men as objects lacking humanity was evident in a clothing ad entitled "Let's Get Lost" that ran in the May 2010 edition of *Interview* magazine. In the ad's photograph, Polish-Canadian White supermodel Daria Werbowy was featured lying atop a group of steamy, sweaty, even faceless dark-skinned Black male models in tribal wear. Their bodies were jammed together in what could be interpreted as a group sex scene. The pale, limp body of Werbowy was depicted with her legs spread open in a sexually inviting way, or perhaps in a way that suggested she had been drugged and/or raped by a gang of Black men. To make clear the sexual insinuation, the accompanying text read:

Let's get lost. The hour is late, the air is thick, and the evening is charged with a steamy sensuality. What works? Tone-on-tone swimsuits, slithers of silk, and plenty of skin, as flesh meets flesh, body meets soul, and Daria gets lost in the heat of the night.

While some saw the image as nothing more than the kind of conceptual "art" commonly used in high-fashion advertising, others were appalled by the sight of heavily perspiring, half-clad, almost lifeless Black bodies being used as nothing more than props—or what some have termed "blacessories"—for a White woman. And then there was the conjured-up imagery of bodies jammed into the well of a slave ship. As one blogger commented, it looked like a "sexualized middle passage."

In response to complaints that African-American models are either not used enough, or, when they are employed, painted as exotic, White editor in chief Franca Sozzani of *Vogue Italia* heard the complaints and disappointments about the treatment of Black models, and decided to do something about it. Cutting no corners, she hired top fashion photographer Meisel for a hundred-page exclusive spread of Black models for the magazine's July 2008 edition. Major distributors across Europe warned that the issue would never sell, since even a single Black model on the cover of a fashion magazine hurts sales. They were wrong: the July 2008 edition sold out immediately.

Nonetheless there were Blacks on both sides of the Atlantic who appreciated the gesture but felt the issue still did not go far enough, as the cover featured models Liya Kebede, Sessilee Lopez, Jourdan Dunn, and Naomi Campbell, all lighter skinned and/or Caucasian featured. Groused one former African-American model lucky enough to get her hands on one of the sold-out magazines, "These Black models represent what Whites in this industry are willing to accept with their light skin, White features, and long silky hair. We cannot even get a more Afrocentric sister on the cover of the 'All Black' issue."

In May 2011, *Vogue Italia* editor Sozzani tried again to get it right with a second special fifteen-page spread paying tribute to Black models. Or maybe she simply recognized the profit potential, as again the special issue sold out. In either case, this time a darker-skinned Black woman was put on the cover and the spread was introduced with the following copy:

With bright eyes peering out under deliciously curled lashes, cheekbones and jawbones contoured as if chiseled from sharp stone, full noses, and sumptuously lush lips, black women are unquestionably beautiful. A tribute is due to the woman whose skin tone ranges from alabaster to mahogany to smooth onyx, who can flawlessly carry any makeup look—from gold-dusted lids to fuchsia blush to ripe purple and pink glosses. These pages pay homage to the versatile woman whose hair can oscillate from a tightly coiled and coifed Afro, to sleek layers, to a slicked-back pixie cut in a matter of minutes. To the divine woman whose enviably full lips, strong white teeth, and delightful smile have been known to electrify the hearts of many. To the siren whose smooth, velvety skin blocks the sun yet remains supple and unblemished with the passage of time. Variable and diverse, black beauty escapes simple classification. But no matter the incarnation—whether the color of molasses, café au lait, bronze, tan, or tinged like desert sand—black beauties radiate with poise and multidimensional splendor.

Although many felt that that *Vogue Italia* issue finally did get it right, some were still discomforted by its segregation, believing it far preferable to integrate Black models with White models throughout all fashion magazine issues. Nonetheless, in specifically showcasing the beauty of Black women, the issue put a spotlight on the often-unconscious and sometimes-deliberate racism and colorism of the fashion industry. And, if nothing else, the fact that the magazine did do well saleswise was yet another strong rebuttal to the belief that "Black don't sell!"

Another image-related arena where a limited view of attractiveness has reigned and Black women have historically been excluded is the American beauty pageant. Barred from entering White beauty pageants, Blacks eventually created their own events to showcase their community's beautiful women. For decades, the winners of these Black pageants tended to be primarily women with light skin and processed hair, but that was not always the case.

According to the sociologist and Black beauty pageant scholar Maxine Leeds Craig, well before the 1960s era of "Black Is Beautiful" consciousness raising, there was pushback from members of the Black community when too many light-skinned women were crowned winners of these contests. In 1914, when a widely read Black newspaper, the *New York Age*, invited female readers to submit photographs of themselves for a chance to be named on a list of the top fifteen most beautiful Black women in the country, pictures poured in. But when the winners were announced and only the light-skinned women had been selected, there was an outcry of disapproval. One reader from Tuskegee, Alabama, wrote to the paper's editor to inquire why all of the women chosen looked "more Nordic than Negro." And in 1947, at the end of the Miss Fine Brown Frame beauty contest held at Harlem's Golden Gate Ballroom, it was down to two women; one was light skinned, and the other, who was darker skinned, was the audience's clear favorite. When the announcer named the lighter-skinned woman as winner of the title, the crowd erupted in protest, to the point where the pageant organizers tried to appease audience members with a tie victory. Still not satisfied, the crowd continued to boo and protest until the darker-skinned contestant alone was crowned Miss Fine Brown Frame.

Perhaps the most fascinating pageant Craig's scholarship unearthed was the short-lived but high-profile Miss Bronze beauty contest. The pageant began in Southern California in the late 1950s, and became so successful and popular that by 1961 a second contest was organized for Northern California. In the final round of the Miss Bronze beauty contest, the two regional winners would face off. The pageant was a lavish affair with well-heeled sponsors, local politicians' endorsements, and celebrity entertainers, such as Lou Rawls and Nancy Wilson. As its name would imply, the pageant was never intended to be yet another showcase for light-skinned beauties. The organizers actively sought women from a range of skin tones, and their mission's success was reflected in the varying skin colors of the winners over the years. The role of Miss Bronze was to showcase the cultural refinements of Black women and to be a positive representative of the Black community. It was also hoped that she would help disabuse Whites of their notions of superiority. But during the 1960s, when the political activism of the Civil Rights Movement spread across the country, enthusiasm for the contest waned; its last pageant was held in 1968.

Coincidently, in that same year, the first Miss Black America pageant was held, organized in protest against the exclusion of

Black women from the Miss America pageant, the most prestigious of all beauty pageants and an event that has been held annually since 1921. But then, only two years later, in 1970, the times they were a-changin', and Cheryl Browne of Iowa became the first Black woman to represent a state in the Miss America contest. The significance of the Miss Black America beauty pageant began to erode and was further reduced in 1983 when the beautiful light-skinned, green-eyed African-American Vanessa Williams was hailed as the "most beautiful woman in America." Her crown predictably sparked controversy in the Black community. While many were proud that one of their own had finally won, others were angered by the particular trailblazer chosen. With her green eyes, light skin, and long, sandy hair, she seemed to resemble a White woman rather than a Black woman. The Congress of Racial Equality (CORE) went so far as to issue a statement declaring Williams not "in essence Black"—a comment that deeply hurt her. That controversy was soon overshadowed by another one when *Penthouse* magazine published a series of nude pictures of Williams. Taking swift action, pageant officials took away Vanessa Williams's crown. Coincidently, that year another Black woman, Suzette Charles, was the runner-up and she stepped in to finish out the last two months of Williams's term. The African-American community now rallied behind Williams, perhaps realizing that no matter how "White" her features, she was still vulnerable to attack by the White mainstream media.

Since Williams's and Charles's victories, Black women have been winning major beauty awards at an astonishing rate. In 1990 alone, African-American women reigned as both Miss USA (Carole Gist) and Miss America (Debbye Turner). Other African-American winners of the Miss America contest would follow, including Marjorie Judith Vincent (1991), Kimberly Aiken (1994), Erika Harold (2003), and Erica Dunlap (2004). Beyond Gist in 1990, other Black women who have won the Miss USA pageant are Kenya Moore (1993), Chelsi Smith (1995), Shauntay Hinton (2002), Rachel Smith (2007), and Crystle Stewart (2008). While all of these women had the requisite long hair of all pageant winners regardless of race, their skin tones at least have varied from light to medium brown.

Another area where images of African Americans are not always "fair and unbiased" is television news. From past patterns in hiring African-American journalists, this industry, too, could be readily charged with color prejudice. Historically, the first Black TV reporter and weathercaster hired for TV news was Trudy Haynes in 1963, and while she was indeed light skinned, she believed producers preferred light-skinned Blacks for a more practical reason. That is, Haynes pointed out that studio lighting was normally set for White journalists, and since African Americans' skin displays many different undertones and their hair has a tendency to absorb light rather than reflect it, it was more difficult to get the lighting right for Blacks. It could be done, though, and Haynes herself noticed that the bigger the name of a Black celebrity in the studio, the greater the effort made to provide good lighting.

Other light-skinned television news journalists would soon follow Haynes, including Carole Simpson, hired as an anchor by NBC News in 1974; Max Robinson, hired as an anchor by ABC News in 1978; and George Strait, hired as ABC's chief medical correspondent in 1984. With improved camera technology and lighting, and a much larger pool of qualified Black television journalists from which to draw, the percentage of medium-to-darker-skinned African Americans, as both anchors and field reporters, should be significantly higher today than it is. CNN has even been mockingly accused of using the "brown paper bag test" in its hiring of African-American journalists, reporters, and anchors—not an unreasonable charge when one considers the network's most visible Black reporters and anchors, such as Fredricka Whitfield, Soledad O'Brien, Jason Carroll, Suzanne Malveaux, Don Lemon, and T. J. Holmes, all of whom are light skinned. On a daily basis, these journalists unintentionally broadcast the message that to be a qualified, believable, and articulate professional, one needs to have light skin. Since Bernard Shaw retired in 2001, Donna Brazile and Roland S. Martin remain the only dark-skinned high-profile political news commentators at CNN.

We now turn to the music industry, which during the 1980s, when television went cable and sound went video, became another influential media source. Image and packaging began to rival, and in some cases overtook, actual talent. When MTV was at its zenith, performers needed great looks, universal sex appeal, and a certain marketable "spin" before they could build a fan base and capture the attention of record producers. With the rise of the Internet, and especially video download sites like youtube.com, the popularity of MTV sharply declined. But what has not waned is the use of a music video to launch a performer's latest song, and if it is a rap or R & B release, then also the hiring of light-skinned women to serve as fantasy love objects.

It would appear that the long-ago vaunted image of the octoroon beauty has been resurrected as today's video vixen. Rarely if ever are dark-skinned African-American women with more Black-like features and natural hairstyles portrayed in these videos, not even in the genre of urban gritty rap. Instead, over and over again, long-haired African-American women with

Caucasian-like features strike provocative poses behind macho Black male performers. Harvard psychiatrist Alvin Poussaint once commented on the practice:

> *The preference for light skin, long straight hair, and keen features comes through most strongly in music videos where dark-skinned Black men frequently choose light-skinned Black women with White features as love interests. Picking this type of woman as an emblem of beauty and desire is a class issue for many urban dark-skinned Black men.*

In fact, popular Black male performers, from old-school rappers like Big Daddy Kane (who wrote the lyrics "Sexy young ladies of a light-skinned breed. You got, you got, you got what I need") to more contemporary rappers like Kanye West, whose song "So Appalled" contains the lyrics "Champagne wishes / thirty white b*tches." Even worse are the words of West's song "Power," where he raps, "Mother******, we rollin' / With some light-skinned girls." To no one's shock in 2012 Kanye began dating Kim Kardashian, who is of Armenian descent but described by some in the Black community as looking like a "mutt." And then there is Lil Wayne's 2010 release "Right above It." In this song, Lil Wayne expresses a desire to lighten the color of an African-American woman when he raps, "Beautiful black woman, I bet that b*tch look better red."

Many of these rappers display outright disdain for dark-skinned African-American women, and understandably many of these women are insulted, including the dark-skinned Lindsay Hunter of Detroit, who proclaims, "I'm sick of these culturally insensitive colorstruck rappers." What strikes Hunter as particularly odd is that, judging by the male rappers' own skin color, most of them probably didn't have mothers who resembled the women they hail as so beautiful in their lyrics. Hunter questions what these rappers really think about their own dark-skinned mothers, grandmothers, sisters, aunties, and even daughters, and whether they ever give a thought to the harm their words might cause.

It is not just dark-skinned women who are angered by these lyrics and videos. A twenty-one-year old, light-skinned African-American woman named Jennifer believes, as Poussaint's comments earlier would suggest, that rappers like Lil Wayne and Kanye West must have "low self-esteem and a problem with their own blackness." This view is supported by a 2006 interview for *Essence* in which West famously asserted that if it weren't for race mixing, there would be no video girls, and that he and most of his friends prefer the "mutts" (i.e., biracial girls). To that, Jennifer has this to say:

> *It is so unfortunate because I have always been a fan of Kanye. From telling the world that George Bush don't like Black people because of what happened in New Orleans during Katrina to standing up for the fact that Beyoncé should have won the Grammy instead of Taylor Swift. I admire the fact that Kanye has always been on the cutting edge of self-expression—but what I don't like is his obsession with light-skinned Black women and the way he seems to dislike dark-skinned Black women. Honestly if I didn't know better I would say that I expect more from him than this.*

But then many in the African-American community would agree that rappers are not the ones who should be looked up to as role models. Why should they be held to a higher standard than anyone else, just because they are entertainers? They are, after all, exposed to the same influences as other African Americans, and consequently not immune to being influenced by the color prejudices that surround us all.

Fortunately, there are contemporary Black musicians like India Arie who seek to challenge colorism, not just with song lyrics but also by projecting the image of a beautiful brown-skinned woman with strong ethnic looks. There are even a few African-American male rappers, most notably Snoop Dogg, who are using their art and celebrity to challenge the aesthetic that "lighter is righter." He has changed his videos so that they now feature both dark-skinned and light-skinned women. In an interview for the urban media site mediatakeout.com, Snoop commented:

> I love ya'll. I got a chocolate daughter at home. I always tell her chocolate is the best thing in the world. Don't think that light skin is in, chocolate ain't never went nowhere. Black is beautiful. I love dark-skinned women. That's why my videos be having dark women in them. I always used to have light-skinned women.

It is encouraging to see artists like Snoop making a conscious effort to minimize skin-color divisions. Yet like weeds in sidewalks, color-coded images keep sprouting back to life to assume new and different forms. Most recently, skin-color divisions have been cropping up on Facebook and Twitter where hashtags like "#TeamLightskin" and "#TeamDarkskin" are gaining popularity. Facebook and MySpace also gradually have become segregated along the lines of color and its second cousin, class. In an interview for NPR, nineteen-year-old

Diego Luna asserted, "I have friends who are White and they are mostly on Facebook. That's why I use Facebook. My brown people are on MySpace." Halie Pacheco, a seventeen-year-old student at the Urban School, an elite private high school in San Francisco, also claimed in the same NPR segment, "No one uses MySpace," adding that she likes Facebook, where "It's safer and more high class."

Yet online sites are also a source of empowerment and change for issues of colorism. Word of the 2011 documentary *Dark Girls* by Black director-producers Bill Duke and D. Channsin Berry spread to thousands from its YouTube preview. The film takes an in-depth and unprecedented look at how colorism is experienced from the perspective of darker-skinned women. In interview after interview, these women recount the emotional suffering and abuse they have endured because of their skin color. The following excerpts capture the pain:

> *"I can remember being in the bathtub asking my mom to put bleach in the water so that my skin would be lighter and so that I could escape the feelings I had about not being as beautiful, as acceptable, as lovable."*

> *"'She's pretty for a dark-skinned girl.' . . . What is that supposed to mean?"*

> *"They used to say, 'You stayed in the oven too long.' It was so damaging. . . . It made it seem like we weren't wanted; that we were less than."*

> *"The racism that we have as a people amongst ourselves is a direct backlash of slavery."*

Whether African Americans are portrayed in print ads, pageants, TV news, or music videos, their images have too often been defined, decided, and determined by their skin color. It may be a while yet before control of the media is wrested away from the dominant White culture, but as the numbers of African-American writers, directors, songwriters, artists, and journalists grow, more and more of them will feel free enough to explore issues of race and color from their own perspective. Ultimately, African Americans need to work together in preventing toxic practices that further misconceptions about skin color and Black features. Media influences are so powerful they can, in the words of one Black woman, "make you like your own features better on someone else"—this comment made in reference to Angelina Jolie with her "sexy full lips," and Kim Kardashian and Jennifer Lopez with their "full shapely asses." But it doesn't have to be that way.

In conclusion, we hope that this chapter—indeed, the book as a whole—has helped to engender individuals who are critical consumers of the media, and who have a willingness to challenge institutionalized colorism. Here are some simple steps to take to help lessen colorism's pernicious effects: If you are disturbed by the fact that the vast majority of Black television journalists are unusually light skinned, send an e-mail to the network, as well as to local news stations, asking, "Why the color casting in choosing anchors and reporters?" Then find another news show to watch or listen to in the meantime. If you are fed up with how a fashion magazine always has to "Photoshop" any African-American woman featured on its cover to make her skin appear lighter, write a letter to the editor to complain about the practice, and don't buy the publication again until the images look better. Angry about rap lyrics that praise light-skinned women and rappers who hire only video vixens who are light skinned with long hair to appear in their videos? Depressed that these women are turned into mere sex objects? Express your views on your Facebook page, or post a blog about it. Use the power of social media. Be inspired by what a collective voice can achieve, from the CRM to the Arab Spring.

Finally, to address the question raised in the introduction of whether colorism had gotten better or worse in the twenty years since the first edition of *The Color Complex* appeared, the answer, unfortunately, is that things have not improved. Instead, skin-color prejudice has gone viral and appears to be infecting ever-greater numbers of people around the world. The pattern is always the same, with most of the discrimination being directed toward those considered too dark to be acceptable, and to a lesser extent, but still occurring, toward those deemed not dark enough to join "the group." But perhaps most insidious of all is the color intolerance that is directed inward toward the self. This form of color prejudice is experienced psychologically and expressed as an intense desire to appear lighter, and is called "the bleaching syndrome."

It would appear that the story of colorism is far from over. That is why we decided to put out a revised edition of *The Color Complex*. However, we sincerely hope that in twenty years' time, we won't be issuing another new edition, for the good reason that we will all finally be living without color prejudice. Only then can we fulfill the promise and live the dream that men and women of all races and colors "will not be judged"—as Martin Luther King Jr. so eloquently expressed it—"by the color of their skin but by the content of their character."

Sources

Introduction

1. On more racially diverse neighbors and work colleagues: Bruce Katz and Robert Lang, eds., *Redefining Urban and Suburban America: Evidence from Census 2000* (Harrisonburg, VA: R. R. Donnelley, 2003).

2. On Alice Walker's coining the term "colorism": JeffriAnne Wilder, "Revisiting 'Color Names' and 'Color Notions': A Contemporary Examination of the Language and Attitudes of Skin Color among Young Black Women," *Journal of Black Studies* 41, no. 1 (2010), pp. 184–206.

3. On "the bleaching syndrome": Ronald E. Hall, "Manifestations of Racism in the 21st Century," in *Racism in the 21st Century: An Empirical Analysis of Skin Color,* ed. Ronald E. Hall (New York: Springer, 2008), pp. 25–44.

4. On "cosmetic Westernism": Cermil Aydin, *The Politics of Anti-Westernism in Asia: Visions of World Order in Pan-Islamic and Pan-Asian Thought* (New York: Columbia University Press, 2007), p. 42.

5. Skin-color-themed play: Dael Orlandersmith, *Yellowman,* in *Yellowman; My Red Hand My Black Hand: Two Plays* (New York: Vintage Books, 2002).

6. Documentary on skin-color prejudice: *Skin* (Washington, DC: National Geographic Society, 2002).

7. Documentary on African-American quilters: *The Skin Quilt Project,* by filmmaker Lauren Cross (Dallas, TX: Lauren Cross and Mae's House Productions, 2010).

8. Documentary on dark-skin colorism: *Dark Girls,* produced and directed by Bill Duke and D. Channsin Berry (Los Angeles: Duke Media, 2011).

9. Documentary on African-American hair: *Good Hair,* produced and directed by Chris Rock (New York: Chris Rock Productions and HBO Films, 2009).

1. The Emergence of Modern Colorism in the Americas

1. On the Age of Discovery: Barry M. Gough, *Distant Dominion: Britain and the Northwest Coast of North America, 1579–1809* (Vancouver, BC: University of British Columbia, 1980), pp. 8–10.

2. On "the White man's burden": Uma Narayan, "Colonialism and Its Others: Considerations on Rights and Care Discourses," *Hypatia* 19 (spring 1995), pp. 133–140.

3. On Brazil as the largest importer of slaves: Rocky M. Mirza, *The Rise and Fall of the American Empire: A Re-Interpretation of History, Economics, and Philosophy, 1492–2006* (Victoria, BC: Trafford Publishing, 2007), p. 125.

4. Ratios of Whites to Black slaves and/or mulattoes: "1735–1835: History Is Marked by Slave Rebellions throughout the Islands of the Caribbean," in *Break Free,* retrieved from http://caribbean-guide.info/past.and.present/history/slave.rebellion.

5. On White men raping female slaves: Edward E. Baptist, "'Cuffy,' 'Fancy Maids,' and 'One-Eyed Men': Rape, Commodification, and the Domestic Slave Trade in the United States," *American Historical Review* 106, no. 5 (December 2001), retrieved from http://www.historycooperative.org/journals/ahr/106.5/ah0501001619.html.

6. On "the mulatto escape-hatch": Carl N. Degler, *Neither Black nor White: Slavery and Race Relations in Brazil and the United States* (New York: Macmillan, 1971; Madison: University of Wisconsin Press, 1986), p. 225.

7. On rebellious slaves: Gelien Matthews, *Caribbean Slave Revolts and the British Abolitionist Movement* (Baton Rouge: Louisiana State Press, 2006).

8. On Brazil's color-caste hierarchy: Denise Oliver-Velez, "Color, Caste and Class in the Americas," *AfriGeneas World Research Forum,* September 28, 2003, retrieved from http://alturl.com/t4asw.

9. Brazilian expressions regarding skin color and money: Marvin Harris, *Patterns of Race in the Americas* (New York: Walker, 1964), p. 118.

10. On the fear that Black features will disappear from Brazil's population: Gilberto Freyre, *New World in the Tropics: The Culture of Modern Brazil* (New York: Alfred A. Knopf, 1959).

11. On "the starving time": Mary Trotter Kion, "First Women of Jamestown: A Wedding and a Baby," *American History @ suite 101,* March 29, 2006, retrieved from http://mary-trotter-kion.suite101.com/article/womenofjamestown-a635.

12. Reference to two Englishwomen in Jamestown: Gail Collins, *American Women: 400 Years of Dolls, Drudgery, Helpmates, and Heroines* (New York: William Morrow, 2003).

13. Reference to the 1619 order for wives: "The Indispensable Role of Women at Jamestown," *Historic Jamestowne,* February 27, 2010, retrieved from http://www.nps.gov/jame/historyculture/the-indispensible-role-of-women-at-jamestown.htm.

14. Reference to the 1620 voyage of ninety women: Archibald Andrews Marks, "The Jamestown Chronicles Timeline," *The Jamestown Chronicles,* 2007, retrieved from http://www.historyisfun.org/chronicles/timeline.html.

15. Reference to Englishmen raping native women: Sara M. Evans, *Born for Liberty: A History of Women in America* (New York: Free Press, 1989), pp. 12–14.

16. On revised history of first Africans to arrive in Virginia: Lisa Rein, "Mystery of Va.'s First Slaves Is Unlocked 400 Years Later," *Washington Post,* September 3, 2006, retrieved from http://www.washingtonpost.com/wp-dyn/content/article/2006/09/02/AR2006090201097.html.

17. On colonial Blacks who lived free: Nathan I. Huggins, *Black Odyssey: The African American Ordeal in Slavery* (New York: Vintage Books, 1990), p. 13.

18. On English indentured servants: Suzanne Lebsock, "No Obey," in *Women, Families, and Communities: Readings in American History,* ed. Nancy A. Hewitt, vol. 1, *To 1877* (Glenview, IL: Scott Foresman, 1990), p. 12.

19. Discussion of legalization of slavery in colonial America: Gloria Hull, Patricia Bell Scott, and Barbara Smith, eds., *All the Women Are White, All the Blacks Are Men, but Some of Us Are Brave* (Old Westbury, NY: Feminist Press, 1982), p. 72.

20. On relations between indentured servants and Black slaves: Joel Williamson, *New People: Miscegenation and Mulattoes in the United States* (New York: Free Press, 1980), pp. 6–14.

21. On race mixing in early America: Lebsock, "No Obey," p. 12.

22. On interracial marriage: Lebsock, "No Obey," p. 15.

23. On natives' referring to Black men as "Mannito" and on the Virginia massacre: Lerone Bennett Jr., *The Shaping of Black America* (Chicago: Johnson Publishing, 1975), pp. 87–88.

24. On romantic relationships between Black slaves and American Indians: Huggins, *Black Odyssey,* p. 21.

25. On Indians absorbed into Black and White populations: Gunnar Myrdal, *An American Dilemma* (New York: Harper & Brothers, 1944), p. 124.

26. On enhanced survival of mixed natives: Plutarco Naranjo, "Epidemic Hetacomb in the New World," *Allergy and Asthma Proceedings* 5 (September/October, 1992), retrieved from http://www.ncbi.nlm.nih.gov/pubmed/1483572.

27. On colonial race mixing: F. James Davis, *Who Is Black?: One Nation's Definition* (University Park: Pennsylvania State University Press, 1991), p. 21.

28. On antimiscegenation laws: Davis, *Who Is Black?,* p. 33. p. 11.

29. On protest by Richard Tilghman: Hull et al., *All the Women Are White,* pp. 88–89.

30. On White owners encouraging rape of White servants: Huggins, *Black Odyssey,* p. xli.

31. On the 1662 law concerning the status of mulatto children: Williamson, *New People,* p. 8.

32. On legal issues concerning the "one-drop rule": Davis, *Who Is Black?,* p. 34.

33. On mulattoes passing as Whites: Davis, *Who Is Black?,* p. 34.

34. On Blacks becoming soldiers in Revolutionary War: Robert A. Selig, "The Revolution's Black Soldiers," *Colonial Williamsburg*, summer 1997, retrieved from http://alturl.com/7uhsk.

35. On owners freeing slaves when America declared its independence: Evans, *Born for Liberty*, pp. 52–53.

36. On three-tiered racial classification preferred by Creoles: Virginia R. Domínguez, *White by Definition: Social Classification in Creole Louisiana* (New Brunswick, NJ: Rutgers University Press, 1986), pp. 163–164.

37. Discussion of skin color and privilege: Bart Landry, *The New Black Middle Class* (Berkeley: University of California Press, 1987), pp. 24–25.

38. Reference to mulattoes' worth on the slave market: Myrdal, *American Dilemma*, p. 66.

39. On friction resulting from skin-color differences: E. Franklin Frazier, *The Negro in the United States*, p. 274; and Na'im Akbar, *Chains and Images of Psychological Slavery* (Jersey City, NJ: New Mind Production, 1984), p. 24.

40. On the rape and molestation of young slave girls: Gerder Lerner, *Black Women in White America: A Documentary History* (New York: Pantheon, 1972; Vintage Books, 1973), pp. 158–159.

41. Reference to White men fantasizing about Black slave women: Huggins, *Black Odyssey*, p. 144.

42. On the case of William Adams: Judith K. Shafer, "Open and Notorious Concubinage: The Emancipation of Slave Mistresses by Will and the Supreme Court in Antebellum Louisiana," *Louisiana History* 28 (1987), pp. 165–182.

43. On Thomas Jefferson's affair with slave woman: Williamson, *New People*, pp. 43–47; and Irma Hunt, *Dearest Madame: The Presidents' Mistresses* (New York: McGraw-Hill, 1978), pp. 51–71.

44. On the 1998 DNA tests and 2000 examination of evidence concerning Sally Hemings: "Thomas Jefferson and Sally Hemings: A Brief Account," *The Jefferson Monticello*, January 2000, retrieved from http://www.monticello.org/site/plantation-and-slavery/thomas-jefferson-and-sally-hemings-brief-account.

45. On White women having affairs with Black male slaves: Mary Frances Berry and John W. Blassingame, *Long Memory: The Black Experience in America* (New York: Oxford University Press, 1982), p. 119.

46. On application of the one-drop rule: Davis, *Who Is Black?*, pp. 35, 49.

47. Options for White women who gave birth to mulatto babies: Davis, *Who Is Black?*, p. 62.

48. On DNA of Melungeons: Roberta J. Estes, Jack H. Goins, Penny Ferguson, and Janet Lewis Crain, "Melungeons: A Multiethnic Population," *Journal of Genetic Genealogy* (April 2012).

49. On declining sexual relations between Blacks and Whites after the Civil War: Davis, *Who Is Black?*, pp. 41, 49.

50. On Angolan Blacks: Davis, *Who Is Black?*, p. 21.

2. The Global Rise of Colorism

1. Origins of color classism in agrarian societies: Ken Chisholm, "Sun Tanning," *Livestrong.com,* April 26, 2011, retrieved from http://www.livestrong.com/article/13930-sun-tanning.

2. On covering skin outdoors: Merrill Singer and Hans Baer, eds., *Killer Commodities: Public Health and the Corporate Production of Harm* (Lanham, MD: AltaMira Press, 2009), p. 151.

3. On "color-class hierarchies": Jennifer L. Hochschild, "The Skin Color Paradox and the American Racial Order," *Social Forces* 86 (February 2007), pp. 643–670.

4. On "the bleaching syndrome": Ronald E. Hall, "The Bleaching Syndrome in the Context of Somatic Norm Image among Women of Color: A Qualitative Analysis of Skin Color," *European Journal of Social Sciences* 17, no. 2 (2010), retrieved from http://www.eurojournals.com/ejss_17_2_04.pdf.

5. On "cosmetic Westernism": Cermil Aydin, *The Politics of Anti-Westernism in Asia: Visions of World Order in Pan-Islamic and Pan-Asian Thought* (New York: Columbia University Press, 2007), p. 42.

6. On populations marked for extermination by Hitler: L. Singer, "Ideology and Ethics. The Perversion of German Psychiatrists' Ethics by the Ideology of National Socialism," *European Psychiatry* 13 (March 1998), pp. 87–92.

7. On 250,000 to 1 million Romanies killed: Ian Hancock, *Responses to the Porrajmos (the Romani Holocaust)* (Boulder, CO: Westview Press, 1995), pp. 39–64.

8. On Scandinavian compulsory sterilization programs: Per Haave, "Sterilization under the Swastika," *International Journal of Mental Health* 36 (spring 2007), pp. 45–57.

9. Numbers of people rendered infertile by Scandinavian sterilization programs: Tor Wennerberg, "Sterilization and Propaganda," *New Left Review* 1, no. 226 (November/December 1997), p. 146, and retrieved from http://www.questia.com/PM.qst?a=o&d=98686687.

10. On prejudice against the Dalits: Wiete Westerhof, "Evolutionary, Biologic, and Social Aspects of Skin Color," *Dermatologic Clinics* 25, no. 3 (July 2007), pp. 293–302.

11. On sales and profits from skin lighteners: Heather Timmons, "Telling India's Modern Women They Have Power, Even over Their Skin Tone," *New York Times,* May 30, 2007, retrieved from http://www.nytimes.com/2007/05/30/business/media/30adco.html.

12. On slowed growth for skin-lightening cream: Sapna Agarwal, "HUL Net Profits Up 18%: Markets Concerned about Volume Growth," *LiveMint.com & The Wall Street Journal,* February 7, 2012, retrieved from http://www.livemint.com/2012/02/06135641/HUL-net-profit-up-18-markets.html.

13. Discussion of male skin-lightening products: "Fairness Cream Market Targets Men," *Rediff Business,* May 20, 2010, retrieved from http://business.rediff.com/report/2010/may/20/fairness-cream-market-targets-men.htm.

14. On Indian women claiming greater control: Eric P. H. Li, Hyun Jeong Min, Russell W. Belk, Junkjo Kimura, and Shalini Bahl, "Skin Lightening and Beauty in Four Asian Cultures," *Advances in Consumer Research—North American Conference Proceedings* 35 (2008), pp. 444–449.

15. Reference to discovery of hydroquinone: Appiah Grant, "Global Implication of Skin Whitening," *Health Digest News*, May 28, 2010, retrieved from http://alturl .com/g9bm8.

16. On white skin as marker of Japanese feminine beauty: Hiroshi Wagatsuma, "The Social Perception of Skin Color in Japan," *Daedalus* 96, no. 2 (spring 1967), pp. 407–443.

17. Reference to prejudice against Japanese Burakumin: Nanette Gottlieb, "Discriminatory Language in Japan: Burakumin, the Disabled, and Women," *Asian Studies* 22 (June 1998), pp. 157–173.

18. Reference to 2007 Nielsen survey on skin-lightener usage: Evelyn Nakano Glenn, "Yearning for Lightness: Transnational Circuits in the Marketing and Consumption of Skin Lighteners," *Gender & Society* 22, no. 3 (June 2008), pp. 281–302.

19. Reference to early history of Philippines: Joanne L. Rondilla and Paul Spickard, *Is Lighter Better? Skin-Tone Discrimination among Asian Americans* (Lanham, MD: Rowman & Littlefield, 2007), p. 54.

20. On light-skin preference: Ronald E. Hall, *Bleaching Beauty: Light Skin as a Filipina Ideal* (Quezon City, Philippines: Giraffe Books, 2006).

21. On color classism in the Philippines: Joanne L. Rondilla, "Filipinos and the Color Complex: Ideal Asian Beauty," in *Shades of Difference: Why Skin Color Matters* ed. Evelyn Nakano Glenn (Stanford, CA: Stanford University Press, 2009), pp. 63–80.

22. Asian plastic surgery statistics: International Society of Aesthetic Plastic Surgery Global Survey, 2011, retrieved from http://www.isaps.org/files/html-contents/ ISAPS-Procedures-Study-Results-2011.pdf.

23. Reference to the first known double-eyelid surgery: Ryan B. Tsujimura, "Asian Double Eyelid Surgery," 2011, retrieved from http://www.plasticsurgery.com/ eyebrow-lift/asian-double-eyelid-surgery-a1540.aspx.

24. On South Korea's rate of plastic surgery: "It's Official: South Korea Has the World's Highest Rate of Plastic Surgery, but . . . ," 2009, retrieved from http:// www.asianplasticsurgeryguide.com/news10-2/081003_south-korea-highest.html.

25. On light-skin preferences in the Arab world: P. van den Berge and P. Frost, "Skin Color Preference, Sexual Dimorphism, and Sexual Selection," *Ethnic and Racial Studies* 9 (1986), pp. 87–113.

26. Moroccan proverb: E. Franklin Frazier, *The Black Bourgeoisie* (New York: Collier, 1962).

27. On skin lightening in the Arab world, and *Al-Ahram*: Samah Sabawi, "Whitening the Arab World: Reinforcing the Arab Inferiority Complex," online site *African*

by Nature, May 2005, retrieved from http://africanbynature.com/eyes/openeyes_whiteningthearab.html.

28. On use of skin lighteners in Africa: Ronald E. Hall, "The Bleaching Syndrome: Manifestations of a Post-Colonial Pathology among African Women," *Nigerian Journal of Guidance and Counseling* 11, (2006), pp. 1–13.

29. On dangerously high levels of hydroquinone: Sylvia Arthur, "Dying to Be White," online *Clutch Magazine,* January 2008, retrieved from http://www.clutchmagonline.com, 2008/01, dying-to-be-white.

30. On poor African women using harmful remedies: Sylvia Arthur, "Dying to Be White," *Jenda: A Journal of Culture and African Women Studies* 2009, retrieved from http://www.africaknowledgeproject.org/index.php/jenda/article/viewArticle/540.

31. On popularity of hair straightening: video clip "Why Women Straighten Their Hair," BBC News, January 28, 2009, retrieved from http://news.bbc.co.uk/2/hi/africa/8330701.stm.

32. Reference to Brazil's poorest having the darkest skin: Edward Telles, "The Social Consequences of Skin Color in Brazil," in Glenn, *Shades of Difference,* pp. 9–24.

33. On Sammy Sosa and Cake Soap: Fred Mitchell, "Sosa Says He's Preparing to Endorse Skin Product," online *Chicago Tribune Breaking Sports,* November 11, 2009, retrieved from http://archive.chicagobreakingsports.com/2009/11/sosa-says-hes-preparing-to-endorse-skin-product.html.

34. Footnote about Blue Cake Soap: Laura Paxman, "So White It's Wrong: Skin Bleaching Products Unveiled for Men," *Femail,* October 11, 2011, retrieved from http://www.dailymail.co.uk/femail/article-2047898/So-white-wrong-Skin-bleaching-products-unveiled-FOR-MEN.html.

35. Reference to ungendering of beauty rites: Donna P. Hope, "From Browning to Cake Soap: Popular Debates on Skin Bleaching in the Jamaican Dancehall," *Journal of Pan African Studies* 4 (June 2011), pp. 165–194.

36. Quote by Kartel: Bim Adewunmi, "Racism and Skin Colour: The Many Shades of Prejudice," *The Guardian,* October 4, 2011, retrieved from http://www.guardian.co.uk/world/2011/oct/04/racism-skin-colour-shades-prejudice.

37. Reference to New Mexico's tourism ad: online news magazine *Santa Fe New Mexican,* March 16, 2012, retrieved from http://www.santafenewmexican.com/Opinion/Our-view-Wanted-the-light-skinned.

38. Reference to buttock-lifting surgery: "Beautiful at Any Cost," *Florida Sun Magazine,* September 28, 2005, retrieved from http://www.cosmeticvacations.us/Press_Room/pressroom_Izzy_Buholzer.php.

39. Reference to Brazil as the country with second-highest percentage of population undergoing plastic surgery: 2009, retrieved from http://www.asianplasticsurgeryguide.com/news10-2/081003_south-korea-highest.html.

40. Reference to the medical tourism trade as lucrative for Brazil: March 2008,

retrieved from http://www.nuwireinvestor.com/articles/top-5-medical-tourism-destinations-51502.aspx.

41. Reference to survey of White college females who dye their hair blond: Melissa Rich and Thomas F. Cash, "The American Image of Beauty: Media Representations of Hair Color for Four Decades," *Sex Roles* 29 (1993), pp. 113–124.

42. Reference to the percentages of natural blondes and people with blue eyes in America: Dennis Clayson and Micol Maughan, "Redheads and Blonds: Stereotypic Images," *Psychological Reports* 59 (1986), pp. 811–816.

3. The Tiers of Color Prejudice in America

1. On definition of racial identity and the one-drop rule: F. James Davis, *Who Is Black?* (University Park: Pennsylvania State University, 1991), p. 34.

2. Reference to lighter-skinned slaves assigned to big house: Jeffrey Gardere, *Love Prescription: Healing Our Hearts through Love* (New York: Kensington Publishing, 2002), pp. 41–42.

3. Reference to darker-skinned slaves assigned to fields: Allison Samuels, "The Ugly Roots of the Light Skin / Dark Skin Divide," *Newsweek,* January 11, 2010, retrieved from http://www.thedailybeast.com/newsweek/blogs/the-gaggle/2010/01/11/the-ugly-roots-of-the-light-skin-dark-skin-divide.html.

4. On backlash of racism against free mulattoes: Kathleen Odell Korgen, *From Black to Biracial: Transforming Racial Identity among Americans* (Westport, CT: Praeger, 1998), p. 15.

5. On the origins of Blue Vein societies: Joel Williamson, New People (New York: Free Press, 1980), p. 82.

6. Fictional credo of a Blue Vein–like club: Wallace Thurman, *The Blacker the Berry: A Novel of English Life* (1929; New York: Simon & Schuster, 1996), p. 21.

7. On the resurgence of Black social clubs: Tamala M. Edwards, "A Twist on Jack and Jill," *Time,* July 2, 2001, retrieved from http://www.time.com/time/magazine/article/0,9171,1000232,00.html.

8. Reference to Jack and Jill of America as open to darker-skinned Blacks: Marianne Rohrlich, "Feeling Isolated at the Top, Seeking Roots," *New York Times,* July 19, 1998, retrieved from http://www.nytimes.com/1998/07/19/style/feeling-isolated-at-the-top-seeking-roots.html?pagewanted=all&src=pm.

9. On some churches' turning away darker-skinned Blacks: Audrey Elisa Kerr, *The Paper Bag Principle: Class, Colorism, and Rumor and the Case of Black Washington, D.C.* (Knoxville: University of Tennessee Press, 2006), p. 106.

10. Description of paper bag test: John Langston Gwaltney, *Drylongso: A Portrait of Black America* (New York: Random House, 1980), p. 80.

11. Discussion of the comb test: Margo Okazawa-Rey, Tracy Robinson, and Janie V. Ward, "Black Women and the Politics of Skin Color and Hair," *Women and Therapy,* 6, no. 1–2 (1987), pp. 89–102.

12. On St. Marks's becoming more integrated: Adam Parker, "Honoring the Past,

Embracing the Future," (Charleston) Post and Courier, May 29, 2011, retrieved from http://www.postandcourier.com/news/2011/may/29/honoring-the-past-embracing-the-future/.

13. On Emanuel American Methodist Episcopal Church: "Welcome to Emanuel," retrieved from http://www.emanuelamechurch.org.

14. Discussion of Strivers Row: Williamson, New People, pp. 162–163; Stephen Birmingham, Certain People: America's Black Elite (Boston: Little, Brown, 1977), pp. 183–193; and Jervis Anderson, This Was Harlem: A Cultural Portrait, 1900–1950 (New York: Farrar, Straus & Giroux, 1982), pp. 339–340.

15. Reference to Harlem's Sugar Hill: Anderson, This Was Harlem, p. 340.

16. Quote from Adam Clayton Powell Sr.: Anderson, This Was Harlem, p. 340.

17. On color-class discrimination at educational institutions: Sidney Kronus, The Black Middle Class (Columbus, Ohio: Merrill, 1971), p. 71; and Gunnar Myrdal, An American Dilemma (New York: Harper & Brothers, 1944), p. 694.

18. On Palmer Institute: Birmingham, Certain People, pp. 1–8.

19. On Dunbar High School: Willard B. Gatewood, Aristocrats of Color: The Black Elite, 1880–1920 (Bloomington: Indiana University Press, 1990), p. 263.

20. On HBCUs: Alexander H. Shannon, The Racial Integrity of the American Negro (1925; Nashville, TN: Parthenon Press, 1951), p. 45.

21. On Daytona School for Girls (later Bethune-Cookman College): Birmingham, Certain People, p. 285.

22. On skin color and career aspirations: Ronald E. Hall, "Impact of Skin Color upon Occupational Projection: A Case for Black Male Affirmative Action," Journal of African American Studies 1, no. 4 (1996), pp. 87–94.

23. Reference to skin-color study by Harvey and colleagues: Richard D. Harvey, Nicole LaBeach, Ellie Pridgen, and Tammy M. Gocial, "The Intragroup Stigmatization of Skin Tone among Black Americans," Journal of Black Psychology 31, no. 3 (2005), pp. 237–253.

24. On Brown Fellowship Society: Gatewood, Aristocrats of Color, p. 14.

25. On Frederick Douglass: William S. McFeely, Frederick Douglass (New York: W. W. Norton, 1991).

26. On light skin color of W. E. B. Du Bois: Davis, Who Is Black?, pp. 5–7.

27. Discussion of Du Bois's "Talented Tenth": Edward Reuter, The Mulatto in the United States (1918; New York: Haskell House, 1969); and John H. Franklin and August Meier, eds., Black Leaders of the Twentieth Century (Chicago: University of Illinois Press, 1982), pp. 63–70.

28. On bleach bath and lemon juice: Abraham Kardiner and Lionel Ovesey, The Mark of Oppression: A Psychosocial Study of the American Negro (New York: W. W. Norton, 1951).

29. On America's skin-bleaching market being worth over $5.6 billion: October 2006, retrieved from http://www.strategyr.com/MCP-2540.asp.

30. On HQ safety concerns: "A Study in Hype and Risk: The Marketing of Skin

Bleaches," a report by the City of New York Department of Consumer Affairs, February 1992.

31. On the claim that Michael Jackson had lupus: Tananarive Due, "Skin Deep," *Miami Herald,* October 2, 1991.

32. Description of dermabrasion: "Repairing the Damage," *Self,* October 1989, p. 142.

33. Quote on contact lenses: Elsie B. Washington, "The Bluest Eyes," *Essence,* January 1988, p. 114.

34. On blue-eyed Black women on magazine covers: Bonnie Allen, "It Ain't Easy Being Pinky," *Essence,* July 1982, p. 67.

35. On W. Earle Matory: "Body, Mind & Soul," *Orange Coast Magazine,* May 1996, pp. 19–20.

4. The Color of Identity

1. Longitudinal study of early identity formation: Phylis Katz and Jennifer Kofkin, "Race, Gender, and Young Children," in *Developmental Psychopathology: Perspectives on Adjustments, Risk, and Disorder,* eds. Suniya Luthar et al. (New York: Cambridge University Press, 1997), pp. 51–74.

2. On doll tests in 1930s and '40s: Kenneth B. Clark and Mamie Clark, "Racial Identification of Negro Preschool Children," in *Readings in Social Psychology, Prepared for the Committee on the Teaching of Social Psychology of the Society for the Study of Social Issues,* eds. Theodore M. Newcomb and Eugene L. Hartley (New York: Henry Holt, 1947), pp. 169–178.

3. On *Brown v. Board of Education*: Richard Kluger, *Simple Justice: The History of* Brown v. Board of Education *and Black America's Struggle for Equality* (New York: Alfred A. Knopf, 1976), p. 4.

4. On methodological criticism of doll tests: Joseph Baldwin, "Theory and Research Concerning the Notion of Black Self-Hatred: A Review and Reinterpretation," *Journal of Black Psychology* 5 (1979), pp. 51–77.

5. On the 2008 FAO Schwarz "Christmas doll adoption campaign": Natasha Sky, "Race Preferences in Adoption," *My Sky ~ Multiracial Family Life* (blog), January 29, 2008, retrieved from http://multiracialsky.wordpress.com/2008/01/29/race-preference-in-adoption.

6. On pilot study of children's beliefs: "Kids' [sic] Test Answers on Race Brings [sic] Mother to Tears," online CNN, May 18, 2010, retrieved from http://ac360.blogs.cnn.com/2010/05/18/kids-test-answers-on-race-brings-mother-to-tears/?iref=obnetwork.

7. On girls' sensitivity to skin color: Cornelia Porter, "Social Reasons for Skin Tone Preferences of Black School-Age Children," *American Journal of Orthopsychiatry* 61 (January 1991), pp. 149–154.

8. On teenagers' preference for medium skin color and gender coding of skin color: S. I. Coard, A. M. Breland, and P. Raskin, "Perceptions of and Preferences for

Skin Color: Black Racial Identity, and Self-Esteem among African Americans," *Journal of Applied Social Psychology* 31 (November 2001), pp. 2256–2274.

9. Personal interviews with Trina, Tiny, and Monique: conducted by Kathy Russell.

10. On mothers who bleach their children's skin: "Black Women and Their Children: Bleaching Their Skin," *The Tyra Banks Show*, NBC, September 10, 2008.

11. Documentary about colorism: Kiri Davis, *A Girl Like Me* (New York: Reel Works Teen Filmmaking, 2005).

12. Reference to study about dark-skinned girls: Tiffany Townsend, Anita Thomas, Torsten Neilands, and Tiffany Jackson, "I'm No Jezebel; I Am Young, Gifted, and Black: Identity, Sexuality, and Black Girls," *Psychology of Women Quarterly* 34 (September 2010), pp. 273–285.

13. Quote about Jeffrey: Itabari Njeri, "Who Is Black?," *Essence,* September 1991, pp. 64–66, 114–116.

14. Quote about "black cool": Michel Marriott, "Light Skinned Men: Problems and Privileges," *Essence,* November 1988, p. 76.

15. Personal interview with Ron Holt: conducted in January 1992.

16. On Stepin Fetchit: Roy Hurst, "Stepin Fetchit: America's First Black Film Star," NPR, March 6, 2006, retrieved from http://www.npr.org/templates/story/story.php?storyId=5245089.

17. Lyrics from "Dark Skin Girls": Del the Funky Homosapien, "Dark Skin Girls," from the album *I Wish My Brother George Was Here* (New York: Elektra Entertainment Group, 1991).

18. Reference to 2002 skin-color study: Eric Uhlmann, Nilanjana Dasgupta, Angelica Elgueta, Anthony G. Greenwald, and Jane Swanson, "Subgroup Prejudice Based on Skin Color among Hispanics in the United States and Latin America," Social Cognition 20, no. 3 (2002), pp. 198–226.

19. On self-esteem of mid-range African Americans: Stephanie Coard, Marianne Breland, and Patricia Raskin. "Perceptions of and Preferences for Skin Color, Black Racial Identity, and Self-Esteem among African Americans," *Journal of Applied Social Psychology* 31 (November 2001).

20. Personal interview with Connie, formerly LeConetria: conducted by Kathy Russell.

21. Workplace discrimination study: Marianne Bertrand and Sendhil Mullainathan, "Are Emily and Greg More Employable Than Lakisha and Jamal? A Field Experiment on Labor Market Discrimination," *American Economic Review* 94 (September 2004), pp. 991–1013.

22. Quotes from Bill Cosby: "Bill Cosby Speech Transcript," *Eight Cities Media & Publications,* retrieved from http://www.eightcitiesmap.com/transcript_bc.htm. See also Christopher John Farley, "What Bill Cosby Should Be Talking About," *Time,* June 3, 2004, retrieved from http://www.time.com/time/nation/article/0,8599,645801,00.html.

23. Personal interview with Theresa H.: conducted by Kathy Russell.

24. On distinctive names and later life outcomes: Roland G. Fryer Jr. and Steven D. Levitt, "The Causes and Consequences of Distinctively Black Names," *Quarterly Journal of Economics* 119 (March 2004), pp. 767–805.

25. On color-based income gap: Nadra Kareem Nittle, "What Is Colorism? The Impact of Skin Color Discrimination in the U.S. and Beyond," *About .com*, February 7, 2102, retrieved from http://racerelations.about.com/od/understandingrac1/a/What-Is-Colorism.htm.

26. Research findings on skin color and Black names: Midge Wilson, Lisa Razzano, and Sherry Salmons, "The Halo Effect Revisited: The Stereotyping of African American Women by Skin Color and Name," paper presented at the 18th Annual Association of Women in Psychology Conference, held in Atlanta, GA, March 1993.

27. Personal interview with African-American woman discussing unique Black names: conducted by Kathy Russell.

28. On renouncing names inherited from slave ancestors: Itabari Njeri, *Every Goodbye Ain't Gone: Family Portraits and Personal Escapades* (New York: Times Books, 1990; Vintage Books, 1991).

29. Personal interview with Jaleel Abdul-Adil: conducted on January 29, 1992.

30. On African Americans' journey toward racial identity and pride: William E. Cross Jr., "The Psychology of Nigrescence: Revising the Cross Model," in *Handbook of Multicultural Counseling*, eds. Joseph G. Ponterotto, Manuel J. Casas, Lisa Suzuki, and Charlene M. Alexander (Thousand Oaks, CA: Sage Publications, 1995), pp. 92–122.

31. Also on African Americans' journey toward racial identity: Janet E. Helms, "An Overview of Black Racial Identity," in *Black and White Racial Identity: Theory, Research, and Practice*, ed. Janet E. Helms (Westport, CT: Greenwood Press, 1990), pp. 9–32.

32. On how African Americans view passing today: Randall Kennedy, "Racial Passing," *Ohio State Law Journal* 62 (2001), pp. 1145–1193.

33. On light-skinned African Americans as "inadvertent passers" and possible responses to their dilemma: F. James Davis, *Who Is Black?* (University Park: Pennsylvania State University Press, 1991), pp. 149–150.

34. On the experience of an "inadvertent passer": Kathleen Cross, "Trapped in the Body of a White Woman," *Ebony*, October 1990, p. 74.

35. On the challenge of establishing self-identity: Rashida Jones, "The Daughter of Q," *American Jewish Life Magazine*, January/February 2007, retrieved from http://www.ajlmagazine.com/content /01/2007/rashidajones.html.

36. On U.S. Census data on multiracial children: Sally Saulny, "Census Data Presents Rise in Multiracial Population of Youths," March 24, 2011, retrieved from http://www.nytimes.com/2011/03/25/us/25race.html.

37. Multiracial bill of rights: Maria P. P. Root, "Bill of Rights for Racially Mixed People," *The Multiracial Experience: Racial Borders as the New Frontier* (Thousand Oaks, CA: Sage Publications, 1996), pp. 3–14.

5. Hair Stories: Politics of the Straight and Nappy

1. On hairstyles of African women: Ekaete Bailey, "South African Hairstyles," May 29, 2010, retrieved from http://www.ehow.com/facts_6566666_south-african -hairstyles.html.

2. On Madam C. J. Walker: A'Lelia P. Bundles, "Madam C. J. Walker: Cosmetics Tycoon," *Ms.*, July 1983, pp. 91–94; A'Lelia P. Bundles, *Madam C. J. Walker: Entrepreneur* (New York: Chelsea House, 1991); telephone interview with A'Lelia P. Bundles, May 1992; and *Two Dollars and a Dream,* produced and directed by Stanley Nelson (New York: Filmmakers Library, 1988).

3. On hair relaxers containing known carcinogens: "Formaldehyde and Cancer Risk," National Cancer Institute, at the National Institutes of Health, June 10, 2011, retrieved from http://www.cancer.gov/cancertopics/factsheet/Risk/formaldehyde.

4. Documentary about hair-straightening products: Chris Rock, *Good Hair* (New York: Chris Rock Productions and HBO Films, 2009).

5. On firing of Tolliver: "Black History Month—Melba Tolliver," *A Taste of Choco-late* (blog), February 3, 2011, retrieved from http://curlychellez.blogspot.com/ 2011/02/melba-tolliver.html.

6. On suspension of Dorothy Reed: blog incorporating the article "TV Reporter Managers in Row over Cornrow Hairdo," *Jet,* February 19, 1981, retrieved from http://alturl.com/c4eig.

7. On wearing weaves: *Brown Sista Online Magazine,* "Women & Their Weaves: A Love Story," October 7, 2009, retrieved from http://brownsista.com/women-their -weaves-a-love-story.

8. Don Imus quoted: "Network Condemns Remarks by Imus," *New York Times,* April 7, 2007, retrieved from http://www.nytimes.com/2007/04/07/arts/television/ 07imus.html.

9. Discussion of *New Yorker* cover with Obama cartoon: "New Yorker Cover Shows 'Muslim' Barack with Gun-Slinging Michelle Obama," *Huffington Post,* July 13, 2008, retrieved from http://www.huffingtonpost.com/2008/07/13/new-yorker -cover-shows-mu_n_112428.html.

10. Blog quote from "The Luscious Librarian": July 2008, retrieved from http://the -luscious-librarian.blogspot.com/2008/07/m-is-for-militant-michelle-and-new .html.

11. Excerpt from Early article: Gerard Early, "Life with Daughters; or, The Cakewalk with Shirley Temple," *Hungry Mind Review* 20 (winter 1992), pp. 6–9.

12. Discussion of motivation for making documentary: Chris Rock, *Good Hair.*

13. On Joey Mazzarino's video clip: "I Love My Hair: A Father's Tribute to His Daughter," NPR, October 18, 2010, retrieved from http://m.npr.org/news/front/ 130653300?page=1.

14. On many Black women having a fear of water/drowning: personal interview conducted by Kathy Russell, May 2011.

15. Quote from Valerie on lack of Black females in water sports: personal interview conducted by Kathy Russell, May 2011.

16. Comments by Whoopi Goldberg and Cicely Tyson: *Arsenio Hall Show*, CBS, December 11, 1990.

17. On Solange Knowles's hair: Dodai Stewart, "Solange Chops Hair, Is Called 'Insane,'" *Jezebel*, July 24, 2009, retrieved from http://Jezebel.com.

18. On lawsuits against Six Flags and FedEx: Ericka Blount Danois, "Six Flags Denies Jobs to 2 Women Based on Natural Hair," *Black Voices*, April 21, 2010, retrieved from http://www.bvblackspin.com/2010/04/21/six-flags-hair-discrimination-dread locks.

19. Article on locing hair: Naadu Blankson, "The Dreaded Decision," *Essence*, October 1990, p. 36.

20. Percentage getting hair permed: Janell Ross, "Natural or Relaxed, for Black Women, Hair Is Not a Settled Matter," *Huffington Post*, October 4, 2011, retrieved from http://www.huffingtonpost.com/2011/08/04/black-hair-natural-relaxed-_n_918200.html.

21. Comments on White women wearing weaves: "Tyra's Fake Hair Academy," *The Tyra Show*, Warner Brothers, November 20, 2009.

22. Reference to expensive weave: "NY Model Pays $46,000 for Hair," *SandraRose* (blog), April 7, 2010, retrieved from http://sandrarose.com/?s=brandi+Irwin.

23. Reference to exercise and hair: Cynthia Tucker, "How to Maintain Your Hair during Exercise, for African American Women," July14, 2011, retrieved from http://www.ehow.com/how_5177077_maintain-exercise-african-american-women.html.

24. Comments by Andre Harrell: Jenna Flanagan, "Hair or History: What's Behind African Americans' Views on Swimming," WNYC, July 20, 2010, retrieved from http://www.wnyc.org/blogs/wnyc-news-blog/2010/jul/20/hair-history-behind-african-american-views-swimming.

25. Comments on touching weaves during sex: "Sex with Weaves: Just Keep Your Hands on the Titties," *A Big Butt and a Smile*, April 9, 2009, retrieved from http://sexandrelationships.abigbuttandasmile.com/2009/08/04/black-women-and-sex-with-weaves-just-keep-your-hands-on-the-titties.

26. Discussion of Justin Bieber touching Esperanza Spalding's hair: Hilton Hater, "Justin Bieber and Esperanza Spalding Bond over Hair, Mothers, Grammys," *The Hollywood Gossip*, February 15, 2011, retrieved from http://www.thehollywoodgossip.com/2011/02/justin-bieber-and-esperanza-spalding-bond-over-hair-mothers-gram.

27. On Malcolm X's first "man perm": Malcolm X with Alex Haley, *The Autobiography of Malcolm X* (New York: Grove Press, 1965; Random House, 1969).

6. Families and Friends: Drawing the Color Lines

1. Discussion of in vitro fertilization: Leslie A. Pray, "Embryo Screening and the Ethics of Human Genetic Engineering," *Nature Education*, January 2008, retrieved from http://www.nature.com/scitable/topicpage/embryo-screening-and-the-ethics-of-60561.

2. On stress over skin color: Nancy Boyd-Franklin, *Black Families in Therapy: A Multisystems Approach* (New York: Guilford Press, 1989), pp. 34–41.

3. Excerpt regarding light-skinned baby in Filipino family: Joanne L. Rondilla and Paul Spickard, *Is Lighter Better?: Skin-Tone Discrimination among Asian Americans* (Lanham, MD: Rowman & Littlefield, 2007).

4. Personal interview with Misha: conducted in May 2011.

5. On adoption practices of some wealthy Black families: Stephen Birmingham, *Certain People* (Boston: Little, Brown, 1977), p. 161.

6. Discussion of foster home placement: Suzanne Daley, "Foster Placement by Skin Tone Seen," *New York Times,* January 18, 1990, retrieved from http://www.nytimes.com/1990/01/18/nyregion/foster-placement-by-skin-shade-is-charged.html.

7. On uses of skin-color information in adoption placements: telephone interview with Sydney Duncan, conducted in October 1991.

8. Reference to NABSW's stand in interracial adoptions: Karen Grigsby Bates, "Are You My Mother?" *Essence,* April 1991, p. 50.

9. Discussion of the Interethnic Placement Act: Joan Heifetz Hollinger and Alice Bussiere, "A Guide to the Multiethnic Placement Act of 1994, as Amended by the Interethnic Adoption Provisions of 1996," U.S. Department of Health and Human Services, 1998, retrieved March 6, 2009, from http://www.acf.hhs.gov/programs/cb/laws_policies/mepa.pdf.

10. On the Adoption and Safe Families Act: Olivia A. Golden, "Testimony on the Implementation of the Multiethnic Placement Act of 1994 and the Interethnic Placement Provisions of 1996," Assistant Secretary for Legislation: Department of Health and Human Services, September 15, 1998, retrieved from http://www.hhs.gov/asl/testify/t980915a.html.

11. Discussion of sperm samples and egg donors: Charis Thompson, "Skin Tone and the Persistence of Biological Race in Egg Donation for Assisted Reproduction," in *Shades of Difference: Why Skin Color Matters,* ed. Evelyn Nakano Glenn (Stanford, CA: Stanford University Press, 2009), pp. 131–147.

12. Experience of African-American graduate student as a "nonresembling" parent: personal interview with student, conducted in July 2010.

13. Mention of Elliot Liebow: Selena Bond and Thomas F. Cash, "Black Beauty: Skin Color and Body Image among African-American College Women," *Journal of Applied Social Psychology* 22, no. 11 (June 1992), pp. 874–888.

14. Findings from focus group: JeffriAnne Wilder and Colleen Cain, "Teaching and Learning Color Consciousness in Black Families: Exploring Family Processes and Women's Experiences with Colorism," paper presented at the Annual Meeting of the American Sociological Association, Atlanta, GA, August 13, 2010.

15. On "post-traumatic slave syndrome": Joy DeGruy Leary, *Post Traumatic Slave Syndrome: America's Legacy of Enduring Injury and Healing* (Milwaukie, OR: Uptone Press, 2005).

16. Quote about mother applying straighteners: Joan Morgan, "The Family Trap," *Essence,* September 1990, p. 82.

17. Eartha Kitt's story: from interview on *60 Minutes,* CBS, August 12, 1990.

18. Discussion of Afrocentric parents' possible view of very light-skinned children: Boyd-Franklin, *Black Families in Therapy*, pp. 34–41.

19. Mention of Malcolm X: Bond and Cash, "Black Beauty," pp. 874–888.

20. Documentary to empower dark-skinned African-American teenagers to resist colorism: Kiri Davis, *A Girl Like Me* (New York: Reel Works Teen Filmmaking, 2005).

21. Paper describing original doll test: Kenneth B. Clark and Mamie P. Clark, "Racial Identification and Preference among Negro Preschool Children," in *Readings in Social Psychology,* eds. Theodore M. Newcomb and Eugene L. Hartley, (New York: Henry Holt, 1947), pp 169–178.

22. Reference to *Brown v. Board of Education*: Richard Kluger, *Simple Justice: The History of Brown v. Board of Education* (NY: Alfred A. Knopf, 1976).

23. Dialogue between Keyonn and Keith in documentary: *A Question of Color,* produced and directed by Kathe Sandler (South Burlington, VT: California Newsreel, 1993).

24. Letter to "The Ebony Advisor": *Ebony,* May 1990, p. 116.

7. The Match Game: Colorism and Courtship

1. On Jennifer Lopez: *People* magazine, April 13, 2011, retrieved from http://www.people.com/people/package/article/0,,20360857_20481259,00.html.

2. Reanalysis of National Survey of Black Americans research: Mark Hill, "Skin Color and Perception of Physical Attractiveness: Does Gender Matter?" *Social Psychology Quarterly* 65, no. 1 (January 2002), pp. 77–91.

3. Study of successful Harlem couples: Melville J. Herskovits, *The American Negro: A Study in Racial Crossing* (New York: Alfred A. Knopf, 1928); reissued (Bloomington: Indiana University Press, 1968), p. 64.

4. Reference to eminent Black men marrying light-skinned women: Elisabeth I. Mullins and Paul Sites, "The Origins of Contemporary Eminent Black Americans: A Three-Generation Analysis of Social Origin," *American Sociological Review* 49 (October 1984), pp. 672–685.

5. Reference to skin color as social capital: Margaret Hunter, "'If You're Light You're Alright': Light Skin Color as Social Capital for Women of Color," *Gender and Society* 16, (2002), pp. 175–193.

6. Historical discussion of preference for light-skinned women: L. Ross, "Mate Selection Preferences among African American College Students," *Journal of Black Studies* 27 (April 1997), pp. 554–569.

7. Quote from Spike Lee: Jill Nelson, "Mo' Better Spike," *Essence,* August 1990, p. 55.

8. Quote from dark-skinned man called "black bastard": Calvin Hernton, *Sex and Racism in America* (New York: Grove Press, 1965), p. 83.

9. Excerpt about Tea Cake and Janie: Zora Neale Hurston, *Their Eyes Were Watching God* (1937; New York: Harper & Row, 1990), pp. 140–141.

10. Analysis of Hurston's book: Alice Walker, "Embracing the Dark and the Light," *Essence,* July 1982, p. 117.

11. Interview with William, a middle-aged Black man from Nashville: conducted by Kathy Russell.

12. Percentage of Black men and women desiring light-skinned partners: Kenneth B. Clark and Mamie P. Clark, "What Do Blacks Think of Themselves?" *Ebony,* November 1980, pp. 176–182.

13. Rates of interracial marriage: Pew Research Center, February 1, 2010, retrieved from http://pewresearch.org/pubs/1480/millennials-accept-iinterracial-dating -marriage-friends-different-race-generations.

14. Percentage of Blacks interracially marrying by gender: retrieved from 2010 Census data, retrieved from http://www.census.gov/population/www/socdemo/ hh-fam/cps2010.html.

15. Discussion of Richard Loving and Mildred Jeter's story: Isabel Wilkerson, "Black-White Marriages Rise but Couples Still Face Scorn," *New York Times,* December 2, 1991, retrieved from http://www.nytimes.com/1991/12/02/us/black-white -marriages-rise-but-couples-still-face-scorn.html?pagewanted=all&src=pm.

16. Reference to interracial dating during Civil Rights Movement: Paul Giddings, *When and Where I Enter: The Impact of Black Women on Race and Sex in America* (New York: William Morrow, 1984), p. 301.

17. Braving guns, hoses, and dogs: "Jill Scott Talks Interracial Dating," *Essence,* March 25, 2010, retrieved from http://www.essence.com/2010/03/26/commentary-jill-scott-talks-interracial.

18. Reference to the feeling of "being passed over at the prom": BeBe Moore Campbell, "Brothers and Sisters," *New York Times Magazine,* August 23, 1992, pp. 6, 8.

19. Discussion of the "wince": "Jill Scott Talks Interracial Dating," *Essence,* March 25, 2010, retrieved from http://www.essence.com/2010/03/26/commentary-jill -scott-talks-interracial.

20. Interview with Nahla: conducted by Kathy Russell.

21. Statistics on African Americans marrying outside race: Jeffrey S. Passel, Wendy Wang, and Paul Taylor, Pew Research Center, June 4, 2010, retrieved from http://pewresearch.org/pubs/1616/american-marriage-interracial-interethnic.

22. Statement attributed to Audrey Chapman: Joy Jones, "Marriage Is for White People," *Washington Post,* Sunday Outlook, March 26, 2006, retrieved from http://www .washingtonpost.com/wp-.dyn/content/article/2006/03/25/AR2006032500029 .html.

23. Discussion of Ralph Richard Banks's book: Imani Perry, review of *Is Marriage for White People? New York Times Book Review,* September 16, 2011, retrieved from http://www.nytimes.com/2011/09/18/books/review/is-marriage-for-white -people-by-ralph-richard-banks-book-review.html?pagewanted=all.

24. Reference to the "Black-nanny syndrome": "Why So Few White Men Marry Black Women," *Abagond Wordpress* (blog), June 25, 2008, retrieved from http://abagond .wordpress.com/2008/06/25/why-so-few-white-men-marry-black-women.

25. Quote from White politician: Dorothy Tucker, "Guess Who's Coming to Dinner Now?" *Essence*, April 1987, p. 133.

26. Interviews with gay and lesbian actors about various skin-color issues: conducted by Midge Wilson.

8. The (In)Justice of Color: Politics, Policies, and Perceptions

1. On possible alteration of Obama's skin color in photos: Michael Roberts, "Did Fox News Darken Barack Obama?" *Denver Westword Blogs*, August 18, 2008, retrieved from http://blogs.westword.com/demver/2008/08/did_fox_news_darken_ barack_oba.php.

2. On *Time* magazine's darkening O. J. Simpson's picture: *New York Times*, June 25, 1994, retrieved from http://www.nytimes.com/1994/06/25/us/time-responds-to -criticism-over-simpson-cover.html.

3. Obama autobiography: Barack Obama, *Dreams from My Father: A Story of Race and Inheritance* (New York: Times Books, 1995, rev. ed., 2008).

4. Toni Morrison on Bill Clinton as "the first Black president": *New Yorker,* Talk of the Town, October 5, 1998, retrieved from http://www.newyorker.com/arch ive/1998/10/05/1998_10_05_031_tny_libry_000016504?currentPage=all.

5. The Reverend Jesse Jackson's criticism of Obama for "talking down to Black people": July 10, 2008, retrieved from http://www.nytimes.com/2008/07/10/us/ politics/10jackson.html.

6. On light-skinned African Americans in Congress: Jennifer Hochschild and Vesla Weaver, "The Skin Color Paradox and the American Racial Order," *Social Forces* 86 (2007), pp. 643–670.

7. On the *New Yorker* cover: Lee Siegel, "We're Not Laughing at You, or with You," July 20, 2008, http://www.nytimes.com/2008/07/20/weekinreview/20seigel.html ?scp=2&sq=the+new+yorker+cover++obama+caricature&st=nyt.

8. Research on perceptions of a political candidate: Eugene M. Caruso, Nicole L. Mead, and Emily Balcetis, "Political Partisanship Influences Perception of Biracial Candidates' Skin Tone," *Proceedings of the National Academy of Sciences* 106, no. 48 (2009), pp. 20168–20173.

9. Study on Obama's perceived suitability for high office: Midge Wilson, Or'Shaundra Benson, and Monika Black, "The Color of Politics: Color and Race in the 2008 Election," conference of the Society for Personality and Social Psychology, Las Vegas, 2009.

10. Study of the perceived electability of candidates: Nayda Terkildsen, "When White Voters Evaluate Black Candidates: The Processing Implications of Candidate Skin Color, Prejudice, and Self-Monitoring," *American Journal of Political Science* 37 (1993), pp. 1032–1053.

11. Report on ABC News–Washington Post survey: "O. J. Simpson—10 Years after Acquittal," October 2, 2005, retrieved from http://abcnews.go.com/GMA/story?id=1177035&page=1.

12. Results of 2006 CNN poll: December 12, 2006, retrieved from http://articles.cnn.com/2006-12-12/us/racism.poll_1_whites-blacks-racism?_s=PM:US.

13. Study of perceptions about "progress toward racial equality": Richard Eibach and Joyce Ehrlinger, "Keep Your Eyes on the Prize: Reference Points and Group Differences in Assessing Progress Towards Equality," Personality and Social Psychology Bulletin 32 (2006), pp. 66–77.

14. On perceptions of racism: Thomas Nelson, Kira Sanbonmatsu, and Harwood McClerking, "Playing a Different Race Card: Examining the Limits of Elite Influence on Perceptions of Racism," Journal of Politics 69 (2007), pp. 416–429.

15. On the Implicit Association Test: Anthony Greenwald, Deborah McGhee, and Jordan Schwartz, "Measuring Individual Differences in Implicit Cognition: The Implicit Association Test," Journal of Personality and Social Psychology 74 (1998), pp. 1464–1480.

16. On mock-jury study: Justin Levinson and Daniel Young, "Compelling (Skin Tone) Evidence: Implicit Racial Bias and Judgments of Ambiguous Evidence," West Virginia Law Review 12 (2010), pp. 307–350.

17. On mock-hiring study: Shilpa Banerji, "Darker-Skinned Black Job Applicants Face More Obstacles," Diverse: Issues in Higher Education, September 21, 2006, retrieved from http://diverseeducation.com/article/6392c2/study-darker-skinned-black-job-applicants-face-more-obstacles.html.

18. On ratio of difference in earnings: Michael Hughes and Bradley R. Hertel, "The Significance of Color Remains: A Study of Life Chances, Mate Selection, and Ethnic Consciousness among Black Americans," Social Forces 68, no. 4 (1990), pp. 1105–1120.

19. Research on skin tone and success: Verna M. Keith and Cedric Herring, "Skin Tone and Stratification in the Black Community," American Journal of Sociology 97, no. 3 (1991), pp. 760–778.

20. Research on color wage gap: Arthur H. Goldsmith, Darrick Hamilton, and William Darity Jr., "From Dark to Light: Skin Color and Wages among African-Americans," Journal of Human Resources 42, no. 4 (2007), pp. 701–738.

21. Reference to 2003 New Immigrant Survey: Joni Hersch, "Profiling the New Immigrant Worker: The Effects of Skin Color and Height," Journal of Labor Economics 26, no. 2 (2008), pp. 345–386.

22. Research on effects of skin tone versus family background: Mark E. Hill, "Color Differences in the Socioeconomic Status of African American Men: Results of a Longitudinal Study," Social Forces 78, no. 4 (2000), pp. 1437–1460.

23. The 1990 Walker v. IRS case, and rise of colorism cases: Henry Findley, Stephen C. Garrott, and Robert Wheatley, "Color Discrimination: Differentiate at Your Peril," Journal of Individual Employment Rights 11, no. 1 (2003/2004), pp. 31–38;

and Marjorie Valbrun, "EEOC Sees Rise in Intrarace Complaints of Color Bias," *Wall Street Journal,* August 7, 2003, retrieved from http://bechollashon.org/data base/index.php?/article/1012.

24. References to multiple color-discrimination cases: U.S. Equal Employment Opportunity Commission, July 3, 2011, retrieved from http://www.eeoc.gov/ eeoc/initiatives/e-race/caselist.cfm#color.

25. On the Mumford Center report: John Logan, "How Race Counts for Hispanic Americans," July 14, 2003, retrieved from http://mumford.albany.edu/census/ BlackLatinoReport/BlackLatino01.htm.

26. On occupational advantage for light-skinned Puerto Ricans and Cubans: Rodolfo Espino and Michael M. Franz, "Latino Phenotypic Discrimination Revisited: The Impact of Skin Color on Occupational Status," *Social Science Quarterly* 83, no. 2 (June 2002), pp. 612–623.

27. On additional color-discrimination cases: U.S. Equal Employment Opportunity Commission, July 3, 2011, retrieved from http://www.eeoc.gov/eeoc/initiatives/ e-race/caselist.cfm#color.

9. The Narrative of Skin Color: Stories in Black and Light

1. On early history of Black writers: Philip Bader, *African-American Writers* (New York: Fact on File, 2004).

2. On the Harlem Renaissance: Jervis Anderson, *This Was Harlem* (New York: Farrar, Straus & Giroux, 1982), pp. 339–340.

3. On Harlem Renaissance writers: Maria Balshaw, *Looking for Harlem: Urban Aesthetics in African American Literature* (Sterling, VA: Pluto Press, 2000).

4. Excerpt from Hughes's poem: Langston Hughes, "Cross" (1926), in *The Collected Poems of Langston Hughes,* eds. Arnold Rapersad and David Roessel (New York: Alfred A. Knopf, 1994).

5. Excerpts from Brooks's poem: Gwendolyn Brooks, "The Ballad of Chocolate Mabbie," in *A Primer for Blacks* (Chicago: Third World Press, 1991), originally published in *A Street in Bronzeville* (New York: Harper & Brothers, 1945).

6. Story of Josephine Baker: Donald Bogle, "Josephine," *Essence,* February 1991, p. 66.

7. On minstrel shows: Daniel J. Leab, *From Sambo to Superspade: The Black Experience in Motion Pictures* (Boston: Houghton Mifflin, 1975), pp. 8–10.

8. On the five basic roles for Black film actors: Donald Bogle, *Toms, Coons, Mulattoes, Mammies, and Bucks: An Interpretive History of Blacks in American Films* (New York: Viking Press, 1973).

9. Discussion of *Birth of a Nation:* Leab, *From Sambo to Superspade,* pp. 23–39.

10. Discussion of D. W. Griffith's films: Langston Hughes and Milton Meltzer, *Black Magic: A Pictorial History of the African American in the Performing Arts* (1956 [with a slightly different title]; Cambridge, MA: Da Capo Press, 1990), p. 303.

11. Reference to Stepin Fetchit's politics: W. Augustus Low and Virgil A. Clift, eds.,

Encyclopedia of Black America (New York: McGraw Hill, 1981; Cambridge, MA: Da Capo Press, 1984), p. 385.

12. Reference to Lincoln Motion Picture Company: Leab, *From Sambo to Superspade*, pp. 64–70.

13. On subversive message about color: Jane Gaines, "The Scar of Shame: Skin Color and Cast in Black Silent Melodrama," *Cinema Journal* 26 (1987), p. 15.

14. References to Oscar Micheaux and his films: Leab, *From Sambo to Superspade*, pp. 78, 173–174, 212–213.

15. Discussion of Lena Horne's career: Gail Lumet Buckley, *The Hornes* (New York: Alfred A. Knopf, 1986), pp. 155–157.

16. References to *Island in the Sun* and Sidney Poitier: Leab, *From Sambo to Superspade*, pp. 209–211, 230.

17. Discussion of "blaxploitation" genre: J. Pines, *Blacks in Films: A Survey of Racial Themes and Images in the American Film* (London: Studio Vista, 1975), pp. 118–127.

18. On "mixploitation" films: Gregory T. Carter, "From Blaxploitation to Mixploitation: Mixed Race, Male Leads, and Changing Black Identities," in *Mixed Race Hollywood*, eds. Mary Beltrán and Camilla Fojas (New York: New York University Press, 2008), pp. 203–220.

19. Book named in film title *Precious: Based on the Novel "Push" by Sapphire*: Sapphire, *Push (A Novel)* (New York: Alfred A. Knopf, 1996).

20. Discussion of Daniels's color complex: Lynn Hirschberg, "The Audacity of Precious," *New York Times Magazine*, October 21, 2009, retrieved from http://www.nytimes.com/2009/10/25/magazine/25precious-t.html?pagewanted=all.

10. #TeamLightskinned: Color in the Media

1. On Victoria's Secret fashion show: "Victoria's Secret is . . . racist?" December 2010, retrieved from http://www.liveleak.com/view?i=1f9_1293749029.

2. On Aunt Jemima and other advertising images: Marilyn Kern-Foxworth, "The Most Battered Woman in America Rises to the Top," in *Aunt Jemima, Uncle Ben, and Rastus: Blacks in Advertising, Yesterday, Today, and Tomorrow* (Westport, CT: Greenwood Press, 1994), pp. 61–108.

3. Discussion of skin color, models, and advertising: Kern-Foxworth, "The Most Battered Woman," pp. 54–58.

4. On colorism and advertising: Courtney Carliss Young, ed., *Color Me Color Struck: How Colorism Marginalizes Women of Color in Popular Culture* (in press).

5. On ad with Beyoncé Knowles in *Elle*: "L'Oréal Denies Lightening Beyoncé's Skin Tone in Ad," August 2008, retrieved from http://www.foxnews.com/story/0,2933,399364,00.html#ixzz1U6S22T5d.

6. On skin lightening of Gabourey Sidibe: "*Elle* under Fire for Gabourey Sidibe Cover," September 2010, retrieved from http://www.cbsnews.com/8301-31749_162-20016677-10391698.html.

7. Reference to 1997 cover of *Elle*: "Alek Wek: Contemporary Black Biography," *Encyclopedia.com*, 2008, retrieved from http://www.encyclopedia.com/topic/Alek_Wek.aspx.

8. Comment made by Oprah Winfrey: Deborah Tannen, "Oprah: TV Host," *Time Magazine U.S.*, June 1998, retrieved from http://www.time.com/time/magazine/article/0,9171,988512,00.html.

9. Source of quote attributed to Stephen Meisel: "About Alek Wek," *Supermodels*, retrieved from http://www.supermodels.nl/alekwek/about.

10. On Sarah Bartmann: *Black Venus: Sexualized Savages, Primal Fears, and Primitive Narratives in French*, T. Denean Sharpley-Whiting (Durham, NC: Duke University Press, 1999).

11. Text for ad featuring Daria Werbowy: *Interview* magazine, May 2010; discussed on multiple blogs and online fashion sites including, Tracy Daniels, *Black Women in Fashion: Bringing You Fashion in Color*, May 12, 2010, retrieved from http://blackwomeninfashion.blogspot.com/2010/05/daria-werbowys-interview-editorial.html.

12. Reference to special *Vogue Italia* issue: Claire Sulmers, "Tribute to Black Beauties," *Vogue Italia*, May 2011, retrieved from http://www.vogue.it/en/magazine/fashion-stories/2011/05/tribute-to-black-beauties.

13. Quote from blog on *Vogue Italia* and Black models: "All Black Italia 'Vogue' Revealed!" *New York Fashion Magazine*, June 2008, retrieved from http://nymag.com/daily/fashion/2008/06/uveiled_italian_vogues_allblac_1.html.

14. On Miss Bronze beauty contest: Maxine Leeds Craig, "The Color of an Ideal Negro Beauty Queen: Miss Bronze 1961–1968," in *Shades of Difference*, ed. Evelyn Nakano Glenn (Stanford, CA: Stanford University Press, 2009), pp. 81–94.

15. Reference to Miss Black America pageant: Elwood Watson, "Miss America's Racial Milestones," *Diverse Issues in Higher Education*, January 2009, retrieved from http://diverseeducation.wordpress.com/2009/01/14/miss-americas-racial-milestones.

16. Reference to Congress of Racial Equality (CORE): David Bradley, "Talking with Vanessa Williams," *Redbook*, February 1984, p.76.

17. Reference to *Penthouse* magazine and Suzette Charles: Elwood Watson, "Miss America's Racial Milestones," *Diverse Issues in Higher Education*, January 14, 2009, retrieved from http://diverseeducation.com/blogpost/86.

18. Reference to Miss USA pageant winner: "Crystle Stewart Crowned Miss USA," April 2008, retrieved from http://thedailyvoice.com/voice/2008/04/crystle-stewart-crowned-miss-u-000448.php.

19. Reference to Miss America winners: Watson, "Miss America's Racial Milestones," retrieved from http://diverseeducation.wordpress.com/2009/01/14/miss-americas-racial-milestones.

20. Discussion of light-skinned CNN journalists: Nadra Kareem Nittle, "CNN's Don Lemon: Anchors of Color on Television Are Light-Skinned," June 30, 2011,

retrieved from http://racerelations.about.com/b/2011/06/30/cnns-don-lemon
-anchors-of-color-on-television-are-light-skinned.htm.

21. Comments on light-skinned women in music videos: telephone interview with
Alvin Poussaint, conducted in February 1992.

22. Lyrics from Big Daddy song: Big Daddy Kane, "On the Bugged Tip" on the album
Long Live Kane (New York: Cold Chillin', 1988).

23. Reference to rapper Rick Ross: "Are Black Men Obsessed with Light Skinned
Women?" *Generation-X*, July 6, 2011, retrieved from http://generation-x.net/
viewVideo.php?video_id=6531&title=Are_Black_Men_Obsessed_With_Light_
Skinned_Women.

24. On rapper Lil Wayne: "Woman Urges Fans to Boycott Lil Wayne over 'Dark-
Skin' Prejudice," *News One from Black America,* January 6, 2011, retrieved from
http://newsone.com/entertainment/newsonestaff2/fansboycott-lil-wayne-dark
-skin-black-women.

25. On rapper Kanye West: "Just Curious: Do Rappers Have a 'Light-Skinned' Preference?" *News One for Black America,* January 7, 2011, retrieved from http://
newsone.com/nation/just-curious-nation/newsonestaff2/lil-wayne-kanye-west
-light-skinned-women.

26. Reaction to Kanye West interview in *Essence*: Carmen Van Kerckhove, "Kanye
West: Mixed Race Women Are 'Mutts and Exist Solely for Music Videos,'"
Racialicious, November 20, 2006, retrieved from http://www.racialicious.com/
2006/11/20/kanye-west-mixed-race-women-are-mutts-and-exist-solely-for
-music-videos.

27. Quote from Snoop Dogg: retrieved from http://mikeresponts.wordpress.com/
2008/03/16/snoop-i-love-dark-skinned-women.

28. Reference to hashtags: Akiba Solomon, "What Colorist Tweet Memes Miss: It's
#TeamStructuralRacism," *Colorlines: News for Action,* July 7, 2011, retrieved
from http://colorlines.com/archives/2011/07/new_study_shows_that_colorism_
isnt_just_a_matter_of_personal_preference.html.

29. Excerpts about dark-skin-color prejudice: *Dark Girls,* produced/directed by Bill
Duke and D. Channsin Berry (Los Angeles: Duke Media Inc., 2011).

Acknowledgments

Collectively, we wish to thank our New York lifelines who made this revised edition of *The Color Complex* possible. Enormous gratitude goes out to Lisa Queen, of the Queen Literary Agency, for believing in our project and securing us a fabulous publisher, Vintage Books of Knopf Doubleday Publishing Group. We also offer our unqualified appreciation for the labor put into this book by associate editor Jeff Alexander, who throughout displayed the right mix of sympathy, encouragement, intimidation, and patience. Without you we would not have reached the finish line—or done so, as we seemingly have, with our mental faculties and friendships intact. It has been a bumpy but ultimately satisfying ride from beginning to end. Also, we want to acknowledge the meticulous copyediting of Janet Fletcher, who did an amazing and nuanced job fact-checking the book.

To those around the world who struggle every day with the pain of colorism, we offer our sincerest wishes that it will get better; we write this book for you. To those who help every day to raise awareness about this insidious form of prejudice, we honor your field activism. And to all our readers, we offer peace through enlightenment.

Kathy Russell-Cole's Acknowledgments

First, I would like to thank God for all of his many blessings. Second, I would like to acknowledge the three most important people in my life.

To my husband, James McArthur Cole II, an amazing man who is not only my life partner but also my best friend: Thanks for your love and support. Thanks for dreaming with me and allowing me to be a part of your dreams. I thank God that he brought us together. I love you, J.

To my mom, Dorothy C. Russell: Thank you for all of the sacrifices that you've made for me. I hope that I've made you proud of the woman I've become. Every day I strive to live my life in a way that honors you. I love you, "Ma"!

To my dear ol' dad, Will R. Russell: I have always loved you, Dad, and I always will. You are the best father in the whole wide world! We're going to ride this one out all the way to the end, Dad—you and me!

Midge Wilson's Acknowledgments

I want to acknowledge those in my life who make all the difference. Without your love, I could not have done what I somehow managed to do. I especially want to thank my closest friends, most notably Cindy Thomsen, Bob Basta, Nancy Webster,

Christine Reyna, and Dael Orlandersmith, who listened to me rant, and then listened more each step of the way; my family, especially my mother, Marge Wilson, my sister Betsy Atkinson, my brother Jeff Wilson, my niece Laura Wilson, and my cousin Nancy Maull, for understanding my loss, and being there for me when I needed you most; and finally thank you, thank you, thank you to all of my DePaul colleagues in the LAS dean's office, but especially Dean Chuck Suchar, for making it possible for me to not just survive emotionally but thrive professionally during a very difficult period in my life.

I also want to acknowledge the contributions of my former graduate research assistant Or'Shaundra Benson, who helped me during the proposal stage of the project, and my office assistant, Natalie Coffin, who assisted with reference citations and other tasks throughout. But most of all, I want to give a big shout-out of appreciation to my research assistant Jocelyn Droege, who was absolutely essential in helping me find relevant articles, putting together a first draft of the sources section, proofreading references to ensure their proper formatting and order, and, in general, being gracious enough to always ask if there was anything more to be done. You rock!

Index

Permissions